"Life is full of difficult choices. It requires courage to take responsibility for your own life and carve your own path. However, that's also the best way to ensure a successful future and a prosperous, healthy society. If I were a young person pursuing a productive and rewarding life, I'd buy a copy of this book and study it carefully."

—John Mackey
Co-Founder and Co-CEO,
Whole Foods Market

"Tom Palmer's new book masterfully integrates the sciences of human life to provide the knowledge of how to care for ourselves and our families and communities without using coercion. If more people knew what this slim book explains, the world would be freer, more prosperous, more just, and happier. That's pretty good for a short book."

—Peter Goettler
President and CEO,
Cato Institute

# Self-Control or State Control?

## You Decide

Edited by Tom G. Palmer
Students For Liberty & Atlas Network

AtlasNetwork.org                    StudentsForLiberty.org

## JAMESON BOOKS, INC.
### Ottawa, Illinois

**JAMESON BOOKS, INC.**

Published by Atlas Network in cooperation with Jameson Books, Inc.

Essays printed with the permission of the authors.

Edited by Tom G. Palmer
Cover Design by Robyn Patterson

For information and other requests, please write
Atlas Network, 1201 L Street NW, Washington, DC 20005.

For bulk orders, please call Jameson Books, Inc., 800-426-1357 or use the mail order form on the last page of this book.

Printed in the United States of America

ISBN: 978-0-89803-177-5

20 19 18 17 16   1 2 3 4 5

# Contents

# Dedication

*Machan Tibor Richard-nak (1939-2016), aki szerette a gondolatokat, a vitákat, a szabadságot és az életet, és aki jobb hellyé tette a világot.*

For Tibor Richard Machan (1939-2016), a lover of thought, discussion, liberty, and life who made the world a better place.

# Preface

"From Maximus: mastery of self and vacillation in nothing; cheerfulness in all circumstances and especially in illness. A happy blend of character, mildness with dignity, ready to do without complaining what is given to be done."[1]
—Marcus Aurelius, *Meditations*

Who am I? What is freedom and how do I achieve it? What is a good life and how do I achieve that? How do I live the life of a free and responsible person? How am I related to others? How should I behave and how should I expect others to behave? For what am I responsible and for what not?

Should some people use force to control others? How does control through the state function and what are its effects? What is self-control, what are its benefits and its costs, and how do I achieve it?

Young people may be especially likely to pose those questions, but those questions are not only for youth—they're for every stage of life.

They're what this short book is about. Such questions aren't topics only for professors of ethics and metaphysics; they're questions for every thinking person. They're questions for you. Moreover, understanding freedom and responsibility involves much more than some narrow intellectual specialization; serious thought on those questions must also draw on economics and history and psychology and neuroscience and sociology and art and spirituality and so much more. You'll find all of that in the book in your hands.

The ideas in this book can help you to live a happier life—to be a better friend, co-worker, student, family member, citizen, thinker, businessperson, in short: to be a better person. You can achieve a life of freedom. Freedom is not aimless irresponsibility, but is inseparable from responsibility. Grasping both is an adventure, an act worthy of a human being.

1

Freedom and responsibility will also help you to create or to strengthen free societies. A key to freedom is to understand that we live freely together, not in isolation, but in societies and communities. It means that just as our freedom is respected, we respect the freedom of others. We accept the responsibility to respect the rights of others. To live freely is to live with respect for the rights of others, as well as for one's own. To live freely is to refuse to submit passively to control by the state, but to be responsible for one's own choices.

This is not a book of secret truths that, grasped in an instant, will solve all your problems. In fact, achieving a life of self-control, freedom, and responsibility takes effort, but it is within your power. Such effort can be heroic, but need not be; normally, it's about slowly acquiring the habits of responsibility. Several chapters discuss the practices and institutions that help us to achieve those habits. They show us the benefits of improving our self-control and contain directly useful insights and tips for achieving self-control, as well as guides to other works that will help you progress further on the path to freedom and responsibility.

Solving social problems requires effort, but effective coordination of effort requires freedom and is generally hindered—not helped—by force. Various chapters explain the history of self-control and how societies of free and responsible individuals have solved and can solve complex problems and how, through freedom, we can achieve peace and prosperity.

Each chapter of this book can stand alone. You can read them in any order; no chapter requires that you have already read another. You can "dip into" the book without having to read it all. You may find some parts engaging and others less so. It's your life and you can spend it as you wish. I do hope, though, that some small part of your life will be spent on the chapters in this book, because what they offer may make the rest of your life better, freer, and—ultimately—happier.

Tom G. Palmer
Amsterdam, The Netherlands
March 30, 2016

# 1

# The Great Choice

*By Tom G. Palmer*

*Can there be freedom without responsibility, or responsibility without freedom? Can we choose to be free and responsible? Why should it matter? Here the terms are clarified, the issues defined, and the case made for choosing the life of responsibility and freedom.*

> "They [the holders of authority] are so ready to spare us all sort of troubles, except those of obeying and paying! They will say to us: what, in the end, is the aim of your efforts, the motive of your labours, the object of all your hopes? Is it not happiness? Well, leave this happiness to us and we shall give it to you. No, Sirs, we must not leave it to them. No matter how touching such a tender commitment may be, let us ask the authorities to keep within their limits. Let them confine themselves to being just. We shall assume the responsibility of being happy for ourselves."[2]
>
> —Benjamin Constant

Each of us faces a great choice. Shall I quietly accept the system of state control or shall I stand up for self-control? Self-control offers a life of freedom and responsibility. It enables us to realize our dignity in peace and harmony with others. It is a life worthy of a human being. It's the foundation for prosperity and progress. State control offers a life of obedience, subservience, and fear. It promotes the war of all against all in the struggle for the power to control the lives of others. Self-control is a clear and simple principle applicable to all: every person gets one and only one life to live. State control has no clear and simple principle and

3

invites conflict as individuals and groups struggle to control the state, and thus each other, or to evade control by others.

Free people are not subservient, but neither are they uncontrolled. They control themselves. Taking control of your life is an act of both freedom and responsibility. In fact, the two are so closely connected that one cannot hold onto one without the other.

Dependent children tend to seek freedom without responsibility; independent adults embrace both. The life of freedom and responsibility offers satisfactions only available to those who take control of their own lives. The life of freedom and responsibility is the life of an adult, rather than a child; of a citizen, rather than a subject; of a person, rather than an object. Our own well being, our happiness, is not something that we can expect from others or that is delivered to us by the state. Governments are properly instituted among men, after all, not to secure our happiness, but to secure our right to the *pursuit* of happiness. We are responsible for being happy ourselves.

**Responsibility and Freedom**
*Responsibility*: For some the word conjures up images of old people lecturing young people about sitting up straight, doing their homework, and writing thank-you notes to elderly aunts. Unsurprisingly, we're expected to think it's boring, tedious, a diversion from our enjoyment of our freedom. The goal of freedom, the images suggest, is to escape responsibilities.

In fact, embracing responsibility is neither boring, nor tedious, nor a diversion from freedom. Being responsible entails at times doing things that are unpleasant or even great sacrifices, but embracing responsibility provides the greatest of human satisfactions. Embracing one's own responsibility is in fact an adventure and an act of daring. We deserve to be free because we can be held accountable for our acts; because we can make choices; because we can exercise self-control. Responsibility is not a burden we must bear to be free; the awareness that "I did that" is what makes freedom a prize worth fighting for. Responsibility is the key to the realization of freedom.

We do not deserve our freedom merely because we have desires or impulses. We deserve to be free—to control our own lives—because we are morally accountable: to each other, to God (for those who believe), and to our own consciences. As one of history's most influential moral philosophers wrote hundreds of years ago,

> A moral being is an accountable being. An accountable being, as the word expresses, is a being that must give an account of its actions to some other, and that consequently must regulate them according to the good-liking of this other.[3]

Adam Smith went on to explain that the development of moral consciousness entails accountability not only to others but to ourselves, for what we seek is not merely *to be praised*, but *to be praise-worthy*, two goals that may resemble each other, but which "are yet, in many respects, distinct and independent of each other."[4]

As social creatures, we seek to become praise-*worthy*, or "admirable," but "in order to attain this satisfaction, we must become the impartial spectators of our own character and conduct. We must endeavor to view them with the eyes of other people, or as other people are likely to view them."[5]

Becoming impartial spectators of our own character and conduct enables us to earn our own self-esteem. As Smith noted, "The man who applauds us either for actions we did not perform, or for motives which had no sort of influence upon our conduct, applauds not us, but another person. We can derive no sort of satisfaction from his praises."[6] Such satisfaction is possible in no other way than by embracing responsibility.

*Freedom*: For some the word conjures up images of "anything goes," of disorder, chaos, immorality, license. Unsurprisingly, they consider freedom frightening. As a consequence, many have believed that order and virtue must be imposed at the expense of freedom. They equate responsibility with submission to the commands of others. Some have even promised that such submission, although it may destroy what we ordinary people consider our freedom, promises a higher freedom, one far superior to what they dismiss as merely empirical or "bourgeois" freedom. They promise an ecstatic freedom that can only be found when our actions are directed by the wise and the good, or at least the powerful.

Freedom is not the same as license; responsibility closely connects freedom with virtue and self-command. The connection was made clear by one of history's greatest champions of freedom, a man who was born a slave in Talbot County, Maryland: Frederick Augustus Washington Bailey, a man who achieved freedom for himself and for millions of others. He is known by the name he chose for himself: Frederick Douglass. Douglass wrote in 1845—as a former slave who liberated himself—of the "holidays" allowed to slaves by their captors. Such moments of seeming freedom were portrayed as acts of benevolence by the slaveholders, but were in fact deployed as "safety-valves, to carry off the rebellious spirit of enslaved humanity."[7] The slaveholders sought to sink their captives in depravity, rather than offer them a respite from slavery:

> Their object seems to be, to disgust their slaves with freedom, by plunging them into the lowest depths of dissipation. For instance, the slaveholders not only like to see the slave drink of his own accord, but will adopt various plans to make him drunk. One plan is, to make bets on their slaves, as to who can drink the most whisky without getting drunk; and in this way they succeed in getting whole multitudes to drink to excess. Thus, when the slave asks for virtuous freedom, the cunning slaveholder, knowing his ignorance, cheats him with a dose of vicious dissipation, artfully labeled with the name of liberty. The most of us used to drink it down, and the result was just what might be supposed: many of us were led to think that there was little to choose between liberty and slavery. We felt, and very properly so, that we had almost as well be slaves to man as to rum. So, when the holidays ended, we staggered up from the filth of our wallowing, took a long breath, and marched to the field—feeling, upon the whole, rather glad to go, from what our master had deceived us into a belief was freedom, back to the arms of slavery.[8]

For Douglass, freedom was found not in the drunkenness and vice encouraged by the masters, but in the dignity of self-assumed responsibility. He learned the measure of freedom when he, as he put it, "got hold of a book entitled *The Columbian Orator*" and was captivated by a dialogue between a master and a slave in which the slave refutes the master's arguments for slavery and persuades the master to emancipate him.[9] The effect of those arguments on Douglass was powerful: "Freedom now appeared, to disappear no more forever. It was heard in every sound, and seen in every thing. It was ever present to torment me with a sense of my wretched condition. I saw nothing without seeing it, I heard nothing without hearing it, and felt nothing without feeling it."[10]

Attempts to substitute state control for self-control generate unintended consequences that are often far worse than the situations that state control is ostensibly intended to improve. The intentions of legislators or administrators are one thing and the consequences of changing incentives are another. To take two prominent examples, Professor Jeffrey Miron of Harvard University exposes the terrible unintended consequences of the "War on Drugs" (crime, overdoses, spread of diseases, and more) in his chapter for this volume and journalist Lisa Conyers in her chapter examines the dependency that is created by welfare state policies, usually, but perhaps not always, as an unintended consequence of those policies.

One can never legislate or choose outcomes directly; all legislators or rulers can do is to change the incentives that participants in social interactions face. Thus, actions may be outlawed because the legislators think they're bad. It does not follow that, after the rulers have spoken, no one will take those actions anymore. Understanding that, rulers specify punishments, from fines to imprisonment to death. It still does not follow that no one will take those actions.

- Freedom to produce, buy, sell, and consume drugs is restricted or completely suppressed in many countries by law. Drugs are illegal in the United States, yet the prisons are full of people who produced, bought, sold, or consumed drugs despite the legislators telling them not to do so. Many millions of people were not dissuaded by the prospect of jail sentences, despite the extraordinary violence and the hundreds of billions of dollars deployed to change their behavior.[11] The experience of alcohol prohibition is being repeated; merely banning a substance does not mean that people will stop consuming it and is likely to generate consequences that the advocates of the ban did not anticipate.[12]

- Responsibility to make decisions about saving for one's retirement all over the world was taken over by governments, ostensibly to invest their earnings wisely, help them to provide for their old age, and create bonds of solidarity among generations.[13] In the United States wages are taxed and the taxes are not invested for the future, but churned into a "Pay As You Go" system that is financially indistinguishable from a pyramid scheme and that accumulates massive "unfunded liabilities" over time. Wage earners were told that their compulsory Social Security payments were being "matched" by "contributions" from their employers, when in fact 100 percent of the "employer contribution" came out of their own pockets, as it was money the employers were paying to hire them and so the money was merely taken from the wage earners by government. The money was paid out immediately and replaced by nothing more than an IOU.[14] Rather than creating intergenerational solidarity, people were encouraged to lobby for more and more payments unrelated to their contributions[15] and unsustainable burdens were shifted to younger people.[16] The system has already turned "cash negative," meaning that the accounting fiction of the "Trust Fund" has been revealed; social security is financed by a pyramid scheme, not through "investments" or "savings."[17] When people are told that their retirement will be taken care of by government, it turns out that they consume more and save less. Moreover, when the costs fall on one group and the benefits on another, the incentives created lead people to seek benefits and avoid costs and generate a myriad of conflicts, including intergenerational conflict. Self-control is never perfect, but state control is no improvement.

## Freedom and Respect for Law

Harmonious social order is possible only when individuals are free to control themselves and to coordinate their actions voluntarily with others. A harmonious society rests on respect for the freedom of each member. Harmonious social order emerges not from commands backed by violence, which are more likely to disrupt order than to establish it, but from respect for the general rules of free societies that delineate spheres of freedom and responsibility for each individual.[18] The institutions of free societies—including manners and mores, markets and prices, persuasion and discussion, debate and deliberation—provide the mechanisms by which people coordinate their behavior voluntarily.

Many have believed, and some still do, that order can only be created by force guided by reason and will. The planet is littered with the graves of the victims of that ideology. The reality of attempts to create heaven on earth through such planning has been not order but what the economist Ludwig von Mises called "planned chaos."[19] Sloane Frost, an expert in health administration policy and a founder of Students for Liberty, showed the irrationality of interventionist "planning" in a study of health care provision. As she discovered in her research, rather than any coherent and rational order,

> We get one intervention piled on top of another, with the bottom so far down hardly anyone remembers how the process started. The systems become embedded in daily life, as well, so much so that people never bother to ask how they got that way. What's worse, because they're not coherently planned, but lurch from crisis to crisis, they are sometimes described not as state interventionism but as "free markets" or "laissez faire" by people who don't take the time to understand the network of interventions and to trace out the incentives they create, how they affect behavior, and how they lead to unintended consequences and then more interventions.[20]

Commands may be suitable for armies, but in the attempts to replicate the planned orders of armies, command-based interventionist policies in fact disrupt existing and emergent functioning patterns of coordination and create not more order, but disorder. Systems of general and stable rules succeed where commands fail, because they allow people to form reasonable expectations of the behavior of others and allow them the flexibility to adapt to changing situations.[21] But even if society could be ordered like a vast army, the order that would emerge would be far less complex than the orders created by free cooperation. If order can be compared to music, the orders of free societies resemble not the cadences of military marches but the emergent orders of jazz ensembles.

The rule of law is an essential ingredient in freedom; each person, including government agents, bears responsibility for observing the rule of law. The rule of law is not the same as issuing or obeying specific edicts, orders, and commands backed up by force, but entails general rules, such that

> under the rule of law the government is prevented from stultifying individual efforts by *ad hoc* action. Within the known rules of the game the individual is free to pursue his personal ends and desires, certain that the powers of government will not be used deliberately to frustrate his efforts.[22]

The rule of law makes possible individual freedom, but its maintenance requires the widespread acceptance of responsibility and self-control within the populations of persons who interact in myriad ways that are virtually impossible for other parties to monitor. There could never be enough policemen in the world to force people to follow and maintain the rule of law if there was not already a substantial degree of self-control among the people, including government agents. When that self-control— that responsibility to uphold the law—is eroded, it undermines the rule of law, the enjoyment of freedom, and social order and coordination. Freedom is the key to the experience of responsibility, as responsibility is necessary for the maintenance of freedom.

John Locke sharply distinguished between the enjoyment of freedom and merely doing what one "lists," that is, what one is inclined to do or merely desires to do, regardless of the consequences for oneself or for anyone else:

*[T]he end of law* is not to abolish or restrain, but *to preserve and enlarge Freedom*: For in all the states of created beings capable of Laws, *where there is no Law, there is no Freedom*. For *Liberty* is to be free from restraint and violence from others which cannot be, where there is no Law: But Freedom is not, as we are told, *A Liberty for every Man to do what he lists*: (For who could be free, when every other Man's Humour might domineer over him?) But a *Liberty* to dispose, and order, as he lists, his Person, Actions, Possessions, and his whole Property, within the Allowance of those Laws under which he is; and therein not to be subject to the arbitrary Will of another, but freely follow his own.[23]

Just as freedom and law are intimately connected, so are freedom and responsibility. They are related functionally and positively: as one increases, so does the other, and vice versa. Responsibility is the very ground of our freedom, as freedom is the ground of our responsibility. Embracing our own freedom and our own responsibility strengthens our moral awareness, makes us mindful of our relations to others and to our own futures, improves our character, develops the habits of the good life in community with others, fosters respect for the freedom of others, and allows us the satisfaction of saying, "I did that; my life is my responsibility and I am accountable for what I achieve."

Our very personal identity is tied up with our freedom and responsibility. Richard Overton, an early libertarian writer and activist in England, wrote from his prison cell in 1646,

To every individual in nature is given an individual property by nature not to be invaded or usurped by any. For every one, as he is himself, so he has a self-propriety, *else could he not be himself*.[24]

Merely to be oneself, each individual must have a "self-propriety," "else could he not be himself." Frederick Douglass independently discovered the same principle:

Only look at the condition of the slave: stripped of every right—denied every privilege, he had not even the privilege of saying "myself"—his head, his eyes, his hands, his heart, his bones, his sinews, his soul, his immortal spirit, were all the property of another. He might not decide any question for himself—any question relating to his own actions. The master—the man who claimed property in his person—assumed the right to decide all things for himself.[25]

As Overton in his lonely prison cell and Douglass meditating on his terrible personal experience of slavery both understood, to be oneself one must have the freedom to say "*my* self."

The Chinese character for liberty, 自由 (*ziyóu*), connotes also "self-determination" or "to be oneself" and contains the character for self, 自 (*zi*). In personal discussions with Chinese scholar-advocates of liberty I have been told that the Chinese characters convey the mutual implication of personal freedom and responsibility more clearly than the English words freedom or liberty. In what follows I will try to tease out the relationship more clearly.

**Freedom or License?**
The philosopher Plato in his book *The Republic* has Socrates disparage the character of freedom in a democratic regime. Socrates asks his interlocutor, Glaucon,

> "In the first place, then, aren't they free? And isn't the city full of freedom and free speech? And isn't there license in it to do whatever one wants?
> "That is what is said, certainly," he said.
> "And where there's license, it's plain, that each man would organize his life in it privately just as it pleases him."[26]

The inevitable outcome of such relations is presented in *The Republic* as chaos and immorality. According to Socrates,

"And the ultimate in the freedom of the multitude, my friend," I said, "occurs in such a city when the purchased slaves, male and female, are no less free than those who have bought them. And we almost forgot to mention the extent of the law of equality and of freedom in the relations of women with men and men with women."

"Won't we," he said, "with Aeschylus, 'say whatever just came to our lips'?"[27]

Slaves would act as if they were just as free as their masters, and women would think they were equal to men, and, well, *that* can't be allowed, can it? People would even say just whatever they feel like saying, and that *certainly* can't be allowed.

Plato (through his mouthpiece, Socrates) suggested eliminating the freedom "to say whatever just came to our lips," as well as abolishing property and the family, at least for the "Guardian Classes"; in place of democratic governance he proposed rule over the city by a "Guardian Class" that would be educated in virtue and thus able to ensure that everyone would know his or her place and be true to it. The polity would be guided to virtue by those with the education that would enable them to know what virtue is; that education is not possible for the many, who must be guided by their betters. Many philosophers have followed in Plato's footsteps, all convinced that they are smarter, wiser, and better than the rest of humanity and thus it is their duty to accept the burden of power and to use that power to guide the behavior and even the thoughts of others to virtue, progress, godliness, purity, order, or whatever higher purpose they see that we cannot. Sadly, for such moral philosophers, perhaps, rarely do those who succeed in the struggle for power turn out to be philosophers, much less moral, and the regimes the philosophers endorse rarely show the neat consistency and coherence they envisaged.[28] They more frequently devour the arrogant intellectuals who proclaimed them in the first place.

Freedom requires establishing not systems of power by means of which educated elites control the behavior and lives of others, but a rule of law, that is to say, *a law of rules*, in which each person can control himself or herself within a set of rules that facilitate cooperation.[29] The rules of the road facilitate the transportation of millions of people to millions of different destinations, all without a central power issuing commands to them; they're not perfect, but rather simple rules of the road help many millions of people to avoid collisions and arrive where they want to be every minute of every day. Frequently the rules themselves emerged without anyone consciously creating and imposing them; even the rules of order emerge without conscious direction and are the byproducts of people interacting to achieve their own diverse ends. The problem is that most people, including intellectuals, despite the evidence before their eyes, find it hard to understand how people can coordinate their behavior merely by following rules that are applicable to all. They can only imagine order when there is someone giving orders. Their eyes are closed to the complex order swirling around them. Free societies are vast systems of countless interlocking spontaneous orders, from language to traffic to moral norms to fashion to markets for groceries, shoes, toothpaste, and furniture. Different legal systems offer a variety of rules of order, but none would function if people were incapable, without conscious external direction or control, of adjusting their behavior to that of others in order to realize their own aims, the aggregate results of which are systems of order that could not be predicted in their particular details.

It's not only philosophers and politicians who extol the use of power to control other people. The belief is rather widespread that authority, power, or even raw force is the only way to "run a society." Everyone else, they believe, must be controlled. Other people are not competent to control themselves or to coordinate their actions with others who are in control of their own lives and actions. It is a false conceit that conscious direction can coordinate the behavior of millions of people better than systems of rules that allow people to make their own choices and to coordinate their behavior voluntarily, to quote Locke, "within the Allowance of those Laws under which they are; and therein not to be subject to the arbitrary Will of another, but freely follow their own."

Free people follow their own wills within the rule of law. They are responsible for the consequences of their actions and they are responsible for respecting the rights of others to live as free persons. Respect for individual rights and the rule of law creates social order and virtuous cycles of cooperation, creation of wealth through mutually beneficial exchange, and harmony. Not everyone sees it that way, of course. From Plato to Putin, advocates of force have called submission to their plans the only way to realize the truly good, orderly, virtuous, or prosperous society. In seeking to relieve us of the responsibility and the freedom to achieve our own happiness, they set themselves over us, degrade us, and to realize their schemes are compelled to resort to violence. Their visions, to the extent they are implemented, realize neither order, nor goodness, nor virtue, nor prosperity. Personal responsibility and freedom succeed where arbitrary power and coercion fail. Benjamin Constant's words are as true today as they were in his day: "Let them confine themselves to being just. We shall assume the responsibility of being happy for ourselves."[30]

# 2

# How Brain Chemistry Explains Human Freedom and Helps Us to Realize It

*By John Tierney*

*Is willpower like a muscle? Can you exercise it? Can you overwork or tire it? Can you nourish it? Experimental psychologists have learned a great deal about willpower in recent decades. The good news is that much of the knowledge gained has very practical value. You can strengthen your willpower, improve your life, and through self-regulation set yourself free. John Tierney is a science writer at the* New York Times *and co-author with experimental psychologist Roy Baumeister of* Willpower: Rediscovering the Greatest Human Strength (*New York: Penguin Books, 2011*).

On July 4, 1776, as his revolutionary declaration of human liberty was being finalized and adopted, Thomas Jefferson also produced some less-exalted prose.

"Pd Sparhawk for a thermometer," he wrote, dutifully recording the precise amount—3 pounds, 15 shillings—he had paid that day at John Sparhawk's shop in Philadelphia. Not even the Declaration of Independence could distract him from his determination to record every purchase. His obsessive recordkeeping was extreme, but the zeal for self-control—for setting goals and monitoring behavior—was common among his colleagues. As an adolescent, George Washington wrote down a list of 110 "rules of civility" covering everything from table manners ("Drink not, nor talk with your mouth full") to morality ("Let your recreations be manful not sinful"). The young Benjamin Franklin kept weekly charts of his progress toward thirteen specific virtues. By marking any lapses in Temperance, Frugality, Industry, Cleanliness, and the other virtues, he aimed to "conquer all that either natural inclination, custom, or company might lead me into." The Founding Fathers believed in the unalienable human right to liberty, but they knew it depended on personal responsibility. To be freed from a tyrant's rule, men had to be able to rule themselves: that truth seemed self-evident.

Today it's even more evident, although it has taken social scientists a while to catch up with their forebears. During the twentieth century, as researchers studied the irrational and unconscious forces in the brain, their faith in self-control waned. It was replaced by faith in state control: more and more rules and programs to protect us from ourselves. But now, thanks to new research, the benefits of self-control have become clear again. Social scientists find that it's the supreme virtue, essential to individual success and to harmony in a free society. They've measured its impact on behavior and begun to understand how it operates in the brain. They've discovered, to their surprise, that willpower is not just a quaint metaphor.

The term "willpower" was introduced by Victorians who shared the Founding Fathers' enthusiasm for self-control. Victorians saw themselves as living in a time of transition as the moral certainties and rigid institutions of feudal Europe died away. Medieval serfs had depended on external forms of control over their behavior: the dicta of the lord, the commandments of the church, and the rigidly enforced norms of the village. But as farmers moved to cities during the eighteenth and nineteenth centuries, they were no longer constrained by village churches and the social pressures of small groups. Christian religious upheavals and conflicts had made religion more individualistic, and the Enlightenment had weakened faith in any kind of dogma. A popular topic of debate among Victorians was whether morality could survive without religion. As they fretted over moral decay and the social pathologies concentrated in cities, Victorians looked for something more reliable than divine grace, some internal strength that could protect even an atheist.

They called it willpower because of the folk notion that some kind of force was involved—some inner equivalent to the steam powering the Industrial Revolution. People sought to increase their store of it by following the exhortations of the Englishman Samuel Smiles in *Self-Help,* one of the most popular books of the nineteenth century on both sides of the Atlantic. "Genius is patience," he reminded readers, explaining the success of everyone from Isaac Newton to Stonewall Jackson as the result of "self-denial" and "untiring perseverance."

The fascination with willpower ebbed in the twentieth century, partly in reaction to the Victorians' excesses and partly due to economic changes and the world wars. The prolonged bloodshed of World War I seemed a consequence of too many stubborn gentlemen following their "duty" to senseless deaths. Intellectuals preached a more relaxed view of life in America and much of Western Europe—but not, unfortunately, in Germany, where they developed a "psychology of will" to guide their country during its bleak recovery from the war. That theme would be embraced by the Nazis, whose rally in 1934 was featured in Leni Riefenstahl's infamous propaganda film, *The Triumph of the Will.* The Nazi concept of mass obedience to a sociopath was hardly the Victorian concept of personal moral strength, but the distinction was lost. If the Nazis represented the triumph of the will . . . well, when it comes to bad PR, there's nothing quite like a personal endorsement from Adolf Hitler.

The decline of will didn't seem like such a bad thing, and after the war there were other forces weakening it. As technology made goods cheaper and suburbanites richer, responding to consumer demand became vital to the economy, and a sophisticated new advertising industry urged everyone to buy now. Sociologists identified a new generation of "other-directed" people who were guided by their neighbors' opinions rather than strong inner moral convictions. The stern self-help books of the Victorian era came to be seen as naïvely self-centered. The new best sellers were cheery works like Dale Carnegie's *How to Win Friends and Influence People* and Norman Vincent Peale's *Power of Positive Thinking.*

The shift in people's characters was noticed by a psychoanalyst named Allen Wheelis, who in the late 1950s revealed what he considered a dirty little secret of his profession: Freudian therapies no longer worked the way they were supposed to. In his landmark book *The Quest for Identity,* Wheelis described a change in character structure since Freud's day. The Victorian middleclass citizens who formed the bulk of Freud's patients had intensely strong wills, making it difficult for therapists to break through their ironclad defenses and their sense of what was right and wrong. Freud's therapies had concentrated on ways to break through and let them see why they were neurotic and miserable, because once those people achieved insight, they could change rather easily. By midcentury, though, people's character armor was different. Wheelis and his colleagues found that people achieved insight more quickly than in Freud's day, but then the therapy often stalled and failed. Lacking the sturdy character of the Victorians, people didn't have the strength to follow up on the insight and change their lives. Wheelis used Freudian terms in discussing the decline of the superego in Western society, but he was essentially talking about a weakening of willpower—and all this was *before* the baby boomers came of age in the 1960s with a countercultural mantra of "If it feels good, do it."

Popular culture kept celebrating self-indulgence for the "Me Generation" of the 1970s, and there were new arguments against willpower from social scientists, whose numbers and influence soared during the late twentieth century. Most social scientists look for causes of misbehavior outside the individual: poverty, relative deprivation, oppression, or other failures of the environment or the economic and political systems. Searching for external factors is often more comfortable for everyone, particularly for the many academics who worry that they risk the politically incorrect sin of "blaming the victim" by suggesting that people's problems might arise from causes inside themselves. Social problems can also seem easier to fix than character defects, at least to the social scientists proposing new government policies and programs to deal with them.

The very notion that people can consciously control themselves has traditionally been viewed suspiciously by psychologists. Freudians claimed that much of adult human behavior was the result of unconscious forces and processes. B. F. Skinner had little respect for the value of consciousness and other mental processes, except as needed to process reinforcement contingencies. In *Beyond Freedom and Dignity,* he argued that to understand human nature we must get beyond the outmoded values in the book's title. While many of Skinner's specific theories were discarded, aspects of his approach have found new life among psychologists convinced that the conscious mind is subservient to the unconscious. The will came to seem so unimportant that it wasn't even measured or mentioned in modern personality theories. Some neuroscientists claimed to have disproven its existence. Many philosophers refuse to use the term. If they want to debate this classical philosophical question of freedom of the will, they prefer to speak of freedom of action, not of will, because they doubt there is any such thing as will. Some refer disdainfully to "the so-called will." Some scholars have argued that the legal system must be revamped to eliminate outdated notions of free will and responsibility.

Meanwhile, though, a few other researchers got interested in the topic of "self-regulation," the term that psychologists use for self-control. The resurrection of self-control wasn't led by theorists, who were still convinced that willpower was a Victorian myth. But when other psychologists went into the laboratory or the field, they kept happening on something that looked an awful lot like it.

Some of the first clues came, by accident, from an experiment in which four-year-old children were offered a marshmallow but told they'd get a bonus (another marshmallow) if they could resist eating it for a few minutes. The point of the experiment, led by Walter Mischel of Stanford, was merely to study how children learned to delay gratification. But many years later, after hearing stories about what had happened to some of the children, Mischel and his colleagues decided to track down hundreds of veterans of the experiments. They found that the ones who had been able to resist the marshmallow temptation at age four went on to get better grades and test scores.[31] The children who had managed to hold out the entire fifteen minutes went on to score 210 points higher on the SAT than the ones who had caved after the first half minute. The children with willpower grew up to become more popular with their peers and their teachers. They earned higher salaries. They had a lower body-mass index, suggesting that they were less prone to gain weight as middle age encroached. They were less likely to report having had problems with drug abuse.

The benefits of self-control looked even more remarkable once other research results were aggregated by Roy Baumeister in *Losing Control,* a scholarly book he wrote in 1994 with his wife, Dianne Tice, a fellow professor at Case Western Reserve University, and Todd Heatherton, a professor at Harvard. "Self-regulation failure is the major social pathology of our time," they concluded, pointing to the accumulating evidence of its contribution to high divorce rates, domestic violence, crime, and a host of other problems. The book stimulated more experiments and studies, including the development of a scale for measuring self-control on personality tests. When researchers compared students' grades with nearly three dozen personality traits, self-control turned out to be the *only* trait that predicted a college student's grade-point average better than chance.[32] Self-control also proved to be a better predictor of college grades than the student's IQ or SAT score.[33] Although raw intelligence was obviously an advantage, the study showed that self-control was more important because it helped the students show up more reliably for classes, start their homework earlier, and spend more time working and less time watching television.

The results were impressive, but how exactly did they come about? What was the mechanism of self-control? How to find out what was going on inside those students' brains? The answer, it turned out, was to start with warm cookies.

### Radishes, Chocolate, and Glucose

Sometimes social scientists have to be a little cruel with their experiments. When the college students walked into Baumeister's laboratory, they were already hungry because they'd been fasting, and now they were in a room suffused with the aroma of chocolate chip cookies that had just been baked in the lab. The experimental subjects sat down at a table with several culinary choices: the warm cookies, some pieces of chocolate, and a bowl of radishes. Some students were invited to eat the cookies and candy. The unlucky ones were assigned to "the radish condition": no treats, just raw radishes.

To maximize temptation, the researchers left the students alone with the radishes and the cookies, and observed them through a small, hidden window. The ones in the radish condition clearly struggled with the temptation. Many gazed longingly at the cookies before settling down to bite reluctantly into a radish. Some of them picked up a cookie and smelled it, savoring the pleasure of freshly baked chocolate. A couple accidentally dropped a cookie on the floor and then hastened to put it back in the bowl so no one would know of their flirtation with sin. But nobody actually bit into the forbidden food. The temptation was always resisted, if in some cases by the narrowest of margins. All this was to the good, in terms of the experiment. It showed that the cookies were really quite tempting and that people needed to summon up their willpower to resist them.

Then the students were taken to another room and given geometry puzzles to work on. The students thought they were being tested for cleverness, although in fact the puzzles were unsolvable. The test was to see how long they'd work before giving up. This has been a standard technique that stress researchers and others have used for decades because it's a reliable indicator of overall perseverance. (Other research has shown that someone who keeps trying one of these unsolvable puzzles will also work longer at tasks that are actually doable.)

The students who'd been allowed to eat chocolate chip cookies and candy typically worked on the puzzles for about twenty minutes, as did a control group of students who were also hungry but hadn't been offered food of any kind. The sorely tempted radish eaters, though, gave up in just eight minutes—a huge difference by the standards of laboratory experiments.[34] They'd successfully resisted the temptation of the cookies and the chocolates, but the effort left them with less energy to tackle the puzzles. The old folk wisdom about willpower appeared to be correct after all, unlike the newer and fancier psychological theories of the self.

Willpower was more than a metaphor. There really was a form of mental energy that provided self-control—and that could be depleted as it was used to resist temptation. This effect, termed "ego depletion," was demonstrated in dozens of studies involving various temptations and tasks.[35] The experiments consistently demonstrated two lessons:

1. You have a finite amount of willpower that becomes depleted as you use it.
2. You use the same stock of willpower for all manner of tasks.

You might think you have one reservoir of self-control for work, another for dieting, another for exercise, and, another for being nice to your family. But the radish experiment showed that two completely unrelated activities—resisting chocolate and working on geometry puzzles—drew on the same source of energy, and this phenomenon has been demonstrated over and over. There are hidden connections among the wildly different things you do all day.

You use the same supply of willpower to deal with frustrating traffic, tempting food, annoying colleagues, demanding bosses, and pouting children. The old line about the frustrated worker going home and kicking the dog jibes with the ego-depletion experiments, although modern workers generally aren't so mean to their pets. They're more likely to say something nasty to the humans in the household. By tracking people from morning through night, researchers in Germany calculated that a person typically spends between three and fours a day resisting desires[36]—the desire to eat, the desire to goof off, the desire to give your true opinion of your boss's latest brainstorm. All these acts of self-control reduce your willpower.

There is also another important way that willpower gets depleted, as Baumeister's lab discovered. After the early experiment with cookies and radishes, a young colleague at the lab, Jean Twenge, came in one day after spending hours with her fiancé deciding what to put in their bridal registry. The decision process left her utterly exhausted, and it gave the researchers an idea. They did experiments with shoppers in a suburban mall and at the online site of Dell computers.[37] Sure enough, the more decisions that shoppers made, the less willpower they had to solve puzzles and do other tasks. Making decisions depleted the same source of mental energy as resisting temptations, leading to a condition that was dubbed "decision fatigue."

After decision fatigue sets in, the brain looks for shortcuts in two quite different ways. One shortcut is to become reckless: to act impulsively instead of expending the energy to first think through the consequences. The other shortcut is the ultimate energy saver: do nothing. Duck the decision. That eases the mental strain at the moment, but it can be costly in the long run, as researchers demonstrated in a study at a German car dealership observing customers ordering options for their sedans.[38] The car buyers—and these were real customers spending their own money—had to choose, for instance, among four styles of gearshift knobs, thirteen kinds of tires and rims, twenty-five configurations of the engine and gearbox, and a palette of fifty-six different colors for the interior of the sedan.

As they started picking features, customers would carefully weigh the choices, but as decision fatigue set in they'd start settling for whatever the default option was. And the more tough choices they encountered early in the process—like going through those fifty-six colors to choose the precise shade of gray or brown for the sedan's interior—the quicker people got fatigued and settled for the path of least resistance by taking the default option. By manipulating the order of the car buyers' choices, the researchers found that the customers would end up settling for different kinds of options, and the average difference totaled more than 1,500 Euros per car (about $2,000 at the time). Whether the customers paid a little extra for fancy tire rims or a lot extra for a more powerful engine depended on when the choice was offered (early or late) and how much willpower was left in the customer.

As they observed the effects of declining willpower, researchers tried to figure out what was going on inside the brain. The answer emerged unexpectedly in an experiment that had been designed to test an entirely different idea called the Mardi Gras theory—the notion that you could build up willpower by first indulging yourself in pleasure, the way that Mardi Gras feasters do just before the rigors of Lent. In place of a Fat Tuesday breakfast, the chefs in Baumeister's lab whipped up lusciously thick ice cream milkshakes for a group of subjects who were resting in between two laboratory tasks requiring willpower. Sure enough, the delicious shakes seem to strengthen willpower by helping people perform better than expected on the next task. So far, so good.

But the experiment also included a control group of people who were fed a tasteless concoction of low-fat dairy glop. It provided them with no pleasure, yet it produced similar improvements in self-control. The Mardi Gras theory looked wrong. Besides tragically removing an excuse for romping through the streets of New Orleans, the result was embarrassing for the researchers. Matthew Gailliot, the graduate student who had run the study, stood looking glumly at his shoes as he told Baumeister about the fiasco.

Baumeister tried to be optimistic. Maybe the study wasn't a failure. Something *had* happened, after all. Even the tasteless glop had done the job, but how? If it wasn't the pleasure, could it be the calories? At first the idea seemed a bit daft. For decades, psychologists had been studying performance on mental tasks without worrying about it being affected by a glass of milk. They liked to envision the human mind as a computer, focusing on the way it processed information. In their eagerness to chart the human equivalent of the computer's chips and circuits, most psychologists neglected one mundane but essential part of the machine: the power cord.

To establish cause and effect, researchers tried recharging the brain in a series of experiments involving lemonade mixed either with sugar or with a diet sweetener.[39] Again and again, the sugar improved self-control, but the artificial sweetener had no effect. Only the sugar provided the glucose necessary to refuel the brain's supply of willpower. The researchers used the sugary drink because it produced quick effects in the lab, but they didn't recommend it for everyday use because sugar produces a cycle of glucose boom-and-bust. The body converts all sorts of food into glucose, and it's easier to maintain self-control by eating foods that release glucose more slowly and consistently (like vegetables and nuts).

As they studied the effects of ego depletion, researchers began to think of willpower as a muscle that got weakened as it was used. But, like a muscle, could it also be strengthened through exercise? They knew that a quick boost of glucose could temporarily strengthen willpower, but was there a way to gradually build up stamina over time? Was there anything to the Victorian notion of "building character," or to Benjamin Franklin's weekly charts and his exercises strengthening self-discipline? It seemed unlikely, but then another happy accident occurred in Baumeister's laboratory.

## Building Character

When they set out to improve people's willpower, Baumeister's team decided to try several strategies.[40] After doing an initial test of students' willpower on some tasks in the lab, they sent the students off with varying instructions. One group was told to work on their posture for the next two weeks. Whenever they thought of it, they were to try to stand up straight or sit up straight. Since most of these (or any) college students were used to casually slouching, the exercises would force them to expend energy overriding their habitual response. A second group was used to test the notion that willpower was exhausting because of the energy required for self-monitoring (like Jefferson's zeal for tracking his spending). These students were told to record whatever they ate for the next two weeks. They didn't have to make any changes to their diet, though it was possible that some of them might have been shamed into a few adjustments. (*Hmm. Monday, pizza and beer. Tuesday, pizza and wine. Wednesday, hot dogs and Coke. Maybe it would look better if I ate a salad or an apple now and then.*) A third group was used to check the effects of altering one's state of mind. They were instructed to strive for positive moods and emotions during the two weeks. Whenever they found themselves feeling bad, these students should strive to cheer themselves up. Sensing a potential winner, the researchers elected to make this group twice as large as the other groups, so as to get the most statistically reliable results.

But the researchers' hunch was dead wrong. Their favorite strategy turned out to do no good at all. The large group that practiced controlling emotions for two weeks showed no improvement when the students returned to the lab and repeated the self-control tests. In retrospect, this failure seems less surprising than it did back then. Emotion regulation does not rely on willpower. People cannot simply will themselves to be in love, or to feel intense joy, or to stop feeling guilty. Emotional control typically relies on various subtle tricks, such as changing how one thinks about the problem at hand, or distracting oneself. Hence, practicing emotional control does not strengthen your willpower.

But other exercises do help, as demonstrated by the groups in the experiment that worked on their posture and recorded everything they ate. When they returned to the lab after two weeks, their scores on the self-control tests went up, and the improvement was significantly higher by comparison with a control group (which did no exercises of any kind during the two weeks). This was a striking result, and with careful analyses of the data, the conclusions became clearer and stronger. Unexpectedly, the best results came from the group working on posture. That tiresome old advice—"Sit up straight!"—was more useful than anyone had imagined. By overriding their habit of slouching, the students strengthened their willpower and did better at tasks that had nothing to do with posture. The improvement was most pronounced among the students who had followed the advice most diligently (as measured by the daily logs the students kept of how often they'd forced themselves to sit up or stand up straight).

The experiment also revealed an important distinction in self-control between two kinds of strength: power and stamina. At the initial lab session, participants began by squeezing a spring-loaded handgrip for as long as they could (which had been shown in other experiments to be a good measure of willpower, not just physical strength). Then, after expending mental energy on another task, they did a second handgrip task to assess how they fared when willpower was depleted. Two weeks later, when they returned to the lab after working on their posture, their scores on the initial handgrip tests didn't show much improvement, meaning that the willpower muscle hadn't gotten more powerful. But they had much more stamina, as evidenced by their improved performance on the subsequent handgrip test administered after the researchers tried to fatigue them. Thanks to the students' posture exercises, their willpower didn't get depleted as quickly as before, so they had more stamina for other tasks.

You could try the two-week posture experiment to improve your own willpower, or you could try other exercises. There's nothing magical about sitting up straight, as researchers subsequently discovered when they tested other regimens and found similar benefits. You can pick and choose from the techniques they studied, or extrapolate to create your own system. The key is to concentrate on changing a habitual behavior. If you're right-handed, you might try using your left hand instead of your habitual right hand for brushing your teeth, using a computer mouse, opening doors, or lifting a cup to your lips. You could try changing your speech habits by forcing yourself to speak only in complete sentences, or to always say "yes" instead of "yeah."

Or you could simply improve your self-control in one aspect of your life, as students did in an experiment in Australia.[41] The researchers, Meg Oaten and Ken Cheng, provided coaching for several forms of self-improvement. Some students were given membership in a gym and help with drawing up a fitness program. Another group was coached to improve their study habits. Others worked on their money management by drawing up a budget and keeping track of what they spent. All of the students came back to the lab from time to time for an exercise that seemed irrelevant to their self-improvement programs. They had to identify patterns on a computer screen while using self-control to avoid a nearby distraction (a video of a comedy routine playing on a television). As the weeks went by, the students got progressively better at ignoring the temptation of the comedy routine. They also made progress toward their various goals. Those in the fitness program got fitter; those working on study discipline got more schoolwork done; the people in the money-management program saved more money.

But—and here was a truly pleasant surprise—they also got better at other things. The students who did the study-discipline program reported doing physical workouts a bit more often and cutting down on impulsive spending. Those in the fitness and money-management programs studied more diligently. Exercising self-control in one area seemed to improve all areas of life. They smoked fewer cigarettes and drank less alcohol. They kept their homes cleaner. They washed dishes instead of leaving them stacked in the sink, and did their laundry more often. They procrastinated less. They did their work and chores instead of watching television or hanging out with friends first.

By strengthening the willpower muscle, they achieved that Victorian goal of building character. The Victorians have a reputation for repression—and they could be quite odd about sex—but they knew that self-control is a form of liberation. That's why it's the quintessential human virtue. By being able to resist immediate impulses, you are free to plan for your own future—and to live in a society where your neighbors are free to plan theirs.

### The Free Society and Its Friends

As psychologists were identifying the benefits of self-control, anthropologists and neuroscientists were trying to understand how it evolved. The human brain is distinguished by large and elaborate frontal lobes, giving us what was long assumed to be the crucial evolutionary advantage: the intelligence to solve problems in the environment. After all, a brainier animal could presumably survive and reproduce better than a dumb one. But big brains also require lots of energy. The adult human brain makes up 2 percent of the body but consumes more than 20 percent of its energy. Extra gray matter is useful only if it enables an animal to get enough extra calories to power it, and scientists didn't understand how the brain was paying for itself. What, exactly, made ever-larger brains with their powerful frontal lobes spread through the gene pool?

One early explanation for the large brain involved bananas and other calorie-rich fruits. Animals that graze on grass don't need to do a lot of thinking about where to find their next meal. But a tree that had perfectly ripe bananas a week ago may be picked clean today or may have only unappealing, squishy brown fruits left. A banana eater needs a bigger brain to remember where the ripe stuff is, and the brain could be powered by all the calories in the bananas, so the "fruit-seeking brain theory" made lots of sense—but only in theory. The anthropologist Robin Dunbar found no support for it when he surveyed the brains and diets of different animals. Brain size did not correlate with the type of food.

Dunbar eventually concluded that the large brain did not evolve to deal with the physical environment, but rather with something even more crucial to survival: social life.[42] Animals with bigger brains had larger and more complex social networks. That suggested a new way to understand Homo sapiens. Humans are the primates who have the largest frontal lobes because we have the largest social groups, and that's apparently why we have the most need for self-control. We tend to think of willpower as a force for personal betterment—adhering to a diet, getting work done on time, going out to jog, quitting smoking—but that's probably not the primary reason it evolved so fully in our ancestors.

Primates are social beings who have to control themselves in order to get along with the rest of the group. They depend on one another for the food they need to survive. When the food is shared, often it's the biggest and strongest male who gets first choice in what to eat, with the others waiting their turns according to status. For animals to survive in such a group without getting beaten up, they must restrain their urge to eat immediately. Chimpanzees and monkeys couldn't get through meals peacefully if they had squirrel-sized brains. They might expend more calories in fighting than they'd consume at the meal.

Although other primates have the mental power to exhibit some rudimentary etiquette at dinner, their self-control is still quite puny by human standards. Experts surmise that the smartest nonhuman primates can mentally project perhaps twenty minutes into the future—long enough to let the alpha male eat, but not long enough for much planning beyond dinner.[43] (Some animals, like squirrels, instinctively bury food and retrieve it later, but these are programmed behaviors, not conscious savings plans.) In one experiment, when monkeys were fed only once a day, at noon, they never learned to save food for the future. Even though they could take as much as they wanted during the noon feeding, they would simply eat their fill, either ignoring the rest or wasting it by getting into food fights with one another. They'd wake up famished every morning because it never occurred to them to stash some of their lunch away for an evening snack or breakfast.

Humans know better thanks to the large brain that developed in our Homo ancestors two million years ago. Much of self-control operates unconsciously. At a business lunch, you don't have to consciously restrain yourself from eating meat off your boss's plate. Your unconscious brain continuously helps you avoid social disaster, and it operates in so many subtly powerful ways that some psychologists have come to view it as the real boss. This infatuation with unconscious processes stems from a fundamental mistake made by researchers who keep slicing behavior into thinner and briefer units, identifying reactions that occur too quickly for the conscious mind to be directing. If you look at the cause of some movement in a time frame measured in milliseconds, the immediate cause will be the firing of some nerve cells that connect the brain to the muscles. There is no consciousness in that process. Nobody is aware of nerve cells firing.

But the will is to be found in connecting units across time.[44] Will involves treating the current situation as part of a general pattern.[45] Smoking one cigarette will not jeopardize your health. Taking heroin once will not make you addicted. One piece of cake won't make you fat, and skipping one assignment won't ruin your career. But in order to stay healthy and employed, you must treat (almost) every episode as a reflection of the general need to resist these temptations. That's where conscious self-control comes in, and that's why it makes the difference between success and failure in just about every aspect of life, as researchers have been reporting in study after study.

In workplaces, managers scoring high in self-control were rated more favorably by their subordinates as well as by their peers. People with good self-control seemed exceptionally good at forming and maintaining secure, satisfying attachments to other people. They were shown to be better at empathizing with others and considering things from other people's perspectives. They were more stable emotionally and less prone to anxiety, depression, paranoia, psychoticism, obsessive-compulsive behavior, eating disorders, drinking problems, and other maladies. They got angry less often, and when they did get angry, they were less likely to get aggressive, either verbally or physically. Meanwhile, people with poor self-control were likelier to hit their partners and to commit a variety of other crimes—again and again, as demonstrated by June Tangney, who worked with Baumeister to develop the self-control scale on personality tests. When she tested prisoners and then tracked them for years after their release, she found that the ones with low self-control were most likely to commit more crimes and return to prison.[46]

The strongest evidence yet was published in 2011. In a painstaking long-term study, much larger and more thorough than anything done previously, an international team of researchers tracked one thousand children in New Zealand from birth until the age of thirty-two.[47] Each child's self-control was rated in a variety of ways (through observations by researchers as well as in reports of problems from parents, teachers, and the children themselves). This produced an especially reliable measure of children's self-control, and the researchers were able to check it against an extraordinarily wide array of outcomes through adolescence and into adulthood. The children with high self-control grew up into adults who had better physical health, including lower rates of obesity, fewer sexually transmitted diseases, and even healthier teeth. (Apparently, good self-control includes brushing and flossing.) Self-control was irrelevant to adult depression, but its lack made people more prone to alcohol and drug problems.

The children with poor self-control tended to wind up poorer financially. They worked in relatively low-paying jobs, had little money in the bank, and were less likely to own a home or have money set aside for retirement. They also grew up to have more children being raised in single-parent households, presumably because they had a harder time adapting to the discipline required for a long-term relationship. The children with good self-control were much more likely to wind up in a stable marriage and raise children in a two-parent home. Last, but certainly not least, the children with poor self-control were more likely to end up in prison. Among those with the lowest levels of self-control, more than 40 percent had a criminal conviction by the age of thirty-two, compared with just 12 percent of the people who had been toward the high end of the self-control distribution in their youth.

Not surprisingly, some of those differences were correlated with intelligence and social class and race, but all those results remained significant even when those factors were taken into account. In a follow-up study, the same researchers looked at brothers and sisters from the same families so that they could compare children who grew up in similar homes. Again, over and over, the sibling with the lower self-control during childhood ended up worse off during adulthood: sicker, poorer, more likely to spend time in prison. The results couldn't have been clearer: self-control is a vital strength and key to success in life.

The rediscovery of self-control has rehabilitated some Victorian notions and caused researchers to reexamine their own "progressive" assumptions. The original Progressives, in the early twentieth century, envisioned an America guided by experts using scientific principles to mold a new kind of society. They believed the future belonged to countries that emphasized collective rather than individual responsibility. Many social scientists eagerly went along with that project—after all, they were the certified experts at shaping human behavior. They provided the rationale for Prohibition, and after that progressive reform failed, they kept on looking for new ways to regulate the rest of the country. The growing nanny state dictated which vices were legal, which temptations could be advertised, which medicines could be sold, which foods were permissible, which sugary beverages were taboo (anything over 16 ounces in New York City).

Critics of those progressive policies were dismissed as unscientific dinosaurs—or worse. Social scientists pathologized rejection of progressive goals and adherence to traditions, which they categorized as conservatism. People who believed in traditional notions of individual responsibility were at best naïfs and at worst oppressors. Psychologists reported that those they identified as conservatives were authoritarian, unscientific, dogmatic, and hostile to new ideas.[48] Their emphasis on the individual over the collective was considered a strategy for preserving their status in the hierarchy. In 2004, when researchers noticed that conservative students got higher grades in economics classes than liberals did, the explanation seemed obvious: conservatives were preserving their privileged social positions.[49] "Academic disciplines which are more likely to provide students with future access to social and economic power tend to favor individuals who hold attitudes that strengthen the existing societal order," the researchers wrote. They couldn't explain exactly how the conservative students were getting higher grades, but it was clear that economics departments were perpetuating the oppressive class system in America by "creating a differential advantage for individuals who can be expected to maintain a system of group-based social hierarchy."

A decade later, some other social scientists took another look at the differences between conservative and liberal students.[50] This time, instead of theorizing about the racist patriarchy, they tested the students' ability to concentrate on mental tasks. It turned out that the conservative students had better self-control than did the liberals, a finding that offers a much more direct explanation for their higher grades. It also helps explain their conservative political beliefs. Those with faith in individual self-control don't automatically look to the state for protection, either for themselves or for their neighbors. Instead, they concentrate on their own self-discipline by using the same basic strategies employed by Thomas Jefferson and Ben Franklin.

The first step in improving self-control is to set a goal, which sounds simple enough. But just about all of us suffer from what psychologists call the "planning fallacy": we routinely underestimate how long a job will take. A project typically takes twice as long as predicted, and often longer. That's why people will often set more goals for the week than they could possibly accomplish all month. You're better off choosing a few important goals—perhaps only one for the week—and then carefully keeping track of your progress. Monitoring your progress toward a goal is just as important as setting the goal. It's essential to any kind of self-control. If you want to cut your spending, keep track of it every week. If you want to lose weight, get on a scale every day—that's one of the few clinically proven ways for taking off pounds.[51]

Another essential strategy, what Baumeister calls "playing offense," emerged from a study tracking self-disciplined people throughout the day.[52] The researchers expected to see them frequently using their strong willpower to conquer temptations. But it turned out these disciplined people actually used willpower *less* often than average. The researchers were puzzled until they figured out these people's secret: they structured their lives to minimize temptations. They stayed away from all-you-can-eat buffets. They didn't keep bowls of candy on their desks or gallons of ice cream in their freezers. If they wanted to focus on a project, they turned off their email notifications. They conserved their limited supply of willpower so that it was available for emergencies and important decisions. They played offense, not defense, and they flourished as a result.

Willpower is vital to any kind of personal success, but ultimately self-control is about much more than self-help. Of all the benefits that have been demonstrated in Baumeister's experiments, one of the most heartening is this: people with stronger willpower are more altruistic.[53] They're more likely to donate to charity, to do volunteer work, and to offer their own homes as shelter to someone with no place to go. Willpower evolved because it was essential for our ancestors to get along with the rest of the clan, and it's still serving that purpose today. Inner discipline still leads to outer kindness.

The Founding Fathers' conception of individual liberty may seem quaint to those clamoring for the state to protect the weak-willed populace from new menaces and temptations. But the rediscovery of willpower offers an alternative vision: a society in which individuals have the brains and the strength to deal with new problems. Our willpower has made us the most adaptable creatures on the planet, and we're rediscovering how to use it for our mutual benefit. We're learning, once again, that willpower is the virtue that sets our species apart, and that sets each of us free.

# 3

## Life in the Nanny State: How Welfare Impacts Those Who Receive It

*By Lisa Conyers*

*What is life like when responsibility for one's own well being has been taken over by the state? How much liberty does one enjoy when subjected to drug testing, controls on alcohol consumption, or compulsory maternity tests? What happens to the pursuit of happiness when that pursuit is largely dictated by bureaucratic imperatives? Lisa Conyers is director of policy studies for the DKT Liberty Project and co-author with Phil Harvey of* The Human Cost of Welfare: How the System Hurts the People It's Supposed to Help (*Santa Barbara: Praeger, 2016*), *for which she interviewed welfare professionals and men and women on welfare across the United States on the streets, in laundromats, shelters, bus stations, homeless tent cities, and on Indian reservations.*

In the late 1980s and the early 1990s, and again from 2012 through 2014, I traveled the United States interviewing a wide sampling of people who were dependent on means-tested public assistance programs, also known as "welfare." I wanted to know whether depending on welfare had an impact on recipients' freedom to pursue happiness, and whether removing responsibility for earning one's keep changed people's perceptions of their lives. Was it possible, I wondered, to be happy without contributing to one's own sustenance?

And what about that crucial relationship between freedom and responsibility—what happens when people give up their freedom in exchange for a life controlled by faceless bureaucracies? Does their sense of personal responsibility fall by the wayside? Do they lose sight of what freedom feels like, and what it means?

Of course, life on welfare is not free of responsibilities, including those required to qualify and re-qualify for the various federal, state, and local programs that provide public assistance. But this is not meaningful work that adds to recipients' wealth, skills, or self-respect.

As I was learning about the links between welfare and work, and freedom and happiness, what surprised me most were the many things I discovered about how the welfare system backfires—actually harming the people it is supposed to help. It turns out that the most enervating aspects of welfare dependency include the fact that the system tends to keep people poor (and sometimes makes them poorer), and that it often makes work a losing proposition instead of a reward. But the most moving tragedy, to me, is the toll dependency takes on one's feelings of self-worth and dignity, and the consequent sense of having lost control of one's own life and destiny.

What follows is some of what I learned on the road about the many ways usurping people's responsibility for their own welfare and making them dependent on government affects those who become dependent. First, though, here's a brief look at how Americans came to have such an expansive welfare state, and how it works for those trapped in it.

## A Brief History of the Welfare State

In the early 1960s, before President Lyndon Johnson launched his "War on Poverty," Americans spent 6.1 percent of their GDP on means-tested social welfare;[54] today, Americans spend close to 14.5 percent.[55] In 1965, when the poverty war was launched, 20 percent of the population—roughly 39 million Americans—lived in poverty.[56] Today a smaller proportion of Americans, 14 percent, are classified as poor; a significant improvement, but that still leaves 44 million Americans in poverty.[57] Further, about $700 billion of our $3.5 trillion federal budget is spent on programs for the poor.[58] Means-tested welfare payments cost the average taxpayer $10,000 a year.[59] One in five Americans now relies on at least one form of public assistance, with 46 million Americans, almost one in six, on food stamps alone.[60]

Johnson's War on Poverty required a definition of poverty to determine who would qualify for benefits. Since 1965, poverty has been defined as living at or below a federally defined "poverty line." The calculation of that number is provided by the Department of Health and Human Services and represents three times the annual cost of an adequate American diet. In other words, you live in poverty if your income is three times or less than the annual cost of an average adequate American diet.[61] That formula has not changed in fifty years. In 1965, that poverty line was $2,000 ($11,600 today in inflation-adjusted dollars per annum).[62] And the poverty line for a single person in 2015 is about the same: $11,770.[63] Until 2008, as long as your income was at or below this poverty line, you were considered poor, and could qualify for benefits.

But in 2008, with the passage of the American Recovery and Reinvestment Act (ARRA, the federal response to the 2008 recession) billions of federal dollars were injected into the US economy on the theory that it was necessary to stave off a full-blown depression. Part of that act extended social welfare benefits to people earning—in some cases—as much as 400 percent of the poverty baseline.[64] The result was an enormous uptick in social welfare spending. America's welfare programs now serve not only the poor, but the middle class as well.

In a recent *National Affairs* magazine article, Daniel Armor and Sonia Sousa write:

Today, more than half of the benefits allocated through programs we think of as "anti-poverty" efforts actually go to people above the poverty line as defined by the US Census Bureau. As a result, our poverty programs—once justified and defended as a safety net for Americans truly in need—exist, increasingly, to make life more comfortable for the middle class.[65]

Meanwhile, those in deep poverty, defined as living on an income of 50 percent or less of the poverty line, have seen the value of their benefits decrease in the last five years. So while the middle class is now benefitting from programs designed to help the poor, those most in need of help are getting less of it.[66]

One thing that has changed positively for those below the poverty line is that their lives have become less materially deprived. A majority of poor households now have microwaves, a car, cable television, and many have air-conditioning and/or personal computers; a far cry from the destitution portrayed in the famous 1964 *Time* magazine article about poverty in Appalachia[67] that was credited with inspiring Johnson to launch the War on Poverty. Those in poverty are certainly less destitute than were the poor of the past; people are clearly materially better off, whether from income transfers or simply the fact of rising prosperity. But poverty rates remain stubbornly high. As Michael Tanner at the Cato Institute remarked recently:

> The poverty rate has been effectively flat for almost fifty years, suggesting that the welfare system has done little to increase self-sufficiency among the poor. In essence, our welfare programs are not fighting poverty by helping people escape to the middle class through work and education; the programs are merely making the terrible situation of living in poverty more endurable. We are throwing these people a life preserver to keep them afloat, but not pulling them into the boat. We are effectively creating and perpetuating a dependent class.[68]

In other words, we have made poverty less uncomfortable for the poor—a worthy achievement—but we're not solving the problem.

### How Welfare Works

One of the first things our welfare system does is make people poorer so that they may qualify for benefits. Qualifying for benefits means spending down assets and savings, and that includes vehicles, which is especially problematic. The ability to move around, make appointments and keep them—much of our daily lives revolves around transportation, predominantly the personal automobile, and yet we make car ownership difficult for those who seek welfare.

"When I went in to apply for food stamps, I had to give them all my bank statements, pay stubs, information on my savings, my bills, my car—every asset I had, every penny had to be disclosed," said Ken. He's a thirty-year-old cook in a suburban strip mall outside Los Angeles who is serving me lunch on Saturday morning. Business is slow, so he settles in for a chat, leaning across the counter, wiping stray crumbs onto the floor.

"I had a car; it wasn't anything fancy, but it was worth about $4,000, and they told me I couldn't have the car and qualify for food stamps. The total value of the assets I could own was $2,000. I had to sell the car, live on the proceeds, and once those were gone then I would qualify. They want you coming in there completely destitute—you can't build up savings, you have to live hand to mouth. That's the deal."

Ken's experience is not unusual. In order to qualify for welfare benefits, applicants must disclose all their assets. Social workers then apply a means test to determine whether applicants are poor enough to meet the criteria to qualify for assistance. Fair enough. We don't want to give money to people who have money; we want to help the poor. But the consequence of that is the system makes people poorer than they already are. They cannot hold on to savings or physical assets worth more than a certain amount; they must dispose of assets that they could otherwise use as collateral for loans or emergency safety nets. This means that they lose control of their own personal backup plan; the government is now the default safety net.

One hot September evening in the Bronx I interviewed Shauna, a young mother of two. We were sitting at a bus stop across the street from a children's playground. We watched adolescent boys chase each other around the jungle gym in the dusk, showing surprising agility given that the burned-out street lights had left the park with only ambient light from passing cars and the buildings across the street. Their shouts got quieter as darkness fell, and eventually they left for home.

Shauna sat waiting for her bus, and she told me of her experience when her grandfather died and left her his car. "It was a Cadillac, and worth about $8,000. Unfortunately, he left it to just me, with the understanding that I'd share it with my sisters—but that doesn't work. In the eyes of the welfare office, I had an asset worth $8,000 and that was going to disqualify me from benefits—I was going to lose my housing voucher, Medicaid, food stamps, cash assistance . . . all of it."

Instead, she and her sisters sold the car and split the proceeds. A car, which could have provided them all with transportation to schools and jobs and trainings, and could have been used to get other relatives to doctor's appointments and other errands, was instead sold, the profits distributed and spent, all so that the welfare office would continue their benefits. "I don't know, maybe that's right, but what it felt like was I was about to get a little freedom, a little step up, and they didn't like that idea, they wanted to keep me right where they had me. So here I am, at the bus stop, waiting for the bus that'll take me an hour to get home. That car would have taken me ten minutes."

The system took away what could have been a tool to gain some self-control and maybe even get out of poverty—a tool to look for a new job in a wider geographic area, or expand the job search to include jobs that require cars. The system made Ken and Shauna poorer.

It is worth noting that some US welfare programs have recently begun to allow an exemption for a personal vehicle or in some cases have raised the allowable value, but not all have done so. As a result, while owning a car might be permissible while receiving benefits from one program, car ownership may disqualify recipients for other programs, and navigating those rules is complicated at best. Once having qualified for assistance, welfare recipients are required to regularly re-qualify. This is a good thing if we are trying to make judicious use of our welfare dollars and make sure only the needy get help. But this one-size-fits-all approach can have burdensome consequences.

One mother in Seattle, whose five children are all on assistance, remarked recently, "Every time I go in to the office there's another form I gotta do, and another, and another. Then I gotta go 'cross town to another office, then they gotta have my baby's birth certificate for something. You know, they got all these computers in there, and I know it wouldn't be that hard to just put me in there once and call it good, but instead I'm just running around in circles trying to make sure I do everything I'm supposed to do."

Asked about work prospects, she rolls her eyes and says, "How you gonna look for a job when at least two to three times a month you gotta be over there, spending hours in line, waiting for your turn to find out what you gotta do next? What boss is gonna let you off work for that?"

If the stakes weren't so high, the regulations wouldn't seem so onerous, but failing to comply with any rule can lead to a loss of benefits, which in turn means going to the back of the line and re-applying, often with a lag in benefits in between. For those on the bottom end of the economic ladder, a month or two without benefits can be catastrophic.

Those who participate most heavily in welfare have the most to lose. If a beneficiary crosses the asset or income line, he or she may lose all benefits at once. That's commonly known as the "welfare cliff," and it's what keeps many mothers from pursuing work. Imagine a young single mother with two children. She is unemployed. She lives in housing paid for by Section 8 housing vouchers; her utilities are paid for with utility subsidies; her medical needs are covered by Medicaid; she gets formula and health supplements for herself through the Women, Infants, and Children program known as WIC; she gets food stamps. If that woman were to suddenly fall off the welfare rolls, she would have to earn close to $40,000 a year in order to replace the value of the benefits she would lose. That becomes an incentive not to work; the risk of losing the benefits is too great. Employment thus becomes, instead of a path out of poverty, a risk to her and her family's wellbeing.

Janie, a mother of three in Chicago, described it this way: "I went in to tell my social worker I was going to take a part-time job and she told me, 'Oh, no, no, no, you can't take that job. If you do you'll lose everything—your housing, your benefits. It's best you stay home.' People say they don't want us on welfare, but they make it so if you get a job and start trying to work your way out they pull the rug out from under you. You can't win."

And this welfare cliff affects the low-income employed as well. One nurse I met, working in a migrant and community health center in rural Washington, explained her situation this way: "I just got offered a nursing supervisor position. It would be great for my career for me to take it. But I can't, because right now, I qualify for public housing because of my low income and number of kids. And I'll lose that if I earn any more money. And I'll lose our subsidized health care and our food stamps. I did the math, and the raise isn't going to cover the value of those benefits." In her case, improving her career was too risky and was going to cost her money.

Keith, a young man I met in New Orleans who was working two part-time jobs, describes his experience when he accidentally broke a food stamp rule. "My aunts asked me what I wanted for Christmas one year, and I told them I'd just lost a roommate, who had stuck me with the utility bills. I asked if instead of buying me stuff they'd just pay the bills, so in that month they paid my utilities and got me caught up. Well, the next month I had to go re-qualify for food stamps, and I told the social worker what had happened."

He paused, took a deep breath, and went on: "I know. I get it. They are just doing their jobs. But what happened is they took away my food stamps; they said the gift was income, that I needed to declare it, and the amount of the gift took me over the income limit. And, on top of that, I had to give back my food stamp money from the previous month, and it took me three months to get back on. I guess it makes sense, but it sure made a mess of my finances." In Keith's case, he was doing the best he could; holding down two part-time jobs, always on the lookout for another, and the food stamps were just enough to make sure he could eat decently most of the time. For those without other income, bumps in the road like that can become sinkholes that trap them in deeper poverty, and make it even harder to escape.

Dora, a young mother in Georgia I met while I was observing a job-training program at a local welfare office, had just been told she couldn't participate anymore because she had been diagnosed with a rare and usually fatal illness, "I wish I could just walk in there and say, 'Here, take your welfare, I don't need it no more.' I want my babies to see me as a proud black mama, working, bringing in the money. I hate them seeing me getting that welfare check every month. My doctor says I can't work, and now they say I can't be in this program, but I'm planning to cut hair in my house, until I'm too sick to keep doing it. Hopefully, by then, I'll have earned enough to get off welfare. It will have to be under the table, because they say I can't work, and I know that is breaking the rules, but I just want the day to come when I can walk in and say to my social worker, 'No thanks; I don't need you anymore. I'm good. I got this.' That will be the day I get my self-esteem back, and can hold my head up again and be proud. I just hope I don't die first."

## Health Costs of Social Welfare Programs

Having no work to do means boredom, and often depression, alcohol, and drugs. While many of those on welfare keep busy, many do not. Several mothers I met at a local park in Harlem described what they do all day. "We hang out with our friends. We eat. We drink," one said. "Then we hang out some more."

Added another, "I'd rather be working, I know that. I get so bored sometimes I start making work for myself, washing clothes that don't need washing, doing my babies' hair up into silly hairdos." Work at a job means, at the very least, doing things that need doing.

Of those I interviewed, a strong majority smoked cigarettes; alcohol use and abuse were common, and many admitted to using drugs. "I smoke cigarettes, and drink, and smoke pot, sure," said Julie. "Why not? This living on the welfare check business is a dead-end road; this way I don't have to think about it too much. Get high, and the day goes by faster and with less stress. I've been selling my food stamps for awhile now, since I can get plenty of food at the shelter. It's crappy tobacco, crappy liquor, crappy pot, but it's better than nothing."

"I go to work high every day," reported Sam, a young man on food stamps who works two part-time jobs and still can't quite make ends meet. "That way I don't stress about it."

It's possible to have some sympathy with such attitudes. Life on welfare can be very hard. For all of those reasons—low self-esteem, constant fear of losing benefits, resentment of a patronizing system that controls their lives—welfare recipients are often desperately unhappy. That they seek a few moments of pleasure or escape, perhaps even joy, seems not only natural but perhaps necessary.

But stories of illicit drug use, expectedly, create backlash. At least thirty-six state legislatures had begun considering laws for mandatory drug testing for welfare recipients by 2011.[69] Florida has gone so far as to require applicants to pay for their own drug tests; those who pass are reimbursed the $40 fee.[70]

Those laws, and many others making their way through state legislatures, are billed as attempts to more effectively target limited resources where they are needed most. Proponents argue that such laws are needed to insure that money from the public coffers is used for true necessities for those in need, not luxuries. Opponents say the laws are yet another unfair intrusion into recipients' lives, holding the poor to a different standard than other Americans.

In addition to practices such as smoking, drug use, and alcohol abuse, all of which are commonplace, there are health consequences that researchers have discovered stem directly from living in poverty.

Recent studies have found that the poor suffer from higher rates of obesity,[71] die at younger ages,[72] and suffer from levels of stress that can lower their IQs.[73] Being out of work has even more drastic consequences, including an increase in suicide rates. A recent study found that during the last recession the loss of self-esteem, self-reliance, and personal dignity that comes with losing a job led thousands of people to kill themselves.[74]

## The Welfare–Work Conflict

Rebecca lives with her disabled father in a run-down hotel outside of Macon, Georgia. She and I sat on the curb outside her hotel room one August day in 2013, after having spent the day visiting food kitchens and churches to see where people go for food donations, as part of my research for a book on welfare.

Speaking in a measured voice, her hands clenched in her lap, Rebecca said, "I hate being on welfare. Hate it. I hate not having control. I grew up believing in the American Dream. If I worked hard, I'd have the house with the white picket fence, the car, the kids, money in the bank. Those dreams—gone. My dad got disabled, my mom took off, and we lost everything. He can't work much. I need to be here for him. He gets some Social Security disability. I get odd jobs on Craigslist, but we are just surviving. Not living, just surviving."

"The American Dream" and "just surviving" were phrases I heard over and over again, all over the country. Americans still believe that if they work hard enough they will achieve the dream. For many that dream is a home and car ownership, a job to pay the bills, and a family. But on welfare the dream fades away. The system creates a form of welfare inertia with beneficiaries focused relentlessly on maintaining their benefits and as a part of that focus, living in fear of earning too much money in a regular job.

As Tiffany, a young single mother in Everett, Washington, told me as we sat on a bench outside a Safeway Supermarket: "Dreams? I don't have any dreams. I used to. Used to have that picture in my head, the white picket fence, the suits, the office job, the kids . . . No, not now. I'm still around because I have a son. I have no hope. Sure, I've got housing, medical, food stamps, and it's just enough to squeak by, get through the month without being homeless and destitute. Just barely. 'Here, survive on this. Now go away, don't bother us,' that's the message I get from welfare programs. It's not about getting me OUT of poverty; it's about keeping me IN poverty."

Those on welfare resign themselves to dealing with cumbersome, redundant bureaucracy as the cost of getting assistance. I didn't meet anyone on the road who didn't have stories to tell about how dysfunctional welfare offices can be, and how difficult to deal with. For some, though, the treatment received is downright humiliating, and there is nothing quite like regular humiliation to make you feel as if you've lost control of your life.

Tanya, a single mother of four children living in a low-income neighborhood on the outskirts of Atlanta, shared this story: "The other day, I went in to my social worker's office to sign up my newborn for services. This lady, she's been my social worker since I started living on assistance. She has known me that long, and she sees me every few months for paperwork."

We sit eating lunch with her newborn infant, Jerome, lying on the couch between us. We are in the welfare office while she takes a break from her job skills training class. Tanya reaches down to rub Jerome's tummy. "This lady, Mrs. Johnson, she tells me she can't sign Jerome up until I get a DNA test to prove he's mine. 'What?' I say. 'You've seen me in here through the whole pregnancy, I was in here a week before I delivered, remember? How could this not be my baby?' 'Doesn't matter,' she says. 'You want welfare for him, you gotta prove he's yours.' So we both had to go across town to the lab to get blood drawn; Jerome cried for hours; and I felt like a criminal."

The caseworker was enforcing a rule that says that all babies must get a DNA test to prove maternity, and possibly paternity if paternity is contested. There may occasionally be fraudulent use of borrowed babies to cheat the welfare system, but a one-size-fits-all approach, which any federal program must maintain, can be hugely humiliating when dealing with people you personally know.

## Work and Happiness

Taking responsibility for ourselves brings meaning to our lives. Moreover, productive work is essential to human happiness. Work gives our lives meaning, not just because we bring home a paycheck, but because we take responsibility for ourselves and get to experience the joys that work—even hard work—brings.

Studies at Santa Clara University's Center for Applied Ethics (2012)[75] and Arizona State University's School of Public Affairs (2011)[76] came to similar and strong conclusions concerning welfare dependence, work, and happiness based on their findings about what happened to the Subjective Well Being (SWB) of single mothers after the 1996 welfare reforms.

Those sweeping reforms, as you may remember, were agreed upon by President Clinton and Congress and were supposed to "end welfare as we know it." Back then, the Aid to Families with Dependent Children (AFDC) program had enabled increasing numbers of young single mothers (and others) to slide easily into a life of welfare without working, and the reforms addressed that problem. The new Temporary Assistance for Needy Families (TANF) program that replaced AFDC required everybody receiving cash assistance to work or train for work; its benefits had a lifetime limit of five years and it resulted in millions of women moving into work and out of poverty.

Comparing data from the years before and after such "workfare" reforms, both studies found that single mothers reported higher levels of subjective well-being after they entered the workforce. Chris Herbst's study at Arizona State concluded that the reforms had mostly positive effects: "These women experienced an increase in life satisfaction, greater optimism about the future, and more financial satisfaction."[77] Herbst also provides indirect evidence that "the mothers' employment after welfare reform can plausibly explain the gains in subjective well-being."[78] Similarly, John Ifcher's report on the Santa Clara University study concluded that results "appear to indicate that the package of welfare and tax policy changes [requiring work] increased happiness."[79] Even relatively menial work, it seems, made these single mothers happier.

These two studies were rigorously executed and they addressed the most notably dependent members of our society—single mothers on Temporary Assistance for Needy Families (TANF). By definition, those women need financial help to meet life's basic necessities for themselves and their children. If they are happier adding the demands of working to their lives, it seems likely that other economically dependent Americans will be happier working as well.

"I don't know if it's happiness," said Cora, a teacher and tribal member I met on the Pine Ridge Indian Reservation in South Dakota. "I just know that something happens to people when they get a job. They sit up straighter. Their chin comes up. They carry themselves with pride. They say hello to me in the supermarket. I know everyone on this reservation, and I can tell when someone is working, because they'll greet me at the store, and brag on what they are doing with their lives."

When governments take responsibility for our welfare, they constrict our freedom of action and generate a cascade of negative consequences. Letting the government control our lives is a recipe for a host of problems, including loss of self-esteem, loss of pride and dignity, loss of aim and focus, and loss of hope. When our lives are dominated by an outside entity rather than by our own wills, the results can be dire. And clearly those most dependent on the state for their sustenance suffer most of all.

Many have forgotten that long before the War on Poverty

of the 1960s, way back in the 1930s, in response to the Great Depression, President Roosevelt launched a massive jobs and welfare program, putting those unemployed and destitute onto federal jobs and make-work programs, and doling out food aid and assistance. In his second inaugural address he spoke to the unintended consequences of those programs. Today, with our vastly expanded welfare state affecting more and more Americans every year, his words should give us pause:

> A large proportion of these unemployed and their dependents have been forced on the relief rolls.... We have here a human as well as an economic problem.... The lessons of history... show conclusively that continued dependence upon relief induces a spiritual and moral disintegration fundamentally destructive to the national fiber. To dole out relief in this way is to administer a narcotic, a subtle destroyer of the human spirit.... The Federal Government must and shall quit this business of relief.... We must preserve not only the bodies of the unemployed from destitution but also their self-respect, their self-reliance, and courage and determination.[80]

So what does work? Work works. One Southern Ute tribal member remembers losing his job. "We went on the assistance for a few months, but I told my wife we either find jobs here on the reservation or we leave. And we left, moved away, got jobs, and later started our own business. I could feel my pride go, and I didn't want to become *that* person. I'm a worker, I have to be able to look back on my life and be proud of the life I built for my wife and my family."

Being needed gives us stature and importance. Parents of young children are needed, for sure, and we may be faced with imperative demands to fulfill needs of other family members or friends. But work also means we are needed. That paycheck is proof of it. One Decatur mother put it this way. "I remember that first paycheck when I went back to work like it was yesterday. One hundred seventy seven dollars. Not much, right? But it was mine, and I took it home and showed it to the kids and it made me feel good inside. My kids, they need so many things—diapers, toys, shoes, clothes. And they need me to provide for them, and it gives me a lot of pride to do that instead of them seeing mama cashing welfare checks."

"I'd rather be able to find enough work to pay my own way all the way. What man wouldn't?" said Ken in Atlanta. "Pay the rent, pay the bills, AND buy food. But I can't find a full-time job so I'm stuck with the food stamps. Every time I go into that welfare office I get treated like dirt by those old ladies in there, and I can't say nothing back to them. I can't wait till I can pay all my bills all on my own."

When I met Rosie in New York City, she told me: "I have to work or I'd go crazy." Homeless and living on the streets of Brooklyn, she continues to string jobs together, under the table. "As long as I can keep busy, then I'm happy," she said.

And Terry, who currently lives in a homeless tent city in Seattle, offered these observations: "When I worked I definitely looked down on all those people on welfare with their food stamps and their hand-me-downs. Then I became that person in the checkout line with the food stamps. I'm the one who is homeless. I'm the one who is taking socks from the church ladies that stop by. Self-esteem? Gone. I would much rather be working, at any job, than living the way I live right now. I know I'll never be a medical tech again, but I'd be happy working at McDonalds. Happy to be working."

As Warren Buffet began in a recent editorial in the *Wall Street Journal*, "The American Dream promises that a combination of education, hard work, and good behavior can move any citizen from humble beginnings to at least reasonable success. And for many, that promise has been fulfilled." But, he goes on to say, "In recent decades, our country's rising tide has not lifted the boats of the poor." Noting that some of this can be blamed on our shift to a knowledge economy he nonetheless argues, and I agree, that the Earned Income Tax Credit (a tax credit for the poor which essentially tops off workers' wages at a certain income level by giving them rebates on their taxes if their income falls below a certain level) should be expanded so that, as he puts it, "America will deliver a decent life for anyone willing to work."[81] I agree; work should never be a risk, it should always be a reward, and anyone contemplating the choice between going on welfare or working (or working part-time) should have an incentive to choose work.

Welfare doesn't end poverty. Work does. And with work comes identity, pride, self-esteem, self-control, and yes, happiness. As I learned from the many Americans I interviewed, the fleeting feelings of security and safety to be had by turning over our lives and destiny to the government pale in comparison to the feelings of freedom and control we experience when we take full responsibility for our lives. As those Americans taught me, the alternative—the lost autonomy and loss of responsibility that comes with government oversight and control—is ultimately destructive to the human spirit.

# 4

# Does Consumer Irrationality
# Justify the War on Drugs?

*By Jeffrey Miron*

*If people are sometimes irrational, or some people are habitually irrational, does it follow that freedom of choice should be overridden by state control? What are the consequences of prohibiting mind-altering substances such as alcohol, narcotics, or nicotine? Is crime caused by drug use, or by prohibition? What are the health consequences for both rational and irrational people of prohibition? Jeffrey Miron is senior lecturer and director of undergraduate studies in the department of economics at Harvard University and director of economic studies at the Cato Institute.*

When—if ever—is state control of individual decisions better than self-control?

In the rational consumer model, the answer is never. That paradigm assumes that consumers know their own preferences, possess all relevant information, process that information correctly, and make consistent decisions over time. Government interference with individual choices—the substitution of state control for self-control—can therefore only harm individuals, who would make optimal decisions on their own.

The rational model has a long history. Many economists still view that model as one useful approach to positive and normative questions. Other economists and non-economists, however, believe many consumers are not fully rational. Their alternative assessment arises both from casual observation of human behavior and from experimental research in behavioral economics and psychology that appears to challenge the rational consumer model.[82]

If consumers are not fully rational, the case for self-control rather than state control might seem less compelling. Government interference would not automatically reduce the well-being of non-rational consumers, since those non-rational consumers might be making sub-optimal decisions on their own behalf.

I argue, however, that consumer irrationality strengthens, rather than weakens, the case for self-control. I make that argument in the context of the "War on Drugs"—the US government's century-long attempt to eliminate marijuana, cocaine, heroin, and other intoxicating or mind-altering substances. If consumers are rational about drug use, prohibition makes them worse off. If consumers are not necessarily rational, prohibition might prevent some "bad" decisions to use drugs unnecessarily, so prohibition may seem worth considering.

As I will explain, however, the War on Drugs is still bad policy—indeed, it's an even worse policy if some consumers are non-rational. Prohibition might deter some ill-advised drug use, but its overall consequences harm irrational consumers more than rational consumers. Self-control as the approach to drugs might not be perfect, but state control is almost certainly worse.

## A Framework for Debating the War on Drugs

Before discussing how consumer rationality affects the merits of prohibition versus legalization, I present what economists call a "positive" analysis of prohibition, meaning one that describes prohibition's effects without addressing whether prohibition is desirable overall.

Prohibition does not eliminate the market for drugs. Evidence from the study of drugs, alcohol, gambling, prostitution, and other services and commodities demonstrates that markets persist even under strongly enforced prohibitions. Instead of eliminating drug markets, prohibition drives drug markets underground.[83]

Prohibition may, however, reduce drug use relative to legalization. On the demand side, prohibition imposes penalties for possession, and some consumers might abstain out of "respect for the law." Others might abstain because of the fear of being caught and punished. On the supply side, prohibition raises production and distribution costs since suppliers must invest resources to avoid detection by law enforcement; that implies higher prices and less use.[84] The net impact of those demand- and supply-side impacts, however, need not be large. Prohibition might spur demand by adding a "forbidden fruit" quality to drugs; if they're forbidden, they must be really good, some seem to think. Because they operate in secret, black market suppliers face lower costs of evading tax and regulatory burdens, which offsets some prohibition-induced secrecy costs. And differences in drug sellers' ability to advertise, the payoffs from advertising, and the extent of market power under prohibition versus legalization might also limit prohibition's impact on use.[85]

Existing evidence indeed suggests that prohibition's impact on use is modest.[86] That holds across different drugs and alcohol and across countries and time periods. The evidence on this question is incomplete, since few societies have moved from prohibition to full legalization, but many have moderated their prohibitions substantially. Those "de-escalations" are associated with small or almost undetectable increases in use. Regardless of the impact on use, moreover, prohibition has numerous unintended effects.

Prohibition increases violent crime. Legal market participants resolve disputes using courts and related non-violent mechanisms. Black market participants use violence instead, since complaining to authorities would reveal their identities and activities and since courts do not enforce contracts involving illegal goods. Relatedly, legal suppliers compete for market share via advertising, but black market suppliers rely on violent turf battles.

Substantial evidence confirms that prohibition generates violence.[87] The use of violence to resolve disputes is common in drug and prostitution markets, as it was in gambling markets before the advent of state-run lotteries and the expansion of legalized gambling during past decades. Over the past century, violence has increased and decreased with the enforcement of drug and alcohol prohibition, as illustrated in Figure 1.[88] Across countries, violence is elevated especially in countries that grow and ship illegal drugs such as cocaine and heroin.[89]

Prohibition also encourages income-generating crime such as theft or prostitution, since prohibition-induced increases in drug prices mean users need additional income to purchase drugs.[90] Prohibition diverts criminal justice resources from deterrence of all kinds of crime.[91]

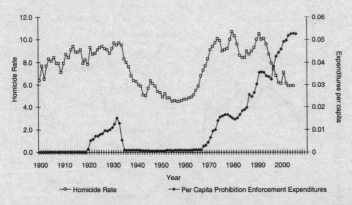

Fig. 1 Expenditures on prohibitions per capita and homicides per 100,000: 1900 to 2006

*Sources:* Homicide rate from FBI UCR (various years). Projected prohibition enforcement expenditures based on Miron (1999) with data from the Budget of the United States Government (various years).

That conclusion—that prohibition causes crime—contrasts with the claim advanced by prohibitionists that drug use causes crime. Little evidence, however, confirms the claim that drug use per se promotes violence or other criminal behavior.[92]

Prohibition also lowers product quality and reliability. In legal markets, consumers who purchase faulty goods can punish suppliers via liability claims, bad publicity, avoiding repeat purchases, or complaining to private or government watchdog groups. In black markets, those mechanisms are unavailable or ineffective, so prohibition causes accidental overdoses and poisonings.[93] US alcohol prohibition provides a classic example, since deaths from adulterated alcohol soared; see Figure 2.[94] Similarly, marijuana users were sickened in the 1970s after the US government sprayed the herbicide paraquat on Mexican marijuana fields but the marijuana was still harvested and shipped to US consumers.[95]

Prohibition generates corruption. In legal markets, participants have little incentive to bribe law enforcement, and they have legal mechanisms such as lobbying or campaign contributions for influencing politicians. In black markets, participants must either evade law enforcement or pay them to look the other way. Similarly, standard lobbying techniques are more difficult.[96]

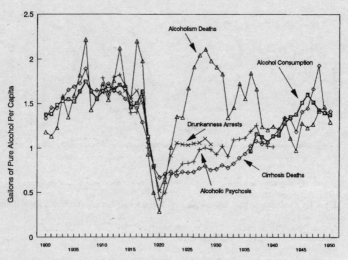

**Figure 2. Estimated Gallons of Pure Alcohol Consumed Per Capita**

The graph displays data on measured alcohol consumption per capita for the non-Prohibition years along with estimated alcohol consumption per capita for all years. The estimates come from regressions of each proxy series (e.g., the cirrhosis death rate) on a constant, a linear trend, and actual alcohol consumption per capita. The data graphed are then the implied values of alcohol consumption per capita for all years implied by inverting the estimated regression to estimate alcohol consumption for the Prohibition years based on the proxy and the estimated relation between the proxy and alcohol consumption. The estimation and inversion procedure converts the units of each proxy into units of gallons of alcohol consumption per capita.

Prohibition enriches those most willing to violate society's laws. In a legal market, the income from drug production and sale is taxed, and the revenue affects everyone via lower other taxes or higher government spending. In a black market, suppliers capture that revenue as profit. Existing estimates suggest that federal, state, and local governments could collect roughly $50 billion per year from legalized drugs.[97]

Prohibition has additional adverse consequences. Because drug crimes involve mutually beneficial exchange, participants do not report them to police, who therefore rely on undercover buys-and-busts, asset seizures, no-knock warrants, stop-and-frisk,

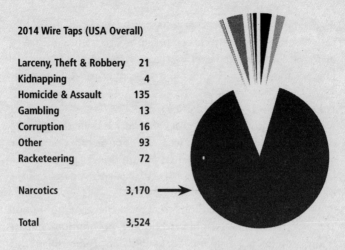

**2014 Wire Taps (USA Overall)**

| | |
|---|---|
| Larceny, Theft & Robbery | 21 |
| Kidnapping | 4 |
| Homicide & Assault | 135 |
| Gambling | 13 |
| Corruption | 16 |
| Other | 93 |
| Racketeering | 72 |
| | |
| Narcotics | 3,170 |
| | |
| Total | 3,524 |

Figure 3. Major Offenses for Which Court-Authorized Intercepts (Wiretaps) Were Granted, 2014 (source: uscourts.gov)

and racial profiling, all of which strain accepted notions of civil liberty.[98] More broadly, the drug war has fueled a broad range of privacy-invading law enforcement tactics, such as domestic wiretaps.[99] (See Figure 3) Because of prohibition, many state governments ban over-the-counter sale of clean syringes, which increases needle-sharing and thus promotes the spread of HIV and other blood-borne diseases.[100] Because of prohibition, marijuana is more tightly controlled than morphine or cocaine and cannot be used for medical purposes.[101] Similarly, doctors face loss of their medical licenses or even jail time for "excess" opiate prescribing, which encourages under-treatment of chronic pain.[102] Prohibition means that foreign policy and free trade negotiations are intertwined with decisions about drug policy.[103] Widespread non-compliance with prohibition, despite draconian enforcement, signals users and non-users that laws are for suckers, undermining the spirit of voluntary compliance that is essential to a free society. And expenditure on police, judges, prosecutors, and prisons to enforce prohibition, summed across all levels of government, totals about $50 billion per year in the United States alone.[104]

To summarize, prohibition may reduce drug use relative to

legalization. But whether that reduction is large or small, prohibition has many other effects compared to legalization, including increased crime, reduced health, greater corruption, diminished civil liberties, foregone tax revenues, and substantial expenditure costs.

## Is Prohibition Desirable Policy?

With that positive analysis as background, I ask whether prohibition is a good policy. This is what economists call a normative analysis: one that asks whether prohibition is preferable to legalization, taking as given a particular positive analysis of the differences between the two policies.

The positive analysis indicates that most effects of prohibition are undesirable. The possible exception is prohibition's impact, if any, in reducing drug use. So, analysis of prohibition versus legalization might appear to turn on how policy should regard that potential reduction and thus on whether consumers make rational decisions about drugs. In fact, the right normative conclusion does not rest on whether consumers are rational.

If all consumers are assumed to be fully rational, then normative analysis of drug prohibition is trivial.[105] In that case, prohibition's effects are all undesirable, since any reduction in use would be a cost, not a benefit, of prohibition. In particular, under full rationality it would not matter whether people consume drugs for the psychopharmacological effects, or the medicinal properties, or to look cool; all that matters would be that consumers voluntarily choose to use drugs. Similarly, under that view, it does not matter whether drugs are addictive or if use negatively affects health or productivity; if rational people choose to accept such risks, they must think the benefits exceed the costs.

The rational model of consumption was long believed to be inconsistent with many observed behaviors related to drug consumption, such as addiction, withdrawal, relapse, and the like. Theoretical work by Gary Becker and Kevin Murphy shows the rational model is potentially consistent with those phenomena, and empirical work has had some success in fitting the model to data.[106] That work does not prove that the rational model describes all drug consumption, but it undermines the presumption that drug use is irrational. Stated differently, it is hard to deny that at least some drug use fits the rational model. Many people claim to enjoy the pleasure associated with marijuana consumption; others value the pain relief or mental calm produced by opiates; still others appreciate the stimulation of cocaine, much as others appreciate the stimulation of caffeine. Thus, at least some drug use is plausibly rational, implying prohibition-induced reductions are a cost of prohibition.

If some consumers make irrational decisions about drug use, prohibition might generate one benefit: preventing such consumers from using drugs. While the harms from drug consumption are often exaggerated, some decisions to use drugs may indeed be ill-advised.[107] That's possible for any good, but the risks may be greater for potentially addictive goods that carry non-trivial health risks. For example, short-sighted consumers might ignore the possibility of addiction and underestimate any associated health risks. A policy that prevents such consumers from trying drugs could, in principle, make them better off.[108]

This argument for prohibition might seem plausible, but further inspection exposes deep flaws. Even if irrationality is rampant and even if policy can prevent irrational drug use, the question for any proposed policy is not just whether it generates benefits but whether these outweigh the policy's costs. So any benefit from policy-induced reductions in irrational drug use must be weighed against the costs of the policy used to achieve that reduction. One potentially large cost is any policy-induced reduction in rational drug use, but there are many others, as well.

The evidence is robust that prohibition has numerous adverse side effects, such as increased crime and corruption, greater HIV infection, diminished civil liberties, forgone tax revenues, and significant direct costs for police, judges, prosecutors, and prisons. Plus, prohibition does not appear to have substantial impacts in reducing drug use. And while hard data are not available, it is plausible that rational users are the ones most likely deterred by prohibition, while irrational consumers ignore prohibition. So it is almost inconceivable that the one possible benefit of prohibition could plausibly exceed its costs. Even if irrationality warrants policies to reduce drug use, prohibition is almost certainly the worst choice among such policies.

Beyond those concerns, the harms from drug use are not only routinely exaggerated but are also not obviously different from those of legal goods such as alcohol, tobacco, saturated fat, and more; indeed, the currently legal substances are the ones whose long-term side effects cause serious illness or death (e.g., cirrhosis, lung cancer, emphysema, heart disease). Yet outlawing marijuana, heroin, cocaine, and other illegal drugs suggests those goods are unacceptably "bad" while legal goods such as alcohol and tobacco are at least "tolerable." Further, policy-induced reductions in irrational drug consumption might induce substitution toward the legal goods that have similar or even more harmful effects.

Perhaps most importantly, prohibition almost certainly harms irrational users more than rational users, given that many irrational users consume anyway. Prohibition means that users must purchase from criminals who are likely to victimize them, often in dangerous neighborhoods. Prohibition means users face not just health risks but also arrest, loss of professional licenses and eligibility for student loans, and more. Prohibition means users face heightened difficulty in assessing the quality of the drugs they purchase, since in underground markets, consumers cannot sue sellers of manufacturers for faulty products, or complain to government watchdog groups, or consistently patronize sellers with reputations for quality, or generate bad publicity for purveyors of adulterated or mislabeled products; thus, prohibition generates increased accidental overdoses and poisonings. Prohibition raises production and selling costs, and therefore also drug prices,[109] so users face elevated incentives to consume via unsafe ingestion methods, such as needle-sharing, and therefore face a greater risk of HIV and hepatitis.

All those negative effects of prohibition harm both rational and irrational consumers, but rational users are more likely to recognize the risks and adjust their behavior to minimize the adverse impacts. To minimize risk of arrest, rational consumers will grow their own marijuana or buy other drugs from known, repeat suppliers. To avoid the risks of impurities, rational consumers will again purchase from reliable suppliers, or try small doses initially, or avoid illegal drugs and substitute legally available and thus reliable alcohol instead. Rational consumers will avoid sharing needles, either ingesting via other methods or substituting other drugs, or they will be more successful in obtaining clean syringes from legal and illegal connections.

Prohibition may also harm irrational consumers by glamorizing drug use in the eyes of those too young, naive, foolish, or myopic to consider the long-term consequences; rational users discount such imagery. Under prohibition, the monetary rewards for working in the drug trade are high, but this is merely compensation for an elevated risk of injury, death, and imprisonment. Rational persons understand that and accept such risks only if the total compensation equals that available in other sectors. Myopic teenagers, on the other hand, focus on the up-front cash and thus expose themselves to excess risk of death or prison. Prohibition suggests to less rational parents that policy can prevent youth drug use; rational parents realize that prohibition has minor impacts on availability, so they must still intervene to protect their children from foolish choices and dangerous influences.

Thus while prohibition may prevent some users from consuming drugs in the first place, prohibition makes use more dangerous and costly for those who consume despite prohibition, and those negative effects are far worse for irrational consumers. And since prohibition's overall impact on use appears modest, it's unlikely that the benefit from reduced irrational use could plausibly outweigh the increased negatives for those who use despite prohibition.

## Conclusion

In comparing self-control to state control the conclusion applies broadly. In many contexts, some consumers make poor decisions, but state control is a blunt instrument for improving those decisions. Rational consumers understand the implications of government policies and can therefore adjust their behavior to moderate the impact. Irrational consumers, however, may respond in ways that make their irrationality more costly. Self-control is not always perfect; nothing guarantees that all individuals make good decisions about their own well being all of the time. But substituting state control for self-control generally yields far worse outcomes; that approach imposes sub-optimal choices on rational individuals and creates perverse incentives that harm precisely the irrational individuals the state control is attempting to protect.

# 5

# Responsibility and the Environment

*By Lynne Kiesling*

*Is responsibility just a faculty of individual self-control, or are there social institutions that assist people in acting responsibly? What institutions and social and legal rules induce people to act responsibly, to consider the long-term consequences of their behavior, and to take into account the impact of their acts on others? Examination of the means used to protect endangered birds of prey helps us understand how the institution of property enables humans to act responsibly. Lynn Kiesling is associate professor of instruction in economics at Northwestern University; her most recent book (co-edited) is* Institutions, Innovation, and Industrialization: Essays in Economic History and Development *(Princeton: Princeton University Press, 2015).*

## Introduction

Our actions often have impacts not only on ourselves, but also on other people. Indeed, they can have impacts not only on other people, but on other species and on the environment itself. Humans have evolved a variety of means of encouraging people to take into account the effects of their behavior on others, known as "externalities" in economics. They include fear of retribution, benefits in repeat games, and norms of care, shame, and sanctity. They also include social institutions that lead people to "internalize" those "externalities," that is, to take into account the effect of their actions on others.

Let's consider a case of behavior regarding an "environmental amenity." Rosalie Edge took action when she saw Richard Pough's photos (taken in 1932) of row upon row of dead birds of prey, killed for sport and money at Hawk Mountain in eastern Pennsylvania. A wildlife conservation activist, Edge saw the threat of extinction facing birds of prey that most humans thought of as expendable vermin because they killed and ate chickens. Thinking of raptors as vermin led to a wildlife policy in many states of paying sportsmen bounties for them; in the 1930s, for example, the Pennsylvania Game Commission paid a $5 per-bird bounty on birds of prey, including the goshawk and the great horned owl. In the Great Depression such a bounty was a welcome income supplement, while also reducing the threat to domesticated animals. Hawk Mountain was a fertile waypoint in the seasonal migration path of many species, thus the name.

In 1934 Edge leased 1,400 acres of land on Hawk Mountain and hired a warden to prevent hunters from shooting birds of prey on that land.[110] Shooting on the land stopped. Edge raised the money to purchase the land, and in 1938 gave the land to the newly created Hawk Mountain Sanctuary Association.[111] The premise was simple: buy the land to ensure control of its use and dedicate its natural resources to wildlife habitat. Over the ensuing decades understanding of the interconnections in complex ecosystems and attitudes toward birds of prey evolved, and initiatives like Hawk Mountain Sanctuary contributed to the revival of many raptor species. Today Hawk Mountain is the world's oldest wildlife sanctuary dedicated to the preservation and observation of birds of prey. It remains privately owned, funded, and operated as a membership-supported conservation organization.

Hawk Mountain provides a vivid example of how property rights affect behavior; in this case, behavior regarding the environment. Imagine how property owners control the use of their land, with barbed-wire fences and signs saying "No Hunting. No Fishing. No Trespassing." If they were to find someone on their land hunting, fishing, or trespassing, they could file a civil lawsuit against them under the common law, and if found guilty, the violators would have to pay monetary damages to the property owner to compensate them for the lost value of the wildlife, fish, or game. If a neighbor were to dump trash or pour toxic sludge onto the owner's land or into the owner's river, stream, or lake, the one causing the harm could be held responsible for the harm. Property rights allow us to be held accountable—responsible—for our behavior. Property rights that are defined and enforced well enough create incentives to maintain environmental quality in the present and for the future, aligning economic and environmental interests across time, space, and uses. Property rights help humans balance the inevitable tradeoff between use and stewardship. They help humans to incorporate into their decision making the wider effects of their actions. They make people attentive and responsible to the interests of others.

## What Are Property Rights?

Property rights are the rights to determine the use and disposal of a resource. If you own a pair of shoes, you decide how to use them—wear them, let them lay idle in your closet, loan them to a sibling, rent them out, or sell them. You also decide on maintenance and upkeep, and when they are worn out and need to be replaced.

According to David Hume, property rights as an institution encompass three elements: stability of possession, transference by mutual consent, and performance of promises.[112] Hume argued that property rights as an institution emerge in societies to enable individuals to coordinate their actions to mutual benefit, and the modern literature on property rights follows Hume's argument. Enforcement of property rights can be formal (common law, contract, legislation that leads to regulation) or informal (conventions, custom, social norms), or both; custom historically has led to law, which is codified in the common law framework in countries such as the United Kingdom and the United States.

Ownership means decision-making authority over how a resource is used, and in many cases those uses can be distinguished as separable and those rights can be transferred separately. Consider owning a piece of land with a cabin on it (e.g., use for house and/or plants, loan, rent, idle). Legal institutions matter too; suppose this land and cabin are in Montana, where state law allows property owners to sell or lease the subsurface rights separately from the surface rights. Being able to separate that right out and transfer it enables the owner to profit from leasing drilling rights to another party that wants to explore for oil or natural gas.

Environmental problems are generally conflicting claims over resources and how they are used. Property rights help to resolve those conflicts by providing a legal institution that prioritizes particular uses—the uses that the owner prioritizes, in the time frame that the owner chooses. For some environmental problems, such as chemical pollution in a self-contained lake, individual ownership of the land that includes the lake is likely to give the owner incentives to maintain the lake's quality, either for his/her own consumption value or because pollution would reduce the market value of the property. Not all environmental problems are that straightforward, though, because defining and enforcing property rights can be costly or even not feasible. That's when the tragedy of the commons becomes an all-too-common phenomenon.

Garrett Hardin famously characterized overgrazing of common pastures in medieval villages as a "tragedy of the commons."[113] In a village with a fixed amount of pasture, if the residents treat the pasture as an open-access resource and allow anyone to graze as many animals as they choose, each person has an incentive to graze another animal as long as the additional individual benefit is above zero. But a pasture has a carrying capacity, or maximum herd size it can nourish, so every additional animal beyond that carrying capacity reduces the food consumed by the other animals below what they need to thrive, even though the benefit to the individual is positive (but less than optimal). Open access amounts to an absence of property rights and leads to overgrazing, erosion, and undernourished livestock. Hardin proposed an alternative: privatize the commons, or define private property rights by dividing up the pasture and having each villager own a plot of land. In this context, though, privatizing the commons is not desirable, because it would have destroyed the economies of scale and risk-spreading that the villagers could exploit through scattered-strip and three-field rotation agriculture. Hardin generalized from this example to modern situations of air and water pollution, in which air and water are open-access resources that are degraded or destroyed because of an inability to define property rights. He concluded that the only feasible alternative was public ownership, nationalizing the commons since it can't be privatized.

Building on Hardin and the economist Ronald Coase,[114] Elinor Ostrom constructed a way of analyzing institutional frameworks in common-pool resources (CPRs) that is valuable for understanding how property rights benefit the environment, even when they cannot be fully defined.[115] Ostrom took Hardin's binary open access/pure private model and expanded it by observing that pure private property is extremely rare; in fact, most of the conditions in which we own property are not really pure private property at all. Instead of thinking of property rights as a dichotomy between open access and pure private, think of property rights as a continuum, and along that continuum are degrees of commons.

Pure private property might be something like your contact lenses, which you and only you own and use and dispose of. But what about that pair of shoes discussed above? If you lend them to a sibling, you create a use right for your sibling, probably complete with (more or less specified) rules about returning them to you in the same condition. Imagine also the possibility that you and your sibling chip in and buy the pair of shoes together to share—the shoes are not pure private property for either one of you, and rules you establish for who gets to wear them when and how to treat them are an example of what Ostrom calls "governing the commons."

Imagine another type of CPR along the continuum: a park with a beach. If it's a municipal park, those in city government can decide whether to charge a user fee for the beach and limit access to those who have purchased access, or treat it as an open-access CPR for all to use. The park is a CPR that is more "commonslike" than the shared pair of shoes. Finally, consider the example of air quality. Defining who owns air and privatizing air is so prohibitively costly that it is not feasible, so air is closer to the open access end of the continuum.

Ostrom's insights were profound. First, it is possible to define and enforce use rights even where property rights cannot be defined well. Second, sometimes the characteristics of a resource make it harder to define property rights, but the decision of whether or not to define use rights is more often a political choice. In cases like CPRs, where people either cannot define property rights or choose not to, they can devise institutions for governing their shared use of the CPR. Those institutions involve specifying use rights, indicating who has use rights, and committing some resources to monitoring and enforcement. Through bottom-up institutional design within communities, Ostrom found investment and sustainable use of resources in communities that defined and enforced use rights within the community, enabling community members to earn increased profits and to thrive over time. Her work shows the role that property rights and use rights can play in sustainable resource use.

## Why Do Property Rights Align Economic and Environmental Incentives?

The coordination that property rights facilitate is economically and socially beneficial. With Hume's three conditions a property owner can be confident that even if s/he is not currently using or inhabiting the property, it will not be taken or used without consent, and if it is, the violator will be required to pay the owner compensation for harm. Those conditions and that degree of relative certainty create a context in which people will produce, invest, innovate, and conserve because the connections between their actions and those benefits and costs over time are clearer.

Better definition of property rights changes time horizons and incentives to think about future outcomes, aligning economic and environmental incentives over time and space, and inducing short-run conservation to enable sustainable longer-run economic gain. Institutional choice affects those incentives and shapes how well property rights are defined and how much into the future people are willing to look in making tradeoffs.

Take the example of the park and beach and whether or not to limit access and charge a user fee. One municipality limits access, the other does not, and that choice affects the quality of the beach, the resources available to maintain it, and the degree of congestion or overuse of the beach. That comparison is not hypothetical—in my own backyard, the city of Chicago does not restrict beach access, while the adjoining suburb of Evanston does, and the two beaches do differ in quality and congestion. Whether the resource is beaches or irrigation systems or air, institutional choice matters.

Note that property rights may not work perfectly to align economic and environmental incentives across time and space, or to mitigate the problems of diffuse private knowledge. Realistically, though, other alternative institutions that we design and use for environmental regulation do not work perfectly either—command-and-control regulation or community self-governance will not achieve perfection. Thus when evaluating the performance of the three different institutional approaches (property rights, community self governance of a CPR, or command-and-control government regulation), it is imperative to compare the likely, realistic effects of the enforcement institutions to each other, not the theoretical or "blackboard" conception of them. It is unrealistic to compare an ideal system of bureaucratic control with a realistic system of regulation by property rights, just as it would be an unjust comparison to compare a realistic bureaucratic regulatory scheme with an idealized property rights alternative and then find the bureaucratic regime inferior. For that reason environmental policy analysis does, and should, require substantial field work that involves social science as much as environmental science.

### Property-Based Environmental Policy in Action

Some of the most effective environmental policies of the past two decades have used those insights to align economic and environmental incentives more closely while avoiding the pitfalls of command-and-control regulation. One notable example in the United States is the Environmental Protection Agency's Acid Rain Program, which created a program of tradable emission permits for the right to emit sulfur dioxide (most from burning bituminous coal to generate electricity).

The effect of this program was unequivocal. In the first year, emissions declined by 25 percent below 1990 levels and by more than 35 percent below 1980 levels. By 2000, emissions were nearly 40 percent below those of 1980. Under the command-and-control approach used before the 1990 amendments, abatement costs would have been more than three times as high—$2.6 billion annually as compared to $747 million under cap-and-trade.[116]

Fisheries provide another example where a property rights approach yields sustainable outcomes unattainable with traditional command-and-control regulation. Ill-defined property rights in fishing created a tragedy of the commons, with overfishing for many species by the 1980s. Traditional regulation led to shrinking of fishing seasons for many species, going from several months to two or three days in a year.[117] A different method of regulation, individual fishing quotas (IFQs, or catch shares), defines a fisher's right to a share of the total allowable catch (TAC), and that right is itself transferable, which makes the IFQ an asset.

IFQs are attractive for two main reasons. First, each quota holder faces greater certainty that his or her share of the TAC will not be caught by someone else ... Second, transferability allows quotas to be reallocated through sales so that they are eventually owned by the most efficient fishermen, that is, those with the lowest costs or highest quality and hence highest-valued catch.[118]

Fisheries using IFQs in places ranging from Iceland to New Zealand have seen fish populations stabilize and even grow along with fishing incomes.

A controversial application of property rights has been implemented in places such as Botswana that use community ownership and hunting rights for wildlife preservation. A policy that defines rights over wildlife as belonging to villagers makes the wildlife an asset—they profit from preserving the wildlife for safaris and ecotourism (and for hunting tourism, where they determine the hunting licenses). That profit induces them to discourage and prosecute poachers. One example of the success of this policy is the rebound in the white rhinoceros population in Botswana compared to the decline in wildlife populations in countries such as Kenya that use traditional anti-poaching regulation to little effect.[119]

## Conclusion

Property rights are consistent with beneficial economic and environmental outcomes because private property promotes good stewardship. But defining and enforcing property rights are costly activities, so even if pure private property rights were feasible, we would not have them in most cases. Property rights need not be perfect in order to be useful at coordinating the actions of individuals and creating incentives that are compatible with sustainability.

In some cases defining property rights is not feasible, and most cases of environmental pollution or degradation are a consequence of either an inability or a political unwillingness to define and/ or enforce property rights. Through collective action ranging from community self-governance to statutory legislation, legal institutions emerge and are designed that help us define and enforce use rights in the CPR, leading to valuable economic and environmental outcomes.

Property rights provide an imperfect, yet powerful, means of connecting behavior with responsibility and of inducing humans to take into account the impact of their actions on others when they make decisions. Property rights both protect the freedom to pursue interests and the responsibility to compensate others when their rights are harmed. They also allow people to pursue interests beyond the narrowly "selfish," such as protecting endangered birds of prey.

# 6

# First Person Singular: Literature and Individual Resistance

*By Sarah Skwire*

*Art reveals truths otherwise hidden from sight. Freedom and responsibility are sometimes best seen in action, and action is often best illustrated in poetry and stories. The struggle for recognition of one's unique identity and enforcement of one's just claims against power is a struggle for freedom and for justice. From the most ancient stories of antiquity to Shakespeare, Mark Twain, and the Hunger Games, art reveals freedom and responsibility to be inextricably entwined. To be a free person is to grasp one's unique identity and to accept responsibility for one's own acts. Sarah Skwire is a fellow at the Liberty Fund and co-author of the popular college writing textbook* Writing with a Thesis *(12th edition, Boston: Wadsorth Publishing, 2014). She earned her PhD in English at the University of Chicago.*

The poet Tom Wayman wrote that good poems mean that "a person is speaking / in a world full of people talking." The measured, individual voice of the poet—of the writer of any literature, really—and the voices of the characters who speak in their works are, as I argued in *Peace, Love, and Liberty*,[120] often some of the most effective ways of reminding ourselves that humans are not an anonymous mass built of indistinguishable and interchangeable parts.

The earliest author whose name we know is Enheduanna, a high priestess of the goddess Inanna who lived between 2285 and 2250 BCE. Among her surviving poems is "The Exaltation of Inanna" a song of praise and supplication. In it, Enheduanna details her long history of devotion to Inanna, and her current state of despair over the destruction of her rituals and her temple. But what is most striking about this poem is what the scholar Roberta Binkley has called "a strong authorial presence that may be unmatched in ancient literary creation until the time of Sappho." Enheduanna's poetry insists on her own importance. Her suffering is not just cultic, or ritual, or on behalf of her people. It is personal.

> I no longer dwell in the goodly place You established.
> Came the day, the sun scorched me
> Came the shade (of night), the South Wind overwhelmed me,
> My honey-sweet voice has become strident,
> Whatever gave me pleasure has turned into dust.
> . . . I, what am I among the living creatures!

Enheduanna's voice is the cry of an individual protesting suffering and injustice.

We hear that same cry in the Book of Job as Job protests God's treatment of him and in the book of Genesis when Abraham argues that God is behaving unjustly by destroying Sodom. But it is not only divine injustice against which our earliest stories protest. In "The Poor Man of Nippur" an Akkadian story from about 1500 BCE, the impoverished Gimil-Ninurta tries to share his only possession—a goat—with the mayor. When the mayor takes the goat and gives Gimil-Ninurta only some scraps of food and third-rate beer, Gimil-Ninurta seeks his revenge through trickery and violence, eventually disgracing the mayor and severely beating him three different times, nearly killing him. Wise or foolish, brave or brutal, Gimil-Ninurta is clearly an individual, and an individual objecting to his unjust treatment by the state.

This kind of protest, the protest of the individual against authority, should be of the greatest possible interest to lovers of liberty. Over a thousand years after "The Poor Man of Nippur," and within a hundred or so years of Job, Sophocles' play *Antigone* presents us with a heroine who refuses to allow a new law to override her religious responsibility to bury her dead brother. Instead, she slips from the city gates, performs rites for him, repeats them when the body is desecrated again, and remains staunchly unapologetic about her resistance to authority. As the arresting sentry observes, "She was not afraid, / Not even when we charged her with what she had done. / She denied nothing." Indeed, she directly confesses her crime to the ruler, tells him his strength is nothing before the gods' laws, and when condemned to death for her actions, announced that "This death of mine / Is of no importance; but if I had left my brother / Lying in death unburied, I should have suffered. / Now I do not." Antigone's defiance is on behalf of her brother's spirit, of course, but it is at least as much on behalf of her own right to practice religious rituals, and the gods' rights to have their laws observed rather than overturned by the state.

The growth of the state and its increasing reach into the private corners of the lives of citizens and subjects spurred an ever-increasing number of such stories of individual protests. Shakespeare's histories and tragedies are filled with small moments where often apparently insignificant individuals speak out for their rights and responsibilities against tyrannical rulers. The gardener's servant in *Richard II,* for example, argues that Richard's deposition from the throne is merely a sign that the king's country has followed the king's example of disorder and tyranny:

> Why should we in the compass of a pale
> Keep law and form and due proportion,
> Showing, as in a model, our firm estate,
> When our sea-walled garden, the whole land,
> Is full of weeds, her fairest flowers choked up,
> Her fruit-trees all upturned, her hedges ruin'd,
> Her knots disorder'd and her wholesome herbs
> Swarming with caterpillars?

The gardener responds Richard should have followed the gardener's example instead. "O, what pity is it / That he had not so trimm'd and dress'd his land / As we this garden!"

The servant who gives his life while fighting against the blinding of Gloucester in *King Lear*; the rebellion of Macduff against Macbeth; Paulina's confrontation of the "most unworthy and unnatural Lord," Leontes, the King of Sicily, for his domestic tyranny—all of these are moments of resistance and of bravery, of the individual spirit against the power of the state.

The modern state spurs similar protests. Dystopian novels of the mid-twentieth century written in response to the rise of various forms of collectivism frequently present precisely this sort of personalized, individual rebellion against command and control. Think of Orwell's Winston Smith hiding from the telescreen, writing in his journal, and finding tiny ways to resist Big Brother throughout *1984*. Consider Zamyatin's novel *We,* set in a society that teaches that, "... the only things that are aware of themselves and conscious of their individuality are irritated eyes, cut fingers, sore teeth. A healthy eye, finger, tooth might as well not even be there. Isn't it clear that individual consciousness is just sickness?" Amid constant attempts to eradicate individual identity, the citizens of *We,* devoid of even names, still find small ways to rebel and to insist on their autonomy—by smoking, drinking, or just loving one another. By the end of the novel, those small rebellions have added up to produce a resistance movement and to begin to crumble that wall that divides the collectivist One State from the wild lands outside of it.

For many readers, the dystopian novel that most expresses the power of individual resistance against a collectivizing, totalitarian state is Ayn Rand's *Anthem.* The society described in *Anthem* has succeeded in the project set out in Zamyatin's *We.* Individuality has been eliminated to the point that singular pronouns no longer exist. It is hard to deny the power of the moment when the female character struggles to express affection for the narrator, but lacks the words to do so.

"We love you."

But then they frowned and shook their head and looked at us helplessly.

"No," they whispered, "that is not what we wished to say."

They were silent, then they spoke slowly, and their words were halting, like the words of a child learning to speak for the first time:

"We are one . . . alone . . . and only . . . and we love you who are one . . . alone . . . and only."

We looked into each other's eyes and we knew that the breath of a miracle had touched us, and fled, and left us groping vainly.

And we felt torn, torn for some word we could not find.

Two chapters later, the rediscovery of the first person singular pronoun with the sentences, "I am. I think. I will." shatters the stifling hold of the state over the mind of the individual, and Rand's narrator knows it. "These are the words. This is the answer."

The current surge in popularity of dystopian novels and films—particularly for young adults—suggests that there is still a thirst for this kind of story of rebellious individuals standing up to an oppressive state. Today the message comes through Katniss Everdeen from *Hunger Games* instead of Winston Smith; Jonas from *The Giver* instead of Zamyatin's D-503; Lena Haloway from *Delirium* instead of the narrator of *Anthem*. It even comes from the television series *Daredevil* in this exchange between the vigilante hero Daredevil and his arch-enemy Kingpin.

Matt Murdock / Daredevil: No, no, I'm not trying to be a hero. I'm just a guy that got fed up with men like you and I decided to do something about it.

Wilson Fisk / Kingpin: That's what makes you dangerous. It's not the mask. It's not the skills. It's your ideology. The lone man who thinks he can make a difference.

The names of the heroes may change, as may the vehicles that bring us their stories. But the message that the individual has the ability to resist the state—and the responsibility to use that power—remains.

Even allowing for the power of these many representations, there is one literary example of the power of individual resistance that is, for me, the most moving. Towards the end of Mark Twain's *The Adventures of Huckleberry Finn*, Jim—the escaped slave who has been Huck's travelling companion, friend, and father figure through most of the novel—is captured. Huck knows, because he has been taught to know it, that Jim is someone else's property. Huck also knows that stealing is a sin that will send him to hell. His struggles as he tries to decide whether he should be good and sinless and tell Jim's owner where to find him, or whether he should be wicked and damnable and help Jim escape, are the most finely wrought explorations I can find of what it means to resist the power of a corrupt state and a corrupt culture.

Initially Huck resolves to write to Jim's owner. He does so, and then pauses.

> I felt good and all washed clean of sin for the first time I had ever felt so in my life, and I knowed I could pray now. But I didn't do it straight off, but laid the paper down and set there thinking—thinking how good it was all this happened so, and how near I come to being lost and going to hell. And went on thinking. And got to thinking over our trip down the river; and I see Jim before me all the time: in the day and in the night-time, sometimes moonlight, sometimes storms, and we a-floating along, talking and singing and laughing.... and then I happened to look around and see that paper.
>
> It was a close place. I took it up, and held it in my hand. I was a-trembling, because I'd got to decide, forever, betwixt two things, and I knowed it.

We hang with Huck, in the balance. He is no hero. He is no great man. He's an unschooled boy, brought up in violence, racism, and poverty. He has just done what he feels is the only good thing he has ever done. He has returned valuable property to its owner. He has done everything that everyone around him—his government, his teachers, his friends—would tell him is the right and the honest and the honorable thing to do.

And he cannot do it. He cannot make himself see the world the way that they do.

And so he tears up the note and cries out, "All right, then, I'll GO to hell."

Huck's choice to defy everything that he has been taught to believe is good and right in order to rescue a man he has been taught to believe is merely a piece of property is surely one of the greatest triumphs of the individual over the powerful compulsion of instantiated cultural and political wrongs.

Margaret Atwood's poem "Spelling" reminds us that "a word after a word / after a word is power." And she tells us—thinking perhaps of the authors before and after Enheduanna whose names we will never know, and perhaps of the nameless narrators of so much dystopian fiction—that we must learn to spell:

> your own name first,
> your first naming, your first name,
> your first word.

To use one's name, to use the first person singular, to claim it as one's right and one's responsibility, is to begin to fight for liberty.

# 7

# Rules and Order without the State

*By Philip Booth and Stephen Davies*

*Is state control the only means of regulating human interaction? Or are there are other mechanisms whereby the behavior of individuals and groups can be regulated to reduce conflict and to generate greater social coordination and harmony? Who provides the rules that regulate exchanges, and how are they enforced? History provides instructive examples of regulatory institutions without the state. It is frequently asserted as a matter of faith that some economic interactions can only be controlled by the state, but historical examination of two of the "hardest cases"—land use and financial risk—shows that non-state regulatory institutions provide regulation without either the coercion or the perverse incentives and rent-seeking of state control. Philip Booth is professor of finance, public policy, and ethics at St. Mary's University, Twickenham and research director at the Institute of Economic Affairs in London. Steve Davies is a historian and head of education at the Institute of Economic Affairs.*

That economic activity of all kinds needs to be regulated is one of those truisms that almost no one denies. Why then is there so much debate around that topic and, even more noticeably, so much confusion, with many people talking past each other? One reason, as will become clear, is a lack of attention to the evidence of economic history and lack of awareness of real-life examples. The more important reason, however, is that the very concept or basic idea of regulation is usually poorly understood and defined. To put it slightly differently, many people assume a definition of regulation that presupposes that such regulation can only be provided by one institution. That, in turn, leads much of the discussion to being framed by a false dichotomy between two alternatives: state regulation or no regulation at all.

Etymologically, if something is regulated, it takes place in a regular manner (as opposed to a random or erratic one) and is guided or constrained by rules. In other words, when applied to human interactions, it means a state of affairs where people cannot simply do whatever they want; their actions are guided by rules and the collective outcomes are the results of the interactions of the choices of individual actors constrained by those rules. That obviously raises a number of questions. In particular, what kinds of rules are needed and who or what is the originator and enforcer of the rules? Confusion over those two questions leads to avoidable misunderstandings. Human cooperation depends on rules. The content, source, and enforcement of rules are thus most important topics that deserve careful study; merely assuming that they can only be provided in one way, without further thought or study, is a serious mistake. State control of behavior is not the only option, as the following case studies show.

As far as the content and nature of the rules is concerned, it is commonly believed that they should have certain characteristics. First, the rules must be known and understood by all or most of the participants in the activities they govern (otherwise they would serve no purpose). Second, there must be institutions, mechanisms, or practices that enforce the rules. Third, there must be sanctions for breaches of the rules as well as positive payoffs for compliance. It is commonly believed that rules should be explicit and spelled out precisely in words that capture and cover all conceivable eventualities. In other words, regulations are codified rules that are written down, comprehensive, explicit, and detailed. Anything less than that, we are told, is a failure of regulation or its complete absence.

It is widely assumed that, if there are to be rules, there must be a ruler: that is, a person or institution (group of persons, in other words) that is the source of the rules. In the absence of a ruler, it is widely assumed, there would be no rules at all. The source of rules is assumed to be the government or one of its agents. If such an entity does not exist or chooses not to issue rules then, so the argument goes, there will be an absence of any rules—essentially chaos.

However, that dichotomy—of state regulation or no regulation—is a false dichotomy. There are other alternatives. Historical research shows that regulation does not always require codified, uniform, and exhaustive written rules. (Such exhaustiveness is theoretically impossible, in any case.) Nor are we limited to a choice between rules created by Hobbes's Leviathan and the lawless war-of-all-against-all of Hobbes's state of nature. The reality is that regulation in the sense described, namely, activity constrained by rules, is possible without the rules and associated enforcement institutions being directly created by the state. It is not only possible, but can be found all around us. Rules can and do arise spontaneously from the efforts of people to achieve their aims in cooperation with others. It is often (though not always) the case that government enables the emergence of such rules, but in such cases government does not actually create the rules or enforce them.

Once one begins to look for rule-governed interactions, one finds that most of human life is regulated in that way. Most rules that govern human interactions were not created by government, although government may create a general framework of the rule of law that facilitates such cooperative creation of rules and enforcement institutions.[121] Obvious examples include language, sports, and codes of social etiquette, but there are many others, as well. The process can be observed today in the emergence of rules governing Internet transactions through eBay, Etsy, and other online trading sites. There is an enormous wealth of empirical examples of non-governmental regulatory regimes in natural resource management (much of the study of those comes from the work of the late Elinor Ostrom and her students[122]).

In such cases the systems of rules typically have features that distinguish them from regulations that are created through political processes. Those that evolve are bottom-up systems in which the systems of rules arise at local levels by spontaneous and unplanned processes, even though the actions that lead to their emergence are themselves purposeful. Others are designed and are agreed to by those whom they govern. The degree of explicitness varies considerably; some incorporate very explicit rules, while others rely more on non-articulated norms. Evolved regulatory systems may vary from industry to industry or locale to locale and may lack the uniformity or standardization that is a feature of designed regimes. They often have the high degree of flexibility and variability that is associated with evolutionary processes; the system as a whole changes over time in response to changed circumstances, but does so in a piecemeal and dispersed or local way as opposed to a general and uniform one. Innovations in one place or system may be tried, found useful, and copied elsewhere, or tried, found unhelpful, and abandoned. They are often connected with wider patterns or orders of social life and their institutions. Their great strength is that they make use of dispersed and tacit or unarticulated (and often inarticulable) knowledge. It is that which accounts for their final feature: they are more effective than their designed government counterparts. (Designed non-governmental regulatory systems that are adopted by those they govern have the advantage of being voluntary and thus can be modified or discarded if they do not succeed in creating or enforcing useful rules. Examples include the rules of condominium associations, clubs, corporate bylaws, and other systems, although even those invariably incorporate many rules that were the results of evolution, rather than design.)

How can we compare the effectiveness of governmental and non-governmental systems of regulation? We can turn to economic history and the many concrete examples it gives of regulatory orders. Historical examples have the advantage in many cases of having been studied and their practices recorded and captured. Also many such regulatory orders appear at certain points in time and then are eradicated or collapse at a later time. Studying the origins and demise of such institutions helps us to understand how and under what conditions they thrive or otherwise. Such studies also correct frequent misunderstandings. Sometimes orderly states of affairs (which are highly regulated by non-governmental institutions) are presented as instances of chaos, randomness, and disorder, because they are not subject to state control.

**State Rules or Market Institutions?**

All markets are regulated, meaning that there are rules that govern them. It is frequently, but erroneously, assumed that only the state can provide the rules or the enforcement mechanisms. The interesting public policy question is not whether there should be regulation, but "who should regulate?" That question is rarely asked. In what follows we will look at two cases that are very commonly assumed to require state regulation. Our evidence will be drawn primarily from the United Kingdom (where we live), but it shows that state regulation is neither inevitable nor always necessary. The two cases on which we will focus are land use and finances.

Of course, those two "hard cases" are not unique. In many regulated spheres of life, it is not the state that provides the regulation. Consider fast food restaurants: many McDonalds outlets are owned and operated by independent investors and managers under a franchise system. To protect its brand name and assure uniform quality, McDonalds regulates in rather minute detail how they operate, what goes onto the menu, the precise ingredients, the precise prices they charge, sanitary precautions, the training of employees, and so on.

It is often assumed that the Catholic Church, because of its social teaching, is committed to high levels of state intervention and regulation. However, in its most authoritative document on such matters, it states: "Another task of the state is that of overseeing and directing the exercise of human rights in the economic sector. However, primary responsibility in this area belongs not to the state but to individuals and to the various groups and associations which make up society."[123] Over time, though, the development of state regulation in many sectors has crowded out institutions of civil society, including private regulatory institutions.

The reaction to the financial crash of 2007–2008 provides an indication of how state regulatory institutions are created and operate. In the wake of the crash, tens of thousands of pages of regulations were written and promulgated. It was estimated that the Dodd–Frank Act in the United States, with its associated regulations, would come to thirty thousand pages.[124] In 2011, some 14,200 new financial regulations were created worldwide. That trend was underway well before the financial crash. It is often asserted that there was a period of deregulation before the financial crash and that the crash was a consequence of deregulation. That is not so, certainly not in the United Kingdom. As Bank of England Chief Economist Andrew Haldane has noted: "In 1980, there was one UK regulator for roughly every 11,000 people employed in the UK financial sector. By 2011, there was one regulator for every 300 people employed in finance."[125] Indeed, if the number of people working in finance and the number of financial regulators in the United Kingdom is projected forward on the same trend from 2011 to 2060, by that date there will be more financial regulators than people working in finance—and that excludes compliance officers and others working on regulatory issues within financial firms themselves. Until very recently within the United Kingdom, responsibility for financial regulation lay with a single body, the Financial Services Authority (FSA). Now that body has had its responsibilities split. It has been calculated that four million words of financial regulation have been generated from just one of the bodies that succeeded the FSA.[126]

The evidence is quite strong that systems of state regulation have not been successful. Not only did the comprehensive systems of financial regulation that developed in the United Kingdom from 1986 and in the United States from the 1930s not prevent the financial crash, but in many ways they were contributory causes that exacerbated and spread the crisis globally.[127] Many forms of mistaken and reckless behavior that led to the failures of banks and other financial institutions in 2007–2008 were encouraged by regulation. Certainly, there is little evidence that regulators had some special insights that would have allowed them to control the behavior of participants in financial markets in beneficial ways. Governments and their regulators encouraged lending to poorly qualified borrowers; they encouraged securitization; they underwrote risky lending; and they distorted the ways in which ratings agencies rated the riskiness of the instruments that accounted for huge financial losses.[128] Paul Tucker, later appointed Deputy Governor of the Bank of England, referred to the process of securitization in a speech as late as April 2007: "So it would seem that there is a good deal to welcome in the greater dispersion of risk made possible by modern instruments, markets and institutions."[129] That statement was made just a few months before the spectacular failure of Northern Rock, an institution that was financing its lending activity through securitizations. Tucker was not necessarily wrong; indeed, he was probably right. However, we should not be confident that state regulators can predict and prevent problems arising within markets. State regulators certainly failed to anticipate the financial crisis.

It is not just that we have too much confidence in state regulators to resolve problems and perfect the world. We also neglect the role—indeed, often deny altogether the role—that private regulatory institutions can play, especially in financial markets.

In other markets, we still see many private regulatory institutions and they are making a comeback as a result of the sharing economy and the use of the Internet for the exchange of goods and services and, of great importance, for the exchange of evaluations of goods and services. They systematically outperform state regulators. For example, Visit England is a body funded by the government to promote tourism. For most of its life it has been a government body, although now it is maintained at arm's length. Whilst a government body it developed a rating system for hotels and other accommodation. If you use Visit England to look for accommodation in the popular English town of Stamford, for example, you can find just two hotels within three miles that have a specific rating, and they both have the same rating, which is not very helpful. TripAdvisor, a private rating service, on the other hand, shows about twenty properties with specific ratings, and between them they have hundreds of visitor opinions. It is difficult to imagine any justification for the maintenance of a government-connected ratings service.

In some sectors, government regulation very clearly crowds out private regulation. One could ask why there are few services such as TripAdvisor in finance. One answer to that is that financial activity is now so highly regulated, that the risks and liability of setting up such services would be enormous. In the United Kingdom, providing financial advice without authorization from a government bureau carries a prison sentence of up to two years.[130] Furthermore, the lines between providing opinion, advice, and information are so thinly drawn that nobody would dare to tread them.

It is clear that regulation can exist in many sectors without the state and that the state has forced out many non-state regulatory institutions and practices. What is perhaps more interesting is that until recently the United Kingdom had a large and thriving financial sector with very little government regulation at all. That will be the subject of one of the case studies below. But first, we take a look at a field that is commonly believed to require state regulation in all circumstances: land use and development.

## Planning without Government Planners: Housing and Development

The systems that developed spontaneously, without the state, to govern urban development in the United Kingdom from the eighteenth century are particularly illuminating. Today land development is heavily regulated by government through statutory law (the Town and Country Planning Act in the British case) and by a huge array of local government regulations (such as zoning laws in the United States and building and planning regulations in the United Kingdom). The dominant historical narrative suggests that, before the twentieth century, urban development was chaotic and that each property owner and developer could do what they wished without regard to the impact of their actions on anyone else.[131] The result, supposedly, was terrible slums, and ugly unplanned development. (A visit to such places as Bath and Bloomsbury might raise doubts about that narrative, of course.) Interestingly, the same people who advance that account also often complain about "suburban sprawl" in the United States without stopping to reflect that such "sprawl" is associated with and largely caused by governmental regulatory regimes.[132] Complaints about the ugliness and poor quality of public and private buildings produced under the pre-1948 regime in Britain are also puzzling when one considers the poor quality of so many buildings that have been produced since that time.

In fact the entire process of urban development in the eighteenth and nineteenth centuries in the United Kingdom was highly regulated, but by a non-political regulatory system. That regime of rules and institutions neither depended on nor derived from statute or government agency rule-making. The state enabled it through the existence of the court system and its enforcement of contracts, but that was as far as it went. Instead of government planning there were often detailed regulations that made use of private contracts and various common law practices. The system was flexible and responsive because it made use of price signals as they were generated by markets for land and improvements.

During that period, although there was much piecemeal and small-scale development, most of the large scale growth of towns and cities after the 1730s was done in large chunks of land. Sometimes, as in Southport or Eastbourne or Cardiff, that involved the building of an entire town. Elsewhere, as in London, Newcastle, and Edinburgh, it was the development of large areas that were parts of growing cities or towns. Sometimes a single estate owned by one landlord was developed in that way, as with the Cadogan estate in Chelsea for example. On other occasions a developer would put together a large parcel of smaller pieces of land, as in some of the developments of Thomas Cubitt.

Those developments were not randomly carried out. Even when, as was normally the case, each individual plot within the larger parcel was developed and built on by a single builder (so that one street would have each house built at a different time by a different builder) the process was governed by explicit and detailed rules. Those were effected through the use of covenants which formed perpetual and binding conditions that were a part of the original lease or sale contract for the land. They bound all subsequent owners or lessors and could be enforced either by the residuary authority of the original developer and his or her heirs or by neighbors. Some were negative and simply prohibited certain things, such as carrying on particular trades and occupations. That meant that there was quite detailed regulation of the economic use made of new buildings and of the impact of the activities of the inhabitants of any one building on their neighbors. (Thus, what we would now call externalities were controlled.) Such matters could also be dealt with through the common law of nuisance, but incorporating them into covenants attached to the act of development made the whole process much cheaper and quicker in the event of a breach of the rules, because it was simply a matter of enforcing an existing contract and there was no need to demonstrate harm or nuisance in a court of law.

Many other kinds of covenant were positive and required things such as standard heights for buildings erected on a plot, size and numbers of rooms, details of decoration and appearance, standards of construction, and the use of certain materials. Those could be, and often were, astonishingly detailed and specific; they set out requirements not just for the use of, say, stone rather than brick, but for a specific type of stone and the exact details of ornamentation, window size and shape, and the like.[133] The result was the harmonious and uniform pattern of development found in places such as Bath. The crucial point, though, was that that was not done through a political process but by interplay and contract between individual developers and customers. That meant that the actual regulations would depend on the individual developer and their situation. There was not a uniform—and hence impossibly complex or prescriptive—set of regulations for an entire district, much less the whole country.

Those private regulatory mechanisms also interacted through the market to adjust and adapt to the preferences and needs expressed through purchasing decisions by consumers. Thus, where the main demand was for luxury housing, the covenants would be extensive and detailed, whereas in places where the demand was for mass cheap housing they would be much more limited and would stipulate requirements of size and provision. The process led developers to provide and lay out the infrastructure of streets, roads, lighting and (often) water supply when they began to develop a site.[134]

In other words you had a predominantly non-state and spontaneously generated system of regulation that covered layout, building standards and materials, design, appearance, quality, usage, and safety and did so in a flexible and responsive way. Moreover, it usually led to coherent communities being created, not least because the typical pattern was for mixed use so that commercial, residential, and leisure provision would all be provided in the same area. There was a comprehensive regulatory system that was decentralized, varied, flexible, and responsive and was independent of the state. It was arguably much more effective than the state system that later replaced it.

What about the terrible slums of the Victorian era about which we read so much? Those certainly existed and they were indeed terrible, but the bleak Dickensian picture needs to be heavily qualified. The great majority of the working class did not live in slums; instead they lived in modest but, by the standards of the day, adequate housing which was within their financial means. The very lowest income groups, especially those on irregular income due to casualized labor, experienced the most serious problems. Movement of people into the older, pre-industrial areas in the centers of the cities created serious problems. Those problems were also well on the way to being resolved by the later nineteenth and early twentieth centuries with the appearance of charitable housing associations such as the Peabody Trust. Such organizations created robust and decent quality but low-cost housing where it was needed most—in the centers of large urban areas and in particular in the "recipient" or "catchment" areas.[135] They also made use of covenants to regulate the behavior of the tenants but that is another story.

What happened and why did that system not survive? It appears at first sight that the system of private regulation described broke down after 1918, most strongly during the 1930s. That decade saw the form and pattern of urban growth and development change dramatically with the appearance of what was called "ribbon development." Instead of the large, integrated developments that had featured earlier, Britain saw the building of residential property along major trunk roads leading out of the main cities. The system of mixed use—commercial, residential, and leisure— seemed to have been abandoned. The development was also of much lower density. The result was a pattern of development that was unattractive and a serious threat to the rural and semi-rural environment and its amenities. That led to the passage of the Town and Country Planning Act in 1947.

What had happened? It clearly was not due to a shortage of large parcels of land becoming available for development; the Great War (World War I) meant that such land parcels were coming on to the market at an unprecedented rate because of the number of deaths among the landowning class during the war and its immediate aftermath and the need to pay death duties. The previous system had been changed via statute in 1910, and it is tempting to blame those changes for what happened. However, the changes were too limited to account for the sudden and dramatic shift that took place. The real reason for the change was a combination of a new technology and an associated change in consumer demand, and a change in government policies that enabled the shift in development patterns.

The new technology was, of course, the motor car. That brought about a radical shift in demand because it enabled people to live a considerable distance away from their places of work. What most people wanted, it emerged, was to have urban housing and amenities in a semi-rural environment, a distance away from the workplace. That created a prisoner's dilemma and a corresponding "market failure": each individual house buyer rationally chose to buy a house built on a major trunk road, but the collective unintended outcome, which ultimately defeated their desires, was the ribbon development described earlier.

That by itself, however, was not enough to undermine the effectiveness of the private regulatory system; ribbon development would have been much more limited had it not been for another factor. Earlier, the advent of the commuter railway had led to the appearance of suburbia, but that was still built in large integrated chunks using the regulatory system described above. (The development of the Edgerton Estate in South Manchester is an example.) The critical new factor was a sudden expansion of the role of government. Before 1850, the road system in the United Kingdom had been run and maintained in large part by turnpike trusts, which were private bodies authorized by a Private Act of Parliament to maintain a stretch of road and levy tolls on it. Much of the paving of urban areas was created by developers while elsewhere it was done and maintained by Paving Trusts and Town Improvement Trusts. From the 1850s onwards both of those functions passed to the control of local authorities (borough councils and counties). Still, there was no involvement on the part of national government. Moreover, the roads of late

Victorian Britain were as quiet as they had ever been because of the domination of medium- and long-distance travel by the railways.

All that changed abruptly in the immediate aftermath of the Great War. In 1919, the Ministry of Transport was created and took over responsibility for all major roads from local authorities. Given the rapid shift to motorized transport (and the inadequacy of the road system as revealed during the war) there was a decision to invest heavily in roads. What that meant, given that those roads were supplied free at the point of use for anybody building houses along them, was that a huge part of the cost to individuals and developers of suburban living and development was now socialized and loaded on to the general taxpayer. That removed the check that had made the kind of private regulation described above function efficiently. In particular, the change created strong incentives to build housing along the "free" roads that had been provided by the state for the purpose of communication and that dictated the pattern of development. The alternative of building estates and nicely planned developments which were linked by roads paid for by the developer with the associated private planning and restrictive covenants was now relatively more expensive than relying on state provision.

The evidence of sub-urbanization linked to the development of the railways is that, if developers and, ultimately, consumers had to pay the full costs of their first choice, the pattern of ribbon development that emerged would have been much less common, and there would still have been a pattern of integrated development regulated by private contract.

What that shows is that what to the modern eye looks like chaos was actually orderly and regulated by mechanisms other than those of the state, and that such systems are vulnerable to government intervention and disruption.

## Regulation without Government Regulators: Banking and Finance

### Self-regulation of finance in the United Kingdom

Until the 1980s, beyond provision of a legal system and protection of property rights, there was very little direct government regulation of either the insurance or the banking[136] industries in the United Kingdom. Today, we have international, European Union, and national regulation of bank capital. Banks are required to hold a level of capital[137] determined through a very complex regulatory process. The capital level is set so as to reduce their likelihood of failure and, thereby, reduce the likelihood of a bank failure undermining the rest of the financial system and possibly the real economy.

In many areas of economic activity, people regulate their own behavior because they face the adverse consequences of reckless actions. Even if people or businesses do silly things, we generally allow them to do so and require them to bear the costs. In a world in which the finance system is so highly regulated, it may be difficult to imagine that that was ever the case when it came to financial institutions. But, in fact, it was. Banks did regulate and restrain their own behavior. Their behavior was also restrained by choices made by counterparties who had capital or deposits invested with the bank and who wanted to deal with responsible financial institutions.

As Capie and Wood conclude in the summary of their 2013 report, *Do We Need Regulation of Bank Capital? Some Evidence from the UK*, dealing with bank capital regulation: "An analysis of bank capital shows that they [banks] adjusted their capital ratios according to the risks that they were taking and that they were well capitalised in comparison with the standards set by regulators under the Basel I and Basel II approaches [the current international regime for statutory regulation of bank capital]. Indeed, when bank capital levels became very thin after the Second World War, banks were prevented by the Bank of England from raising more capital, despite their appeals to the Bank." Crucially, they also note: "During this long period of prudent management of the banking sector, there was no clear expectation that the state would have stepped in to save an insolvent bank in Britain."[138]

In other words, banks behaved responsibly when they were financially accountable for their own decisions. Of course, banks occasionally did fail. The Bank of England, as regulator, regarded it as its role to protect the banking system as a whole when an individual bank failed, but it would not have saved the bank itself. Certainly that approach was much more successful than the far more governmentally regulated US banking system, in which banks were fragile because they were prevented from diversifying. Between 1870 and 1979 there were no major banking crises in the United Kingdom and only two minor crises. Non-state regulatory mechanisms worked well. That system of regulation appeared to break down after the state injected systematic moral hazard into the system through state guarantees; when banks, creditors, and depositors knew that risky decisions would, at least to some extent, be underwritten by the state, increasingly risky behavior was the predictable result. That was even more evident in the United States. Central bank (ab)use of lender of the last resort facility;[139] the bailing out of bond holders; deposit insurance; the underwriting of mortgage securitization by the US government; weak bankruptcy law; and the way in which monetary policy was managed; all of that changed the risk climate within banks and changed their incentives and thus their behavior.[140] That happened to a lesser extent in the United Kingdom, although a limited degree of deposit insurance was introduced in 1979.

Other aspects of financial services were also largely free from state intervention or regulation during the period from 1870 to 1986. Again, that contrasted with the United States. In the United Kingdom, life insurance was regulated in a manner broadly consistent with freedom of contract.[141] The 1870 Life Assurance Companies Act required the publication of accounting information. That information was, in effect, released to the market via the Board of Trade (a government department). Over time, the government became slightly more involved with the analysis of that information but, for much of the period, it simply published the information and any correspondence it wished to exchange with the company. Crucially, there was also a special set of procedures for winding up life insurance companies so that, if they failed, they could be wound up safely with all creditors obtaining what was due to them.

That whole legal framework was very successful and remained more or less intact for a hundred years. The regulatory regime surrounding pension funds was also liberal and designed in the best traditions of British common law until the 1980s.

In the case of banks, pension funds, and life insurance companies, institutions evolved within the market to deal with consumer concerns. Pension funds were largely free of state control or regulation, but the assets were always held within trusts, the trustees of which had a fiduciary duty to act in the best interests of the members of the trust and to invest as a prudent person would invest. That meant that an employee was not at risk of losing his or her whole pension if his or her employer became bankrupt. Unit trusts (the UK equivalent of mutual funds) also operate using trusts for the same purpose. Within insurance markets, professions developed which would only admit members with high levels of technical expertise and who had to put their professional duties ahead of any obligations they might have had to their employers when it came to management of solvency and the general behavior of the company.[142]

It is important to note that, in the insurance and pensions industry, those professions were entirely self-regulating bodies that had no state protection and no state involvement with the setting of qualifications. Different forms of corporate ownership also evolved. Mutuals, for example, were common in both insurance and banking. They are often technically less efficient than proprietary companies.[143] However, they manage conflicts of interest between owners and customers better.[144] In both banking and insurance markets, mutuals thrived in that period of limited state regulation. In the case of the banking industry, mutual building societies developed their own system of capital regulation. As well as mutuals, 100 percent reserve deposit banks also existed. Institutions operating according to different conventions provided wider consumer choice and obviated the need for state regulation.

Moreover, accounts by contemporaries suggest that the health of insurance professions was much stronger in the United Kingdom than in the United States, where state regulation of the insurance industry was much more prominent.[145] In that environment, insolvencies of life insurance companies were very rare. There were two significant events between 1870 and 1970, and neither of those adversely affected policy holders.[146]

It is worth noting the kinds of institutions and forces at work here: responsibility exercised by owners, creditors, and customers;

the development of private regulatory organizations such as professions; and the development of special forms of corporate ownership. All were important in ensuring that markets promoted responsible behavior. Not all of those were market regulatory devices (though the professions were), but they led market participants to regulate and take responsibility for their own behavior. Market participants do not wish to lose their investments or be subject to fraud, so it is hardly surprising that markets should have developed such regulatory processes.

## Rule-making institutions in financial markets

What surprises many today is that formal regulatory institutions developed within financial markets to perform roles that, these days, are widely believed to be exclusively the responsibility and function of the state.

Orderly markets develop when individuals and corporations have to take financial responsibility for their own decisions. However, there are some situations where more formal rule-making institutions are needed. That is especially important if there are "externalities" from particular forms of market behavior. For example, if the behavior of one individual or institution undermines market confidence in other institutions or, if there are benefits from standardized terms and conditions of trading, there is a need for institutions to provide the rules for all those market participants who wish to join (and who meet the conditions that the rule-makers set).

Perhaps surprising to some, there are a number of non-state institutions within financial markets that govern the behavior of participants. The International Swaps and Derivatives Association (ISDA), for example, was established in 1985 to "make the global derivatives markets safer and more efficient." As ISDA put it: "ISDA's pioneering work in developing the ISDA Master Agreement and a wide range of related documentation materials, and in ensuring the enforceability of their netting and collateral provisions, has helped to significantly reduce credit and legal risk."[147] Stock exchanges, even given the high levels of state regulation that now exist, still provide rules and regulations in order to create orderly conditions for markets on which companies can have their shares quoted.

However, it is perhaps more interesting to examine historical examples of where private sector organizations were the only regulators of securities and derivatives markets, as was the case in the United Kingdom until as recently as 1986. It is clear that ISDA does an important job, but it might be thought that it can only do that in the context of tight government regulation. That is simply not true, as history indicates.

The world's first modern stock markets developed in Amsterdam and London in the seventeenth and eighteenth centuries.[148] Those markets provided a secure environment for trading in securities. Trading on account was possible and forward markets developed. Sometimes those markets facilitated the trading in and enforcement of contracts that were not even enforceable in national courts. In the United Kingdom, the London exchange developed rules for the trading of securities, for members of the exchange and for the companies the securities of which were traded on the exchange. By 1923, the reputation for propriety was such that the motto of the exchange became "my word is my bond." In the early stages, of course, rules were informal, though they were effective. For example, when trading on account was introduced, those who had not settled had their names chalked up on a board under the heading "lame duck." In time, rules became more formal, as did enforcement mechanisms.

In the United Kingdom, unlike in the United States, the trading of securities was more or less entirely regulated by the stock exchange—a private institution—with almost no involvement from the state until 1986. In 1986, the government effectively prohibited many of the regulations that that private body had developed and enforced and, from 1998, began to develop a highly bureaucratic system of state regulation.[149]

The first codified rule book covering topics such as default and settlement was developed by the London exchange in 1812. That rule book included provisions for settlement, arbitration, and dealing with bad debts. There were also rules about general behavior that were designed to increase transparency. At the beginning of the twentieth century, more onerous conditions were developed for companies that wanted their securities listed and traded on the exchange. Until 1986, apart from a few pieces of primary legislation, nearly all regulation of securities markets was undertaken by private institutions such as the stock exchange. Some of the rules imposed on members were onerous (and not without controversy). For example, from 1909, members were prohibited from both broking (buying shares on behalf of clients) and trading on their own book (that is taking risks and positions themselves). That reduced the likelihood of conflicts of interest but would also have reduced opportunities for members to develop their businesses.

A Royal Commission enquiry in 1877–78 illustrates the importance of those mechanisms in London's financial markets. The Royal Commission noted that the exchange's rules "had been salutary to the interests of the public" and that the exchange had acted "uprightly, honestly, and with a desire to do justice."[150] It further commented that the exchange's rules were "capable of affording relief and exercising restraint far more prompt and often satisfactory than any within the read of the courts of law." That is to say, the exchange was better able to solve problems than were the courts of law.

There was no legal requirement to deal through members of the exchange or to have shares quoted on the exchange. The London Stock Exchange did not have a monopoly. However, the exchange was perceived to use its powers in a cartelistic way. That arose from its ability to decide who was a member and how members should operate, which is vital if it is going to be effective as a regulatory body.

The exchange's most important self-regulatory powers were, in effect, removed when the government decided that they were a form of unfair restriction on trade; that happened in 1986. Ironically, the change occurred at the very time technology would probably have led to international competition between different non-state regulatory bodies which would have removed any perceived problem of restrictive practices disadvantaging other participants in financial markets. The state regulator now has the absolute power to decide who operates in financial markets and under what conditions; that is to say, the state regulator now has a total monopoly.

It is now impossible to operate in securities markets in the

United Kingdom without permission from the state regulator (even if one holds very high level academic or professional qualifications). There are, however, despite all the constraints, important areas where non-state governance still prevails. The London Stock Exchange no longer is the main determinant of rules for trading, deciding how quoted companies should behave and so on, but it does provide various mechanisms such as clearing facilities that are important for orderly and liquid markets. Furthermore, there are other bodies and markets, such as ISDA and the Alternative Investment Market (AIM), which have their own rules systems as determined by the kind of business they do. AIM, for example, is a more lightly regulated market that tends to host trading of smaller companies. Indeed, variety in regulation and adaptability to differing circumstances are two of the advantages of private regulatory institutions.

The United States evolved similar institutions, but the state actively involved itself much earlier than in the United Kingdom. In 1817, a group of people created the New York Stock and Exchange Board, which developed formal rules for trading, the paying of commissions and so on, and demanded financial guarantees from members. Indeed, arguably, its formal rule-making capacity developed earlier than that of the London exchange. The New York exchange evolved over time until after the crises of 1929–1933. In 1934, the Securities and Exchange Commission (SEC) was founded. Under that new arrangement, for quite some time, the New York exchange was allowed to regulate itself without a great deal of interference. Gradually, that changed—especially from 1975. Effectively, the exchange is now accountable to the state regulator, the SEC.[151]

State regulation is hardly necessary in investment markets, as the UK experience has demonstrated. Companies want a well-regulated exchange because regulation ensures investor confidence and more liquidity and thus leads to a lower cost of capital. The members of the exchange demand that the companies that have their shares traded are subject to certain forms of regulation because that reduces risks to members and their clients. That makes trading more attractive, thus reducing the cost to a company of raising capital, and so on. There is a symbiotic relationship.

## Conclusion

Throughout history, banks, other financial institutions and securities and derivatives markets developed their own highly effective regulatory structures. And since the regulation of securities markets in the United Kingdom was taken over by the state in 1986, it is very difficult to argue that the number of scandals has fallen. Formal exchanges are just one of many types of institutions that emerged to regulate behavior in complex financial markets. It is worth noting that regulation does not just come from formal institutions. As long as participants in financial markets bear the cost of their decision-making, they have incentives to regulate their own behavior and develop special forms of cooperation to handle conflicts of interest, financial risk, and other problems more effectively.

The same is true in land-use planning where the state's role is so ubiquitous that most people are hardly aware that it is not necessary. Some of the most highly regarded developments in the United Kingdom arose through voluntary non-state planning systems.

Voluntary non-state regulatory institutions can provide the benefits promised, but rarely delivered, by state regulatory bodies. Indeed, we are again witnessing the reemergence of such systems. New non-financial markets (such as Uber and eBay) already have a wide range of non-state regulatory mechanisms attached to them. That openness could be extended to other kinds of markets, as well. As new forms of finance develop (such as crowd-funding and peer-to-peer lending) the state could choose to step back and allow markets to coordinate borrowers and lenders, investors and entrepreneurs, in an environment where market participants and institutions provide the regulation. Those new innovations could even be clearly labeled "UNREGULATED BY THE STATE." Nobody would be excluded from financial services as existing products, channels, and services would still exist. Unfortunately, in the United Kingdom, the financial regulator has chosen to regulate those new innovations just like it regulates traditional finance.

Regulation is a desirable quality of market exchanges. The central question is, regulated by what and by whom? Markets regulated by the rule of law, rather than by detailed and minute commands and prohibitions, have existed and do exist now and thus are possible. It is time to jettison the thoughtless assumption that only the state, in the form of politicians and bureaucrats, can provide the rules, the regularity, and the oversight that can be such valuable features of cooperative ventures. Given the framework of the rule of law, it may be far wiser to let people exercise their own self-control, rather than surrendering that control to the state.

# 8

# The Welfare State and the Erosion of Responsibility

*By Nima Sanandaji*

*Do welfare states generate high degrees of trust, social cohesion, and norms of responsibility, or do they require high degrees of pre-existing trust, social cohesion, and norms of responsibility to avoid systematic social conflict and dysfunction? A study of the welfare states of the Nordic countries shows the irreplaceable role of norms of responsibility in avoiding dysfunction. The responsibility precedes the welfare state, and not the other way around. Moreover, evidence gathered over decades shows that welfare states systematically undermine the norms of responsibility and with that social trust and cohesion. Dr. Nima Sanandaji is a Swedish-based fellow of the Center for the Study of Market Reform of Education. He is the author of* Scandinavian Unexceptionalism: Culture, Markets, and the Failure of Third-Way Socialism (*London: Institute of Economic Affairs, 2015*) *and other works. He received his PhD from the Royal Institute of Technology in Stockholm.*

The "New Deal" that President Franklin D. Roosevelt presided over can be considered the birth of the American welfare state. It was those laws and executive orders that created the central institutions and programs that have formed the modern welfare state as we know it today. The architect of the American welfare state, Roosevelt, was, however, concerned about the long-term viability of the programs he had created, because he believed that welfare payments might impact societal norms.

Two years into his presidency, Roosevelt addressed the United States Congress and praised the expansion of welfare programs. During the same speech, however, he noted that many of the individuals who had lost their jobs during the Great Depression still remained unemployed. Roosevelt commented that "the burden on the federal government has grown with great rapidity." His greatest concern was not, however, the sustainability of public finances, but rather that public dependency also created a profound spiritual and moral problem. With foresight the president reached the conclusion:

> When humane considerations are concerned, Americans give them precedence. The lessons of history, confirmed by the evidence immediately before me, show conclusively that continued dependence upon relief induces a spiritual and moral disintegration fundamentally destructive to the national fiber. To dole out relief in this way is to administer a narcotic, a subtle destroyer of the human spirit. It is inimical to the dictates of sound policy. It is in violation of the traditions of America.[152]

In today's political climate, Roosevelt's view on public benefits might be denounced as quite radical. History, however, has borne out his warnings. Not only advocates of small public sectors but—perhaps even more so—proponents of large welfare states should carefully consider how policies change people's norms and behavior over the long term.

### Roosevelt's Concern

President Roosevelt's views were at the time more common than one might suppose today. In the beginning of the twentieth century even the proponents of the welfare state were worried that the build-up of welfare programs might strain the social fabric. To understand why, one must bear in mind that for the welfare state to function properly, it is not enough that most individuals follow the norm of paying taxes. Nor does it suffice that most individuals follow the norm of not overusing welfare services. Rather, for the system to be viable over the long term, the vast majority of individuals must obey both norms and must believe that others are doing the same. In other words, they must obey the social contract.

However, as transfer schemes become more generous and taxes are raised, it becomes increasingly lucrative to shift from working and paying taxes to not working (or working less) and receiving benefits. If everyone in society were to follow the norms of working and paying taxes, only relying on welfare programs when in true need, even a large system of transfers could be sustained. However, if some individuals start to defect from the norms, others are likely to follow suit. If a critical mass of people change their behavior, either by dodging taxes or overusing benefits, the erosion of welfare norms can accelerate as the social contract falls apart.[153]

This is not merely speculation based on abstract game-theoretical reasoning. Researchers Erns Fehr and Urs Fischbacher have found that legal rules and legal enforcement mechanisms typically lack effectiveness if not backed by social norms. Social norms can in this sense be seen as rules of "conditional cooperation." Critically, "defection of others is a legitimate excuse for individual defection."[154] In other words, if an individual perceives that her neighbors stick to the norm, she will be likely to follow it as well. If the neighbors begin abandoning the norms, she is likely to change her behavior as well. An erosion of the conditional cooperative foundation of a sustainable welfare state can have grave societal effects. The result can be deteriorating work ethics, increased public dependency and bitter social strife.

To further complicate the matter, it's not enough merely to implement stricter enforcement of rules to restore a sustainable system of norms. Administrative measures to control use of public programs might signal to law-abiding citizens that violations have become common. Friedrich Heinemann has studied how generous welfare systems can—over time—undermine the very norms that make those welfare systems possible. He explains that the imposition of sanctions for improper receipt or use of benefits can "be perceived as limiting citizens' self-determination and will then further crowd out the intrinsic motivation to respect the law."[155]

If society reaches a point where over usage of welfare programs becomes common practice, the deterioration of norms may prove difficult to stop. Imposing restrictive regulations or administrative measures may be inadequate to stop the erosion of norms and may in fact accelerate the process. In that light, one can better understand why President Roosevelt himself viewed doling out relief as "a narcotic, a subtle destroyer of the human spirit."

## Unintended Consequences

With time, welfare state proponents forgot Roosevelt's warning. The advocates of welfare policy grew more confident that generous government services and handouts could, in fact, be introduced, and funded by high tax rates, without the social norms that made such transfers possible being undermined in the process. However, the actual societal development showed that there was indeed reason to keep the long-term effects of welfare policy in mind. The same welfare policies that were intended to, and to some degree succeeded in, alleviating material poverty also unintentionally created persistent "social poverty." Concerns about the welfare dependency that arose in marginalized communities lead to a shift in political thinking.[156] President Ronald Reagan articulated this concern in 1986, during his radio address to the nation on welfare reform:

> From the 1950s on, poverty in America was declining. American society, an opportunity society, was doing its wonders. Economic growth was providing a ladder for millions to climb up out of poverty and into prosperity. In 1964 the famous War on Poverty was declared and a funny thing happened. Poverty, as measured by dependency, stopped shrinking and then actually began to grow worse. I guess you could say, poverty won the war. Poverty won in part because instead of helping the poor, government programs ruptured the bonds holding poor families together.[157]

President Reagan provided a textbook example of how the social capital of families can be eroded by welfare programs ostensibly intended to help them:

Perhaps the most insidious effect of welfare is its usurpation of the role of provider. In states where payments are highest, for instance, public assistance for a single mother can amount to much more than the usable income of a minimum wage job. In other words, it can pay for her to quit work. Many families are eligible for substantially higher benefits when the father is not present. What must it do to a man to know that his own children will be better off if he is never legally recognized as their father? Under existing welfare rules, a teenage girl who becomes pregnant can make herself eligible for welfare benefits that will set her up in an apartment of her own, provide medical care, and feed and clothe her. She only has to fulfill one condition—not marry or identify the father.[158]

Ronald Reagan's critique resonated with the public. Americans supported policies to limit the scope of welfare programs, with the motivation of curbing the unintended consequences of welfare dependency. Not only Republicans, but also some Democrats, supported those policies. Crucially, in 2006, President Bill Clinton signed the Personal Responsibility and Work Opportunity Reconciliation Act. He promised "to make welfare a second chance, not a way of life." In an opinion article published ten years later in the *New York Times*, Bill Clinton argued that the bipartisan legislation had indeed been successful:

The last 10 years have shown that we did in fact end welfare as we knew it, creating a new beginning for millions of Americans. In the past decade, welfare rolls have dropped substantially, from 12.2 million in 1996 to 4.5 million today. At the same time, caseloads declined by 54 percent. Sixty percent of mothers who left welfare found work, far surpassing predictions of experts.[159]

The United States is not the only nation where eroding social norms have led people to re-examine welfare programs. The same issue has been raised in many other parts of the world. Yet there has been a persistent conviction amongst the modern proponents of welfare states that it is somehow possible to create stable systems that combine high benefits and high taxes. Proponents typically point to the Nordic countries—Sweden, Norway, Denmark, and Finland—as evidence. The welfare states in this part of the world seem, at least at first glance, to have succeeded in providing extensive services and cash benefits without eroding personal responsibility. If generous welfare works in the Nordics, why not also in the rest of the world?

This issue is quite interesting for me. One reason is that I have written some twenty books and over one hundred policy reports, mainly dealing with various societal issues in Sweden and other northern European countries. Another reason is that I myself grew up in an immigrant family in Sweden, supported mainly with welfare. Thus, I have had firsthand experience of the short-term benefits that such programs provide to less-fortunate families. I have also seen the long-term disadvantages of a system that traps entire families and communities in dependency.

## The Lutheran North

The four Nordic nations—Sweden, Denmark, Finland and Norway—are often regarded by proponents of the welfare state as prime role-models whose policies should serve as models for others. *New York Times* columnist and Nobel Prize-winning trade economist Paul Krugman, for example, has written, "Every time I read someone talking about the 'collapsing welfare states of Europe,' I have this urge to take that person on a forced walking tour of Stockholm."[160] The Nordic countries are perceived by many as having successfully implemented large-scale welfare states, with generous and broad-ranging public programs, while avoiding the moral hazards associated with welfare policy.[161]

The reality is that not only policy but also culture sets this part of the world apart. The Nordic countries—and to some extent other similar northern European countries such as Germany and the Netherlands—are characterized by social norms that place unusually strong emphasis on individual responsibility and not "free riding" on the efforts of others. Religion, climate, and history all seem to have played a role in forming these unique cultures.

Over a hundred years ago, the sociologist Max Weber observed that Protestant countries in northern Europe tended to have a higher living standard, more highquality academic institutions, and overall stronger social cohesion than Catholic and Orthodox countries. Weber believed that the cause of the success of Protestant nations was to be found in a stronger "Protestant work ethic."[162] Swedish economist and welfare state researcher Assar Lindbeck later built upon that theory by considering factors other than religion. Lindbeck explains that it has historically been difficult to survive as an agriculturalist without working exceptionally hard in the hostile Nordic environment. The population therefore out of necessity generated a culture that placed great emphasis on individual responsibility and hard work.[163]

What is unique about Nordic nations is not only that they are cold, but also that throughout most of their recent history they have been dominated by independent farmers. Hard work has historically been a necessity in the cold north. The rewards of hard work also accrued to individuals and their families due to widespread private ownership of land. In addition, the homogenous Nordic societies have adopted cultures characterized by strong social cohesion and the highest levels of trust in the world.[164] A study of sixty countries by Jan Delhey and Kenneth Newton shows that the Nordic countries[165] combine all the features traditionally associated with high levels of trust. The authors write: "High trust countries are characterized by ethnic homogeneity, Protestant religious traditions, good government, wealth (gross domestic product per capita), and income equality." Delhey and Newton go on to explain, "This combination is most marked in the high-trust Nordic countries, but the same general pattern is found in the remaining 55 countries, albeit in a weaker form."[166]

**Welfare States Rely on Norms**
High levels of trust, a strong work ethic, and social cohesion are the perfect starting points for a successful economy. They are also the cornerstones of sustainable social democratic welfare policies; a pre-existing high level of social cohesion allows welfare programs and high taxes to be implemented without the same impact on work habits as such policies might have in a different

environment. Thus the Nordic countries and other parts of northern Europe have had optimal conditions for introduction of welfare state policies.[167]

The measured level of reluctance to claim government benefits without legal entitlement is referred to as "benefit morale." Benefit morale is measured through the World Value Survey, a global attitude study where respondents are asked, among other things, whether they believe that it can sometimes be justified to claim government benefits to which they are not entitled. By examining thirty-one different developed economies between the period of 1981 and 2010, Daniel Arnold demonstrated that high benefit morale reduces the incidence of absence and sick-pay entitlements.[168]

Once we realize that benefit morale affects welfare states, our understanding of modern welfare policies can be expanded. A common notion is that politicians in the United States have opted to introduce less-generous public programs, perhaps since they care little for the needs of the poor, whilst politicians in the Nordic countries have chosen a more generous route. Ideological differences are, however, not the entire truth. We must account for the fact that welfare state policies have been more suited for Nordic societies than for America. The historical evolution of current policies supports that notion. Nordic countries did introduce early welfare state projects. But Nordic Social Democrats at the time had a pragmatic approach, and were careful not to disrupt the successful small-government systems that existed at the time. Therefore the size of government remained small for a long time.

As late as 1955, the tax burden in Sweden was at the same level as in the United States (taxes amounted to 24 percent of GDP in both countries) while those in Denmark were slightly lower (23 percent of GDP).[169] When the Great Depression hit the world, politicians such as Franklin D. Roosevelt responded by introducing massive public programs, viewing state involvement as the best stimulus. Somewhat surprisingly, Nordic countries reacted differently. These trade-dependent nations were initially hit hard during the Great Depression. However, they recovered rapidly by relying on a market-oriented approach. During the crisis years, Nohab Flight engines (today known as Volvo Aero), was born. Shortly after the crisis, Securitas and SAAB were founded. A new method for creating paper pulp was invented, leading to the creation of Sunds Defibrator (today Metso Paper, a leading developer of paper industry equipment).[170]

A common myth holds that early on the United States chose a free-market path while the Nordic countries rapidly moved toward large welfare regimes. In reality, the American welfare system developed parallel to that of the Nordic countries. But there was a major difference: the American welfare system met with early criticism, precisely because the unintended consequences of deteriorating norms and family break up was so evident. In homogenous Nordics, that early criticism did not materialize—at least not on anywhere close to the same scale.

The uniquely strong norms associated with personal responsibility and work in the Nordics made those societies particularly well suited for avoiding the moral hazard of large public sectors. The Nordic cultural affinity for collectivist policies was certainly quite different from that of the American melting pot. The same reasoning can explain why northern European countries have been more successful in introducing welfare states than their southern European neighbors, which are not as exceptional when it comes to trust and ethics related to personal responsibility.

### The Chicken or the Egg?

Well before scholars had shown the link, Franklin D. Roosevelt and Ronald Reagan had the foresight to understand that norms and the viability of welfare regimes go hand in hand. The important question that arises is which way the causation points. Which did come first, the chicken or the egg? From a theoretical perspective, one could certainly argue that a generous welfare state might even *strengthen* norms such as trust and benefit morale. If the general public desires welfare policy, and knows that welfare state programs rely on norms such as widespread trust, people might act to reinforce those norms. Similarly, the state could launch various programs aimed at promoting system compliance. As is often the case with the chicken and the egg problem, it is not so easy to distinguish which factor strengthens the other. The Swedish researcher Andreas Bergh and his Danish colleague Christian

Bjørnskov apply sophisticated research methods to examine the issue, by looking at levels of trust.

As Bergh and Bjørnskov note, a long tradition in psychology indicates that a basic level of trust in strangers is instilled in individuals in early childhood. That basic sense remains relatively stable for the rest of the individual's life, if it is not disturbed by major events. Indeed, high levels of trust seem to span over generations, as they are passed from parent to child. An important observation is that the trust levels of American citizens closely follow the trust levels of the countries from which their ancestors came. And as it turns out, no group in the United States has trust levels as high as those with Nordic origins.[171] Americans of Nordic descent even have slightly higher levels of trust than their cousins who currently inhabit the Nordic countries themselves.[172] That suggests that the origin of the Nordic culture of trust pre-dates modern welfare states. After all, large-scale migration of Nordic populations to the United States occurred during the late nineteenth and early twentieth centuries, well before the shift toward large public sectors in the countries of origin.

Bergh and Bjørnskov use a number of different statistical techniques to examine historic trust levels. They reach the conclusion that historic trust levels are not caused by the welfare state itself, since such welfare states are relatively recent phenomena and the historic trust levels predate the establishment of the welfare states. The authors reach a clear conclusion: "trust is high in universal welfare states, not because welfare state universality creates trust, but because trusting populations are more likely to create and sustain large, universal welfare states."[173]

So we can, in fact, separate the egg from the chicken. High levels of trust among Nordic populations existed before the introduction of the contemporary welfare states. Additionally, the same strong norms that led to high living standards and low poverty in the Nordics thrive—even more so—in the United States. Other indicators of work ethics are not measured in the same way as trust. However, few would argue against the claim that Americans of Nordic origin also have very strong norms concerning work and individual responsibility. As a consequence, American descendants of Nordic origin in the United States today have half the poverty rate of the American national average, a pattern that has held constant for decades. Nordic Americans even have lower poverty rates than their cousins in the Nordics. It seems that Nordic norms coupled with American capitalism leads to even lower poverty than Nordic norms coupled with Nordic-style democratic socialism.[174] Lastly, the US Census shows that the individuals who identify themselves as having Nordic origins have a median yearly household income higher than the American average and also considerably higher than in the Nordic countries.[175]

This simple comparison hopefully shows the fallacy of trying to replicate a Nordic welfare state in the United States, and the mistaken belief that those policies alone will bring about the same low poverty level as in Nordic countries. If Nordic Americans already have reached the same (or in fact, higher) social success than in the Nordics, perhaps culture should also be factored in. Similarly, as Philipp Doerrenberg and his co-authors show, when it comes to taxes, the nice guy does finish last. The authors find that governments exploit groups with high relative levels of tax morale by taxing them more.[176] It is no coincidence that taxes are higher in countries with stronger tax morale. To sum up, simply copying Nordic tax policy or welfare policy will not lead to the same outcomes as in the Nordics if the cultural support for such policies is lacking.

### The Theory of the Self-Destructive Welfare State

So far, we have established that the welfare state critically relies on pre-existing norms, and that large welfare states have been implemented in countries which over the course of history have developed strong norms. But how does welfare policy in itself affect norms? What of Franklin D. Roosevelt's warning that welfare dependency is "a subtle destroyer of the human spirit"?

Previously mentioned scholar Friedrich Heinemann has studied whether Roosevelt's warning "of the moral disintegration effect of welfare dependency" is supported by evidence. The study is based on the same World Value Survey that Daniel Arnold used in his work. Heinemann examines whether benefit morale is affected in the long run by welfare policy. He reached the conclusion that a self-destructive mechanism exists in welfare states: generous welfare payments over time undermine the reluctance to over-utilize public support. That is to say, they undermine the same norms on which the welfare state rests. High rates of unemployment, which can result from policies hindering wellfunctioning labor markets, can have the same effect. Heinemann explains: "In the long-run an increase of government benefits and unemployment is associated with deteriorating welfare state ethics."[177]

The World Value Survey gives strong support for the erosion of norms in the Nordics. In the 1981–1984 survey, for example, 82 percent of Swedes and 80 percent of Norwegians agreed with the statement "claiming government benefits to which you are not entitled is never justifiable." The citizens in the two countries still had a strong ethical approach to government benefits until the 1980s. However, as the populations adjusted their cultures to new economic policies, benefit morale dropped steadily. In the 2005–2008 survey, only 56 percent of Norwegians and 61 percent of Swedes believed that it was never right to claim benefits to which they were not entitled. The 2010–2014 survey only includes Sweden out of the Nordic countries. It shows that benefit morale has continued to fall in Sweden: only 55 percent answered that it was never right to overuse benefits.[178]

### Norms Change Slowly, Over Generations
The architects of the welfare state believed that the risks of moral hazard posed by high transfer payments and high taxes could be avoided, at least in the social democratic utopias that Nordic countries were intended to be. Why was Roosevelt's warning not taken more seriously? The simple answer is that norms change slowly, even over the course of generations. When the government raises taxes or makes living on benefits more advantageous, most people continue to act as they did previously. Therefore, at least initially, it seemed that policies did not change people's behavior. But norms are not set in stone. Over time even the Nordic populations have adapted their norms to the incentives created by contemporary welfare states.

Jean-Baptiste Michau studied the link between government benefits and cultural transmissions of work ethics. He notes that parents make rational choices regarding "how much effort to exert to raise their children to work hard," based on their "expectations on the policy that will be implemented by the next generation." Therefore a significant lag should exist between the introduction of certain policies, or even a public debate regarding future policies, and changes in ethical views. Building a model with a lag between those two factors, Michau argues that generous unemployment insurance benefits can explain a substantial fraction of the history of unemployment in Europe after the Second World War.[179]

In another study, Martin Halla, Mario Lackner, and Friedrich G. Schneider conduct an empirical analysis of the dynamics of the welfare state. The authors hypothesize that individuals do not respond to changes in economic incentives right away. The reason is that individuals are constrained by social norms for some time. "Therefore, the disincentive effects may materialize only with considerable time lags." Interestingly, the authors find that a high level of public social expenditure can even have a small positive immediate impact on benefit moral. This would fit with the theory that individuals initially adjust their norms to follow the intent of public benefit programs. However, in the medium- and long-term, high levels of expenditure lead to reduced benefit morale. That is in line with the theory that individuals over time adjust their behavior to economic incentives. Halla, Lackner, and Schneider warn: "our results suggest that the welfare state is at risk to destroy its own (economic) foundation and support the hypothesis of the selfdestructive welfare state."[180]

**Even Nordic Welfare Norms Follow Roosevelt's Prediction**
The Nordic countries still today retain much of their uniquely strong norms. Yet, it is quite evident that norms have indeed deteriorated as the populations have gradually adjusted their behavior to reflect high taxes and generous welfare regimes. The theory of the self-destructive dynamics of welfare states has, to a significant degree, been developed by previously mentioned Assar Lindbeck, one of Sweden's leading modern economists. Lindbeck has stated that changes in work ethics are related to a rising dependence on welfare state institutions.[181] Additionally, he believes that the evidence of explicit benefit fraud in Sweden,

where, for example—some individuals receive unemployment benefits or sick-pay whilst working in the shadow economy—leads to a weakening of norms against overusing various benefit systems. Reforms to limit fraud are therefore necessary in order to maintain the welfare system.[182]

A number of attitude studies in Sweden show that a significant portion of the population has come to consider it acceptable to live on sickness benefits without being sick. A survey from 2001, for example, showed that 41 percent of Swedish employees believed that it was acceptable for those who were not sick but who felt stress at work to claim sickness benefit. Additionally, 44 and 48 percent respectively responded that it was acceptable to claim sickness benefits even by individuals who were not sick, if those who did so were dissatisfied with their working environment or had problems within their families.[183]

Other studies have pointed to increases in sickness absence due to sporting events. For instance, absence due to sickness increased by almost 7 percent among men at the time of the Winter Olympics in 1988, and by 16 percent in connection with TV broadcasts of the World Championship in cross-country skiing in 1987.[184] During the 2002 soccer World Cup, the increase in sickness absence among men was an astonishing 41 percent. The stark difference between the events during the end of the 1980s and the beginning of the 2000s might be seen as an indication of the deterioration of work ethics over time—though all three figures are remarkably high.[185]

During recent years, governments on both the right and the left in Sweden have reduced the generosity of the welfare system. Additionally, gate-keeping functions have been introduced, mainly in the sick-leave system to limit overutilization. Interestingly, a recent paper suggests that the reforms may need to be quite farreaching to reverse the long-term effect that the welfare state has had. Economist Martin Ljunge suggests that politicians who wish to increase the generosity of the welfare state must take into account the long-term costs of such policies. The abstract reads:

> Younger generations use sickness insurance more often than older generations. Amongst the younger generation twenty

113

percentage points more take a sick leave day compared with those born twenty years before, after other circumstances have been adjusted for. The higher demand for sick leave pay amongst the younger generations can be seen as a measure of how rapidly the welfare state affects attitudes towards the use of public benefits. The results have implications for economic policy. The demand for social insurance increases, even if the rules do not become more generous. Policy evaluations based on behavioural changes shortly before and after a reform can strongly under-estimate the long-term changes that are relevant for the financial integrity of a welfare state.[186]

Similarly, the Danish researcher Casper Hunnerup Dahl has reached the conclusion that: "The high degree of distribution in the Danish welfare state does not merely reduce the concrete incentives that some Danes have for taking a job or to work extra in the job that one already holds. Much evidence suggests that the welfare state also has a very costly and long-lasting effect on the working ethic of Danes."[187] There can be little doubt then that the erosion of norms due to longterm adaptation to welfare policy is an observable phenomenon rather than just theory.

**Nordic Policies Aim to Reverse Erosion of Norms**
For the outside world, the Nordic countries still seem today to be shining examples of how large public sectors can be created without the moral hazard of welfare states predicted famously by Roosevelt. Those who have greater insight into Nordic policies can, however, observe that much of the recent development has centered on the issue of deteriorating norms and overutilization. As stated above, reductions of the generosity of the welfare state— as well as significant tax cuts—have already been introduced in Sweden. Particular focus has been given to curbing overutilization of sick leave. The current trend in the country, where sick leave rates are again rising rapidly to high levels (although the population is amongst the healthiest in the world), suggests that more needs doing.

Sweden no longer holds the title of the nation with the highest tax rate in the world. Today Denmark holds that distinction.

Although Denmark has yet to introduce reforms as broad-ranging as those in Sweden, the realization that change is needed is strong. Somewhat surprisingly, the debate about how welfare policies have created overuse of and entrapment in the benefit systems has not been limited to the conservatives or libertarians in Denmark. The Social Democrats have joined in. Bjarne Corydon, at the time the country's Social Democrat finance minister, made international headlines in 2013 by discussing the need to reduce the generosity of transfer systems in the country. Corydon explained that it was no mere coincidence that the government was reforming taxes, welfare aid, and the system for early retirement: "The truth is that we are in full swing with a dramatically positive agenda, which is about strengthening and modernising the welfare state, and the result of the change will be a much better society than the one we have today." The leading Social Democrat went as far as formulating a new vision for the future of the welfare state: "I believe in the competition-state as the modern welfare state. If we are to ensure support for the welfare state, we must focus on the quality of public services rather than transfer payments."[188]

## Toward a New Welfare Contract?

Americans who still believe that the moral hazard risk is avoided in the Nordic countries would do themselves a service by reading (with the help of Google Translate perhaps) a report published by the Danish Social Democratic government in 2013. The report reached the conclusion that 400,000 Danish citizens at the time had few economic incentives to participate in the labor market. Those individuals lost 80 percent or more of their incomes when entering the labor market, since they lost benefits and had to pay taxes. Through extensive reforms of taxes and benefits the previous Social Democratic government hoped to reduce the group to 250,000 individuals. Even that would be a large share of the working age population, which is below 3 million.[189]

In June 2015, the Danish left-of-center government lost the election to a new right-of-center coalition, which has an even greater emphasis on welfare reform. Interestingly, the Social Democrats themselves increased their support in the election, regaining the position as the country's largest party. Power shifted since the coalition partners of the Social Democrats, who had criticized the vision of the competition state, lost considerably during the election. It would thus seem that the Danish electorate supports the vision of a system with more self-reliance and less welfare-reliance. That shift in political attitudes has occurred as welfare dependency has grown, particularly amongst the population with foreign background.

Other northern European welfare states have followed a path similar to Denmark's and Sweden's. For a long time the Netherlands had one of the most generous welfare systems in the world. During the beginning of the 1980s, the Netherlands ranked as a top spender in terms of welfare policy, on par with the (at the time) famously generous Swedish public system. With time, however, the Netherlands scaled back its welfare system, reducing the scope of public spending, privatizing social security, and introducing elaborate market mechanisms in the provision of health care and social protection.[190] Although not geographically a part of the Nordics, the Netherlands has cultural, economic, and political features very similar to its northern neighbors. A difference is that the Netherlands was earlier in shifting away from a very generous welfare system to a more limited model. The ambition to provide social safety nets, health care, and schooling to its underprivileged citizens has remained. Through scaling down the generosity of the system and creating insurance markets which combine universal coverage with competition and individual responsibility, the Netherlands has found a new social contract. Arguably, this new social contract has more long-term stability since it encourages individual responsibility more than the previous system.

Germany and Finland have never introduced welfare regimes quite as ambitious as Denmark's and Sweden's, but they have also moved in a similar direction as the long-term effects of norms on public behavior have become apparent. Even the United Kingdom, with its more moderate welfare model, is experiencing an extensive debate about the need to re-strengthen norms. In the beginning of 2014, for example, the documentary *Benefit Street* was aired and ran for five episodes. The show filmed the lives of residents of James Turner Street in Birmingham, where reportedly 90 percent of residents claim benefits. *Benefit Street* sparked a massive debate about the British welfare system, benefit claims, and lack of motivation to seek employment. Recent political trends indicate that the route to welfare reform is favored by many amongst the general public.[191]

## Collapsing Norms in an Oil-rich Welfare State

There is a possible exception to the new welfare contract being formulated in northern European welfare states: Norway. Thanks to its massive Atlantic oil wealth, this mountainous country has long retained the social democratic ideal of very generous public programs. However, as Roosevelt so elegantly put it, welfare dependency is not only an economic but also a human issue. Certainly the oil funds have made it possible for Norway to afford to pay for substantial public benefits. It is an entirely different question whether the nation can afford the human cost associated with the same policies. One consequence of the generous welfare policies in Norway is deterioration in work ethic. The TV series *Lilyhammer*, starring *Sopranos* actor Steven Van Zandt as an American expat to Norway, regularly makes fun of the lack of work discipline in the country.

That phenomenon is also apparent outside popular culture. In 2014, the *Financial Times* reported: "Norway's statistics office says many people have started to call Friday 'fridag'—'free day' in Norwegian. The state railway company says commuter trains serving the capital are less full on Fridays, and the main toll road operator says traffic is noticeably quieter on Fridays and on Mondays."[192] It's not only the adults who have stopped focusing on work. The youth—born and raised in a system with little reward for work—have gone even further. In a recent survey, three out of four Norwegian employers answered that Swedish youth working in the country have a better work capacity than Norwegian youth. Out of those questioned, merely 2 percent believed that young Norwegians between the ages of sixteen and twenty-four years old have a high work capacity. Stein André Haugerund, the president for the employment company Proffice, which carried out the survey, argued that the Norwegian welfare model has created a situation where incentives for hard work are limited, which in turn affects the behavior of youth.[193]

Those who doubt that generous welfare systems can affect working norms should think hard about the case of Norway. It is difficult to disregard the fact that Norwegians, just a few generations ago, had some of the strongest working ethics in the world. Without high trust, social cohesion, and a culture focused on individual responsibility Norway would never have grown so successful. The country's oil wealth boosted the economy further. However, it proved a double-edged sword since the massive oil revenues to the state made it difficult to limit the generosity of public programs and cash transfers. From a progressive viewpoint, one could of course argue that the Norwegian situation—that is, being able to afford a very generous welfare state thanks to natural resources wealth—is admirable. However, much like in oil-rich Arab countries, welfare handouts have not simply created social good; as an unintended consequence, the same systems have fostered a class of the socially poor.

## A Class of the Socially Poor
On the surface of it, it seems that Norway has low unemployment. In reality, however, much of the unemployment is hidden in early retirement statistics. This is true amongst native-born Norwegians in general and amongst immigrants in particular. One study looks at the individuals aged 30–55 who were granted a disability pension at some point between 1992 and 2003. That group includes 11 percent of men and 16 percent of women with Norwegian background. For those born in the Middle East and North Africa the figures were even higher: 25 percent amongst the men and 24 percent amongst the women.[194]

Disability pensions are of course aimed at people who are truly disabled. It might therefore seem puzzling why such a high share of the population in one of the healthiest countries in the world is granted this benefit. One explanation is that this benefit is used to hide the true unemployment level—if an unemployed person is given disability benefits, he or she is no longer counted as being part of the labor force and thus vanishes from the unemployment statistics. Another explanation is that many individuals misuse the system. Being granted disability pension benefits is often more lucrative than being supported by unemployment. Thus, many who are unemployed, but not too sick to work, strive for being granted a disability pension. Some even combine this with black market work, which of course proves that they are indeed not too sick to work.

Nordic countries are notoriously bad at integrating foreign-born individuals into their labor markets. The combination of high taxes, generous public benefits, and rigid labor markets makes it difficult even for highly educated groups of refugees to enter the workforce. Welfare dependency and norm-deterioration in particular thus affect immigrants and their children. It is, however, important to point out that welfare dependency is not only an issue for minorities. Ethnic Nordics are also affected. A good example is given in the "The Confessions of a 'Welfare Freeloader,'" published in the Norwegian daily paper *Dagbladet*. There a young man wrote about how he had been supported by welfare for the last three years, although he was healthy and in his prime years. In this, he was not alone:

> I know several people—talented, gifted people—who do not take a job. They do not do much else either, seen from a societal standpoint. No studies, no clearly defined plan for the future and no cunning plans to create wealth of any kind. The interest to "participate" or to "help" is minimal within this group, and poses no motivation to talk about. The feeling of responsibility when it comes to an abstract entity as "society" is low.[195]

The article spurred a national debate about the need to adjust the generosity of the welfare state even in oil-rich Norway, as it became obvious that the welfare state was undermining its core goal of combating poverty—by inadvertently creating a class of the socially poor.

### Is There Such a Thing as Too Much Welfare?
A central political question is, can there can ever be such a thing as too much welfare? Is it possible that individuals might in some

circumstances be better off receiving less generous public support? That question is tricky to answer, since it is difficult to prove how a certain policy affects people on an individual or family level. Gordon B. Dahl, Andreas Ravndal Kostøl, and Magne Mogstad use an ingenious method to arrive at a conclusive answer. In social sciences, it is often difficult to prove that one thing actually causes the other. The best way to separate causation from correlation is to use so-called "natural experiments."

Dahl, Kostøl, and Mogstad write: "Some policy makers and researchers have argued that a causal relationship exists, creating a culture in which welfare use reinforces itself through the family. Others argue the determinants of poverty or poor health are correlated across generations in ways that have nothing to do with a welfare culture." Those claims are difficult to test empirically because many factors can explain the link between children's behavior and parents' tendency to rely on welfare. However, the authors find a natural experiment that makes it possible to isolate the effect of welfare generosity. In the Norwegian welfare system, judges are sometimes appointed to look at disability insurance claims that have initially been denied. Some appeal judges are systematically more lenient when it comes to granting benefits. From the perspective of claimants, being appointed a strict or lenient judge is a random event. The researchers can therefore compare those who are granted disability insurance by a lenient judge with those who are denied the benefit by a strict judge. The conclusion is clear. The authors find:

> [S]trong evidence for a causal link across generations: when a parent is allowed [disability insurance] at the appeal stage, their adult child's participation over the next five years increases by 6 percentage points. This effect grows over time, rising to 12 percentage points after 10 years. Although these findings are specific to our setting, they highlight that welfare reforms can have long-lasting effects on program participation, since any original effect on the current generation could be reinforced by changing the participation behavior of their children as well.[196]

Thus, we can resolve the long-standing political debate about welfare dependency by looking at the most generous welfare state in the developed world. The conclusion is clear: overly generous welfare can indeed create a poverty trap for families, creating a social marginalization which is transferred from parent to children.

## A Way Out Of or Into Poverty?

As the Nobel laureate Robert Fogel has suggested, many of the traditional sources of poverty have been alleviated in modern societies. In previous generations, those born in impoverished families were often hungry, had poor or no housing, could not afford education, and even lacked the means to buy the decent clothing they needed for a job interview. Those were all obstacles for individuals who were attempting to create good lives and to become self-sufficient. Today, in most if not all modern societies, underprivileged citizens can rely on various public programs to get their basic needs, such as housing and food, covered. Basic education is free of charge, and scholarships are available to fund higher degrees. Global capitalism has created a system where it is difficult to determine from a distance if a shirt is made by an expensive Italian tailor or bought cheaply off the racks of H&M or Zara. But that does not mean that the obstacles to escaping poverty have vanished. Still today, those born in poor circumstances often remain there, and in turn pass social marginalization on to their children.

Fogel suggests that poverty exists in modern societies to a large degree because of an uneven distribution of "spiritual resources" such as self-esteem, a sense of discipline, and a sense of community.[197] Basic welfare institutions can help in alleviating material poverty, in providing schooling for all. Thus, they can provide various benefits to disadvantaged families. However, the spiritual poverty which Fogel points to can be exacerbated when individuals who could otherwise be self-reliant become dependent on public support. That is what Ronald Reagan meant when he said that the "most insidious effect of welfare is its usurpation of the role of provider," pointing to how "government programs ruptured the bonds holding poor families together."

### Reagan and Roosevelt Were Both Right

To sum up, both Roosevelt and Reagan had good reasons to fear how the social fabric and human wellbeing could inadvertently be harmed by welfare dependency. Although Nordic welfare states in particular seemed to avoid that moral hazard problem initially, we know today beyond doubt that that has not been the case in the long term. Norm deterioration due to adjustment to generous welfare states is an observable phenomenon, not least in the Nordics. The only thing that Roosevelt did not foresee was that norms change slowly. Even the northern European welfare states—founded in societies with exceptionally strong working ethics and emphasis on individual responsibility—have with time caught up to his dire predictions.

Although the ideals of the welfare state remain strong in northern Europe, political leaders from both left and right in countries such as the Netherlands, Sweden, and Denmark are seeking to formulate a new social contract—with greater emphasis on incentives, personal responsibility, and insurance markets. The motivation behind that political shift is not only to curb public spending or even to strengthen working ethics. The basic idea of welfare policy is to help disadvantaged groups to create a better future for themselves and their families. Evidently, overly generous welfare is not the best route for accomplishing that goal. Even proponents of large welfare states should strive to find this balance. More generous welfare is not always the same as better conditions for the less well-off.

# 9

# The Self-Controlling Individual
# in Society and Community

*By Tom G. Palmer*

*How do self-controlling individuals coordinate their actions with others to generate social order? Do individual human beings come with self-control, freedom, and responsibility built in, or does self-control have a history? Is self-control unique to any particular cultures or even perhaps incompatible with some cultures or religions? Sociology, economics, history, and political science illustrate how individuality, self-control, and freedom are connected, while various attempts to link freedom uniquely to one or another culture are examined and debunked; concepts, practices, and tools all have histories, but it does not follow that only the heirs of certain cultures may embrace or utilize them. Freedom is a universal human right and carries with it the universal human responsibility to respect the freedom of others. (Note: In this essay the term liberalism is used to refer to "classical" liberalism.)*

Some people, when they think about self-controlling individuals, conjure up images of rugged, lone figures who leave society to "go it alone," or of selfish and self-obsessed persons who reject all shared connections of family, friendship, and community. Such people assume, without argument or evidence, that self-controlling individuals are somehow averse to or unsuited for social interaction, when, in fact, the more "social" people become and the more complex societies become, the more the individuals who constitute them need to exercise and assert self-control.

Greater differentiation (or individuation) is itself a product of social interaction; the greater the complexity of the social order, the greater the ability of the members of society to distinguish themselves through their complex, intersecting, and overlapping forms of affiliation and identity.[198]

Individuality is also intimately connected to responsibility and accountability. We "own" the choices we make and their consequences. John Locke grounded the moral agent, the self, on the ability of the self to "own" its actions:

> Any substance vitally united to the present thinking Being, is a part of that very *same self* which now is: Any thing united to it by a consciousness of former Actions makes also a part of the *same self*, which is the same both then and now.
>
> *Person*, as I take it, is the name for this *self*. Where-ever a Man finds, what he calls *himself*, there I think another may say is the same *Person*. It is a Forensick Term appropriating Actions and their Merit; and so only belongs to intelligent Agents capable of a Law, and Happiness and Misery. This personality extends it *self* beyond present Existence to what is past, only by consciousness, whereby it becomes concerned and accountable, owns and imputes to it self past Actions, just upon the same ground, and for the same reason, that it does the present.[199]

The self does not exist in a mere instant, existing momentarily and winking out of existence, to be replaced by another succeeding self. The "self"—the "person," the "individual"—exists temporally, across its experiences. Ownership is not merely a concept applicable to physical possessions; you own your actions, through which you have become the person you are and through which you can become the person you want to be.

The sociologist Georg Simmel distinguishes between two meanings of individuality: "individuality in the sense of the freedom and responsibility for oneself that comes from a broad and fluid social environment. . . . The other meaning of individuality is qualitative: it means that the single human being distinguishes himself from all others; that his being and conduct—in form, content, or both—suit him alone; and that being different has a positive meaning and value for his life."[200] Both senses will be deployed, but also further distinguished, in this essay.

Individualism, as a political theory of the proper relationship among individuals and between individuals and the state, is virtually the opposite of "atomism," the idea that humans exist without social connection, like atoms bouncing off each other in a void.[201] Individualism means both an understanding of the uniqueness of each individual and a moral theory of human association based on recognition of common features that deserve respect, namely, the right of every person to make choices governing his or her own life.[202]

Individuation, i.e., the development of a unique self to which one can be true, tracks the development of self-control; greater coordination and harmony in a complex social order require not more powerful and detailed systems of command by those with authority or power, but higher degrees of individuation and individual self-control.[203] Greater self-control is a central part of the process of civilization. The more complex and differentiated the social order, the greater the corresponding need for self-control; alternatively put, greater social coordination among large numbers of people, such as characterizes modern civilization, can only come about when people possess and exercise greater capabilities of self-control. The history of civilization is one of greater and greater attention to the impact of our actions on both ourselves and on those with whom we interact, an awareness that becomes habitual.

The sociologist Norbert Elias found evidence of greater self-control through his careful examination of books of etiquette and social manners from the thirteenth to the nineteenth centuries; the results were surprising, as such books admonished *adults* to avoid behavior that would today be considered quite disgusting even among children and that are taught not to adults (who are presumed to have already learned them), but to very small children. [204] (Memorable examples include not blowing one's nose on one's hand and then reaching with that hand to get bread from a common bowl, not gnawing on a bone and then putting it back into the common serving dish, not picking one's nose while eating, not blowing one's nose on the tablecloth, not spitting across the table, and so on.) Moreover, normal human interaction often entailed what we would consider astonishing brutality and violence, but which was considered at the time so common that it barely merited notice.[205]

No mind is capable of issuing the commands necessary to direct all the actions needed for large numbers of people engaged in complex undertakings to coordinate their behavior harmoniously; generals may command armies, which are organizations, but generally no one can command societies, which are far more complex than organizations and which are not subordinate to any particular purpose or goal, but are the result of the interactions of many people pursuing many goals. Complex social orders depend primarily on following abstract rules (i.e., rules that are independent of particular aims, purposes, interests, or persons) and the observance of such abstract rules requires a high degree of self-control, by which individuals can control transient (and frequently harmful or aggressive) impulses and adjust their behavior to act in accordance with the same rules followed by others. In Elias's words,

> As the interdependence of people increases with the increasing division of labour, everyone becomes increasingly dependent on everyone else, even those of high social rank on those people who are socially inferior and weaker. The latter become so much the equals of the former that they, the socially superior people, can experience shame-feelings even in the presence of their social inferiors. It is only in this connection that the armour of restraints is fastened to the degree which is gradually taken for granted by people in democratic industrial societies.[206]

Peaceful social coordination and prosperity depend not on dictatorship, but on the liberty of the self-controlling individual to make his or her own choices within the framework of generally applicable rules, which John Locke referred to as "a Liberty to dispose, and order, as he lists, his Person, Actions, Possessions, and his whole Property, within the Allowance of those Laws under which he is; and therein not to be subject to the arbitrary Will of another, but freely follow his own."[207]

Traffic rules provide a simple and easily grasped example: millions of drivers have their own myriad destinations and purposes, but a fairly simple set of rules allows them under normal circumstances to reach their destinations and to achieve their purposes without detailed instructions from a central power.

Many thinkers yearn for guarantees that things will always turn out for the best and believe that "if only someone were in charge" or "if only there were a law," mistakes, frailty, bad luck, and dead ends would be avoided. That is a fatal conceit. Self-control does not generate perfect results, of course; not everyone succeeds in achieving self-control and happiness, sometimes because of their own failures, and sometimes because of factors outside of their control.[208] Voluntary social coordination does not guarantee perfect efficiency or the best imaginable outcomes. That is no argument against self-control, however, because *no* system of state control, from the mildest to the harshest dictatorship, achieves its ostensible goals of perfect social harmony and universal happiness. It is not enough to imagine an ideal outcome and then imagine an ideal dictator creating it; life isn't like that. Bitter experience shows that substituting state control and direction for self-control rarely generates positive outcomes and more generally is a cover for predatory exploitation in the interests of those who actually exercise power over others.[209]

### The Myth of the Purely Rational Individual

The lone and self-sufficient individual who makes a rational choice to "enter society" for his or her own benefit is a myth.[210] For people to come together to agree on rules to govern themselves already presupposes a set of relationships, not to mention the norm that agreement is the proper foundation for social cooperation. Without such relationships and norms, they could not negotiate or agree on a contract to found "society."[211] The myth of lone individuals generating morality and norms through agreement is not only *un*helpful to the advancement of individual self-control and of social and political orders that protect individual liberty, but it is positively harmful to the cause of liberty, limited government, and self-control. It is a convenient straw man for advocates of state control over individuals (which is why they perpetuate it at virtually every opportunity), and it misleads us about the nature of voluntary cooperation in free societies. It is so obvious that individuals are dependent on each other, and not only for survival (consider flying in airplanes and being able to watch movies and otherwise enjoy the amazing luxuries of the modern age), that if the public can be falsely convinced that liberal individualists deny something so obvious, liberalism can be made to appear foolish. Families, tribes, schools, clubs, temples, villages, cities, and so many other inherently social entities are obviously necessary for transmission and cultivation of the values, norms, habits, language, and other elements of character that make us human. Individualism is itself a product of social interaction; humans with widely varied individuating features, interests, needs, and capabilities could not survive, much less flourish, without social cooperation, as classical liberal/libertarian social scientists have taught for centuries.

The social thinker F. A. Hayek emphasized (not that his critics bothered to read him) that "individualism" is not wedded to the idea of man "as a highly rational and intelligent" being, but saw the human being instead "as a very irrational and fallible being, whose individual errors are corrected only in the course of a social process. . . ."[212] Each individual is limited in the knowledge on which he or she may draw. There is no mind to whom all of the relevant information is available; among limited and fallible human beings institutions have emerged by which individuals may share information without even being aware of the existence of those with whom they are interacting. Consider prices; some of Hayek's most important work in economics focuses on the role that prices play in providing encapsulated forms of information that help millions or billions of people, who share different interests and are generally unaware of each other, to coordinate their actions.[213] Hayek focused on the evolved rules by which human beings coordinate their actions without relying on an omniscient central planning authority; he associated "true individualism" not with super-human resolve, strength, intellect, or powers—characteristics that might suggest that coherent social planning by an intelligent, capable, and informed leader or elite would be possible, but with humility and a recognition of the limits of individual minds.[214] As social psychologist Jonathan Haidt puts it, "we must be wary of any *individual's* ability to reason ... We should not expect individuals to produce good, open-minded, truth-seeking reasoning, particularly when self-interest or reputational concerns are in play. But if you put individuals together in the right way, such that some individuals can use their reasoning powers to disconfirm the claims of others, and all individuals feel some common bond or shared fate that allows them to interact civilly, you can create a group that ends up producing good reasoning as an emergent property of the social system."[215]

Hayek considered the key insight of Enlightenment-era classical liberal thinkers to be the importance of limiting the damage individuals could do and deflating their ambitions to impose their self-proclaimed genius on society: "It would scarcely be too much to claim that the main merit of the individualism which he [Adam Smith] and his contemporaries advocated is that it is a system under which bad men can do least harm. It is a social system which does not depend for its functioning on our finding good men for running it, or on all men becoming better than they now are, but which makes use of men in all their given variety and complexity, sometimes good and sometimes bad, sometimes intelligent and more often stupid."[216] (The insight was not limited to Smith, but was shared by many figures in the history of liberalism, e.g., James Madison, Benjamin Constant, Frédéric Bastiat, and many others.)

Everyone is a unique individual (a statement so trite as to be almost not worth writing) and almost everyone (there are pathological exceptions) can exercise self-control. Yet a variety of influential ideologues who have sought to vest greater and greater powers in the state have argued that "true freedom" can only be realized through giving up self-control and enhancing state control. Others, less extreme in their ideology, argue that experts with superior knowledge, wisdom, and foresight should be granted the power to control the decisions of the rest of society for their own good; sometimes they suggest that such submission realizes a higher freedom, but more commonly they argue that it is justified on utilitarian grounds, because the experts have the special knowledge that the common people (i.e., you and I) lack.[217] Of course, trained specialists generally do know more than others about their areas of specialization, but it is a far cry from that fact to believing A) that politicians are the people among whom such expertise is to be found, B) that politicians have more skill in identifying qualified experts than those who will directly bear the consequences of good or bad decisions, or C) that one decision will be the best decision for everyone and thus should be uniformly imposed on all. (There is a vast literature on the economics of "public choice" that documents the effects of such overestimation of the capabilities of political decision-makers, as well as the perverse incentives created by substitution of state control for self-control.[218])

## Are Individual Freedom and Responsibility Culturally Specific?

Assumptions about super-rational individuals forming societies de novo should be rejected, but what of those who claim that individual autonomy and responsibility are products of a particular culture and thus any claims one might make regarding responsibility and freedom are limited to that culture? That claim is frequently made as if it were self-evident and not to be questioned. It deserves to be questioned, because it is hardly self-evident. In fact, it is false and has been very harmful, for it has been invoked to justify the imposition of—or indifference to—incalculable suffering and injustice. ("They don't value freedom;" "They cannot be held to the same standards regarding respect for women, children, or the vulnerable;" "They don't feel pain and loss like we do.")

Before rebutting the claim that the capacity and the right to individual self-control are limited to just one culture (or just those that have generated such beliefs), it is worth looking at the claim in its most general form, namely, that ideas carry little flags that limit their applicability. Antoine Lavoisier, one of the great pioneers of chemistry and the identifier of oxygen, was born in France and wrote in French. Someone inclined to limit the application of ideas to their cultures of origin might conclude that oxygen (or at least the theory of oxygen) cannot be useful to people from other countries, or speaking other languages. Koreans and Canadians (except, perhaps, for the Québécoises) could not invoke the theory of oxygen, because the applicability of the concept is limited to the French. And the same would go for the use of zero as a placeholder for mathematical calculation and the use of yoga as healthful exercise. (Hindus only, please!) The fact that an idea has a history, with names, places, and times specified, is no reason to limit its applicability or usefulness to people with those names, or to people who live in those places, or to people who lived at those times.

The idea of individual freedom and self-control, rather than control by slave masters, warlords, potentates, or politicians achieved its most thorough formulation in Europe and in societies that derived their political institutions from Europe. The term for the philosophy built around the "presumption of liberty" is liberalism.[219] (Because of peculiar historical circumstances, the term liberalism acquired a different meaning in the United States, where the philosophy of liberty is now sometimes referred to as "classical liberalism"; the term "libertarianism" is also used, although it is sometimes reserved for more radical or consistent versions of liberalism.) Freedom is thus the touchstone of liberalism, but is freedom a uniquely "European" idea? Certainly, the idea of self-direction and freedom from coercion is hardly unknown in other societies. Moreover, the ideas of liberal individualism have spread around the world, such that advocates of liberalism are now present in every country (including North Korea, Iran, Saudi Arabia, and other tyrannical states), even if their voices may be muted or suppressed by violently intolerant authoritarians, whether acting through government or organized as mobs, vigilante committees, or other kinds of criminal associations. Against liberalism, it is frequently asserted that, *because the rulers of those countries do not embrace the idea of liberty for their subjects, it is justified for those rulers to deny freedom of religion, or trade, or movement, or speech to their subjects*. The conclusion does not follow. The claim rests on a hidden premise, namely, that those exercising power represent the wishes or thoughts of the people, which may not be the case; or, it presumes that merely *because* tyrannies do in fact exercise power over their subjects, they are therefore *justified* in exercising all the powers they exercise, which is not an argument, but a mere assertion. (The statement "Those people don't believe in freedom like we do" and the conclusion "therefore it's ok to arrest, jail, or punish them for disobeying their rulers" presupposes that the individuals or groups who are punished—and not only the rulers who punish them—don't believe in or value their own freedom; that is generally not the case. Moreover, even if that were the case, by itself it would not be sufficient reason for oppressing them; not only those who explicitly embrace their freedom deserve their freedom.[220])

Just as the fact that yoga originated in India does not mean that no one else can learn or practice it, the fact that the theory of the right of self-control was articulated among certain groups of people earlier than among others, or that the latter may have adopted some ideas of rights from the earlier, does not limit the range of applicability of rights only to the descendants of the originators.

## Historical Dimensions of Individual Freedom and Responsibility

Nonetheless, history matters. Historical understanding offers a powerful lens through which to understand scientific theories, philosophical concepts, legal enactments, and other social phenomena. It generally helps to understand an idea if one understands its history. Ideas, concepts, and theories can be understood as tools that we use to solve problems and thus an understanding of their histories—of the problems to which they were presented as solutions—can help us to understand those ideas, concepts, and theories. That said, offering a historical account of an idea need not imply that the idea is limited in validity to certain people, times, or places. Nor need it imply that it could only have been developed under those conditions; certainly it is common for people widely separated in time and space to develop similar or identical tools, including ideas, and it is also common for tools and concepts to spread to other groups through persuasion and emulation.

The recognition of individuality, of the uniqueness of each

individual, is commonplace in all cultures. It's simply undeniable that persons are individually distinct; indeed, specific organs and regions of the human brain are functionally necessary to distinguish and recognize human faces, without which sustained patterns of human cooperation would be impossible.[221] Each human person is unique, even if rulers may consider us interchangeable and expendable. What is less commonly grasped is that we all share in common something morally significant and that therefore all human beings have legitimate claims to rightful treatment by each other, that is, to respect for their human rights. Only in modern times has such an idea achieved widespread, albeit far from universal, acceptance.

The theoretical appreciation of individuality at both the level of individual uniqueness (or "individuation") and of individualism as a foundation for legal and political claims emerges at different times in different places. Those streams of individualistic ideas that merged to form liberalism mostly emerged from Europe, although the core elements of liberal individualism can be found in Chinese, Islamic, Indian, and other civilizations. They emerged in Europe for a number of historically contingent reasons, including: Europe's post-classical radical decentralization of political authority (which resulted in both feudal society and later civil society, the former mainly rural and the latter mainly urban and commercial, but both were decentralized responses to violence and predation that facilitated experimentation and competition among jurisdictions);[222] the separation and rivalry of the institutions of organized religion and state;[223] the competition of political authorities (including city republics, kingdoms and principalities, archbishoprics, manors, and other political entities) to attract workers, skills, and capital, and the ensuing growth of industry and commerce;[224] and the rediscovery and frequently very selective re-appropriation of the heritage of classical (mainly Greek and Roman) philosophy and law.[225] (The emergence of liberalism is itself a spontaneous order, not the product of one or a few brilliant minds; it emerged from the confluence of a number of different processes to form a coherent and evolving mutually reinforcing body of ideas in law, moral philosophy, economics, sociology, psychology, history, and other humane sciences.[226])

**Historical Contingency**

History is full of contingencies, of things that could have been otherwise. Had the Mongol armies continued into Europe after the poisoning of the great Khan Ögedei on December 11, 1241, European history would likely have taken a radically different course. As it was, the Mongol war lords returned to Karakorum to elect a new Khan and central and western Europe were spared the Mongol conquests that so profoundly influenced the trajectories of the societies of Russia, Asia, the Caucasus, Central Asia, India, and the Middle East. Historical accident and contingency give us reason to be wary of essentialist claims about cultures.

Inferring necessary development from initial starting points is risky, but that rarely stops people from doing it. Some years ago I participated in a colloquium on the comparison of Confucian and Aristotelian thought, at the end of which one participant concluded that a culture with Aristotle at its base resulted in the US Constitution, the Industrial Revolution, and the abolition of slavery, whereas one with Confucius at its base resulted in Mao Zedong, the tens of millions of deaths of the Great Leap Forward, and the Cultural Revolution. It was as if nothing else had happened in the time between the lives of Aristotle and Confucius and the present; according to that all-too-common approach, history is just a linear trajectory from an idea to a set of outcomes. What shapes society is exclusively the Idea (with a capital "I") and, because different Ideas have different implications, it's just a matter of tracing out those implications to deduce the present from the ideas of the past. One reads the Bible or Aristotle or the Quran or the Analects or the Mahabharata and, without interpretive apparatus or context, deduces its implications. (Sometimes the associations are especially absurd, as with the association sometimes made between "Asian culture" and collectivism. When such claims about the inevitability of tyranny in Asia are made, Chinese libertarians point out that Karl Marx, Friedrich Engels, Vladimir Lenin, and Joseph Stalin, whose posters are still hung in the buildings of Chinese state institutions, are rather implausibly classified as Chinese or Asian thinkers.[227] The horrors of collectivist tyranny in Asia had far more to do with ideas articulated by European thinkers than with "Asian culture," which, in any case, is hardly monolithic.)

One can find statements of libertarian ideals in classical times,[228] and expressions of individuality and personal freedom in Arabic and Islamic civilization[229] (the last itself also an heir to classical civilization), in Chinese civilization,[230] and in Indian civilization,[231] but the intellectual and institutional sources of what became global liberalism converged mainly in Europe.

The historical trajectory could have been otherwise, but it wasn't. While individualistic thinking can be found in other cultures—and, had some things gone differently, liberalism might have emerged instead, or more strongly, in those other cultures (and not in Europe)—that's not what happened, which is why historians focus on the origins of liberal individualism in Europe. (A number of the physical sciences were also disproportionately pioneered by European thinkers, as well, but few would claim that modern biology, chemistry, physics, and mechanics are only for Europeans, simply because some of the pioneering inventions and discoveries in those fields were made in Europe.)

### Individuality and Moral/Political Individualism

Awareness of one's distinct individual identity and attention to the individuality of others is related to political individualism, in the sense of a legal and political order based on respect for the rights of individuals, but individuality and individualism are not, strictly speaking, the same. Both recognize the uniqueness of the individual, but the latter combines that recognition of individuality with claims about a common feature ascribed to all human beings, namely, that they have equal basic rights (e.g., "life, liberty, and the pursuit of happiness"). When did those ideas begin to take clear form and to gain more widespread acceptance?

The historian Colin Morris identified the twelfth century as "a peculiarly creative age" for "the development of self-awareness and self-expression . . . the freedom of a man to declare himself without paying excessive attention to the demands of convention or the dictates of authority."[232] Morris focused on the importance of humanist thinking (particularly the rediscovery of the writings of Cicero and Seneca the Younger, two important Roman philosophers), the theological shift from seeking the salvation of mankind to focusing on individual salvation, and the depiction of human individuality in art and literature.[233] Artistic and cultural appreciation for individuality increased through that period and beyond. John Benson has focused our attention on such elements as the development of biography and portraiture, diversification of names, monasticism, the substitution of conceptions of individual guilt for social shame, and the focus on the distinction between childhood and adulthood as elements in the increasing appreciation of individuality.[234]

The recognition of the equal rights of all is complementary to the recognition of the individuation of persons, who are not merely interchangeable units. Each human being is a unique individual, but all bear common features, among them equal rights. (In the words of the American Declaration of Independence, "All men are created equal . . . they are endowed by their Creator with certain unalienable rights . . .") A key document in the history of the legal recognition of universal rights was a Decretal, or legal pronouncement, issued by the lawyer Pope Innocent IV, about the year 1250. It concerned the rights of non-Christians.

> I maintain . . . that lordship, possession and jurisdiction can belong to infidels licitly and without sin, for these things were made not only for the faithful but for every rational creature as has been said. For he makes his sun to rise on the just and the wicked and he feeds the birds of the air, Matthew c.5, c.6. Accordingly we say that it is not licit for the pope or the faithful to take away from infidels their belongings or their lordships or jurisdictions because they possess them without sin.[235]

It's worth pausing to consider the role played by religion in that story. Pope Innocent IV quotes the Book of Matthew from the Christian New Testament, as well as alluding to the scholastic/Aristotelian idea of the commonality of rationality. He cites a Christian Gospel text, so was it simply Christianity that was playing the key role? And if so, which of the many Christian theologies, or which elements of the various Christian doctrines, were essential? And what role is played by the insistence that "these things were made not only for the faithful but for every rational creature as has been said"?

In a thoughtful and provocative book, full of novel ideas, the political theorist Larry Siedentop has provided an answer that reminds me forcefully of the story I told above of the colloquium participant who concluded that the American Constitution was a result of Aristotle's ideas and China's disastrous "Great Leap Forward" was the result of Confucius's, that each result was an implication of texts written thousands of years ago. It's worth examining Siedentop's account, because understanding how mistaken it is may help us to appreciate better the universality of the ideas of liberal individualism. In his recent book *Inventing the Individual: The Origins of Western Liberalism*, Siedentop hints that Christian doctrine, in the form of the ideas set forth by St. Paul (hereafter "Paul"), is *the necessary foundation* for liberal individualism and that the ideas of rights not only emerged from a particular context, but could *not* have emerged elsewhere, and perhaps could not be realized without the necessary theological context. Siedentop argues that it was Paul's message that made liberal individualism possible. According to Siedentop, Paul's

> understanding of the meaning of Jesus' death and resurrection introduced to the world a new picture of reality. It provided an ontological foundation for "the individual," through the promise that humans have access to the deepest reality as individuals rather than merely as members of a group.[236]

Starting with the writings of Paul in an account of "the invention of the individual" may seem somewhat unpromising, because Paul's writings seem to suggest not the recognition of the individual as a unique moral being, but the submergence of the individual in a collective identity through her or his incorporation into the greater body of the Church: "For just as the body is one and has many members, and all the members of the body, though many, are one body, so it is with Christ" (1 Corinthians 12, Revised Standard Version).[237] Moreover, in his letter to the Romans, Paul instructs them that all political authority is vested with the authority of God: "Let every person be subject to the governing authorities. For there is no authority except from God, and those that exist have been instituted by God. Therefore he who resists the authorities resists what God has appointed, and those who resist will incur judgment" (Romans 13, Revised Standard Version). (Learned scholars have pored over those texts and concluded that they can indeed be reconciled with liberal individualism, but the wording of Paul's letters suggests that substantial interpretive apparatus is required to do so.) Siedentop does not deal with those issues, but instead provides a not very clear account of how faith undermined rationality, which—surprisingly—he understands not as a universal characteristic (recall Innocent IV's comment about how "these things were made not only for the faithful but for every rational creature as has been said") but *instead with aristocracy, moral and legal inequality, and privilege*! According to Siedentop, in the ancient world and for very long thereafter, "Reason or rationality—logos, the power of words—became closely identified with the public sphere, with speaking in the assembly and with the political role of a superior class. Reason became the attribute of a class that commanded. At times reason was almost categorically fused with social superiority." He invokes throughout the book an alleged "ancient association of rationality with inequality."[238] It is a very perplexing account and reverses the usual understanding of the relationships.

But even without going into the subtleties of theology, the proper interpretation of Paul's views on the church as the body of Christ, the presumptive legitimacy of established political powers, or whether reason should be understood to be egalitarian or hierarchical, there is a gaping and obvious hole in Siedentop's historical account: Paul's letters are also accepted as part of the Bible by Orthodox Christians, among whom liberal individualism did not emerge and flourish as it did in Latin ("Western") Christianity. Yet Siedentop, who puts emphasis squarely on the words of Paul, never bothers to consider why the same texts in other contexts did not produce the same outcome.

Siedentop quite unfairly tars any objections to his thesis as mere "anti-clericalism" and insists that "texts are facts. And the texts remain."[239] Indeed, for Siedentop, it's just a matter of ideas unfolding and revealing their implications:

> Centuries would be required for the implications of Christian moral beliefs to be drawn out and clarified—and even more time would pass before long-established social practices or institutions were reshaped by these implications.[240]

Why were "the implications" of the same texts "drawn out and clarified" in some contexts and not in others? Siedentop seems oblivious to the problem. (Throughout the book Siedentop also refers to "Christian moral intuitions," a term which is far more vague than the implications he thinks he has discovered in the writings of Paul. He even asserts that the Gregorian Reformation and the freedom of the Church, which was accomplished in Roman Christianity but not among the Orthodox, was a case of Pope Gregory VII "drawing out the deepest moral intuitions of the church."[241]) One might ask why it took thousands of years for the implications that allegedly led to toleration to be made explicit.[242] Further, the emergence of liberal individualism cannot be merely the drawing out of the implications of texts or even intuitions when the same texts (and presumably the same intuitions) did not seem to have the same implications elsewhere. Rather, different ideas became dominant for a long time in countries in which Orthodox traditions were the norm.[243] When liberal individualism reached those countries it was more often adapted from ideas that had germinated in Europe. Siedentop's story of the "texts" of Paul's Epistles (or the rather vaguer "Christian intuitions") grounding liberal individualism fails utterly to account for its emergence on this account alone: Paul's letters are not only considered part of the Christian Bible among Latin (or Western) Christians, but among other Christian traditions, as well, including the Coptic and Orthodox Churches, yet the ideas and intuitions that Siedentop claims were implicated or intuitable did not result in liberal implications or intuitions being drawn from them in those other traditions that also embraced Paul's Epistles.

To his idiosyncratic theological and historical accounts Siedentop tacks on a controversial and untenable philosophical one, namely, that the philosophical tradition of "nominalism" (i.e., the idea that what exists are individuals and not timeless essences and that universals are mere names) of the great European medieval thinkers Peter Abelard and William of Ockham was another necessary foundation for individualism. Nominalists are held to believe that what exists is the individual entity "Larry," and not the essence "man." If "essences" do not exist, but only a multitude of individuals (Moe, Larry, and Curly, for examples) do, then—*voilà!*—individualism. Ockham was both a nominalist and a pioneer in the development of modern theories of individual rights; he was also a "voluntarist" in theology, meaning that he explained God's creation of the world and its laws by recourse to God's will, rather than to God's timeless essence or intellect. The problem with Siedentop's account is that Ockham's ideas on individual rights neither rest on nor invoke either his nominalism or his voluntarism, as Brian Tierney (ironically, Siedentop's main source on Ockham) makes very clear: "Ockham is presented in my [Tierney's] work as an important figure in the development of natural rights theories; but I argue that his characteristic teachings were not derived from his nominalist and voluntarist philosophy, but rather from a rationalist ethic applied to a body of juristic doctrine available to him in the canon law collections that he knew well and cited frequently."[244] As Tierney and other scholars have demonstrated, parallel theories of individual rights were being developed by thinkers who did not share either Ockham's nominalism in philosophy or his voluntarism in theology. Siedentop cites Tierney as a source, but seems not to have followed, or perhaps even read, Tierney's argument.[245]

None of that is to suggest that either Christianity or nominalism were unimportant in the history of thought (which would be absurd), nor to denigrate any particular interpretation of either nominalist philosophy, theological metaphysics, or the ideas of Paul, but merely to point out that Siedentop's attempt to establish his curious interpretation of Paul and his claims about nominalism as necessary and sufficient conditions for the emergence of liberal individualism fails.[246]

Why is all of that important? For three reasons:

A) Because respect for the universally valid rights of each and every unique individual is compatible with a wide array of philosophies, religions, and cultures and the limitation of liberalism to only one cultural context is incompatible both with the historical evidence and with the universal claims of liberalism itself;

B) Because Siedentop's account ignores or downplays important institutional innovations that were significant conditions for the development and triumph of individual liberty and because those institutional innovations may be necessary for the maintenance of liberty; the innovations of greatest concern include constitutional limits on government power, checks and balances among competing powers, freedom of trade and freedom of exit, respect for property, and accountability of authorities to the law and to their publics;

C) Because Siedentop implies that Christianity, or at least his understanding of it, is a necessary element in the defense of civil liberty and, moreover, that "Islam" (rather than intolerant political Islamists) is "challenging" Europe, which he identifies with liberty. Siedentop rather excitedly claims that "Europe is now faced with the challenge of Islam" and asks "Will Europeans come to understand better the moral logic that joins Christianity with civil liberty?"[247] thus suggesting that defending civil liberty requires the embrace of that which is joined to it by "moral logic," i.e., a particular interpretation of a particular religion. That unjustified claim is in conflict with liberalism itself.

Siedentop's puzzling reconstruction of liberal individualism's origins may in fact be quite harmful to the very liberalism he seems eager to defend, for it suggests a closed club of cultures that are open to liberalism; others need not apply. Liberal individualism is not an exclusive property of European Christians; nor is it an inevitable consequence of "Christian intuitions," nor a necessary implication of an eccentric interpretation of Paul's writings, nor an outcome of European philosophical disputations over realism and nominalism. It is a philosophy open to people of all faiths or none who embrace the moral principles of respect for the rights of others.

## Origins of Liberal Individualism

The historian Walter Ullman presented a strong rebuttal to Siedentop's thesis, long before Siedentop formulated it. Ullman traced the transformation of the passive "subject" to the active rights-bearing and rights-asserting citizen of liberal society and did *not* find it in implications of the texts of Paul: "Most, if not all, of the basic principles relative to the individual as a subject to higher authority are contained in the Bible, notably in the Pauline letters."[248] For example, the transition from subject to citizen, from obeying laws that were imposed on one to following rules that in the creation and maintenance of which one had some role, is not an obvious implication of Paul's letter to the Romans, which maintains that all earthly authority is ordained by God. In Paul's account, the power of kings comes not from the consent of the people, but from God:

> The king received his powers as a concession from divinity— another Pauline principle was concretely applied: there is no power but of God—and what he had received through the grace of God in the shape of public power, he could concede to his subjects. The individuals as subjects had no rights in the public field. Whatever they had, they had as a matter of royal grace, of royal concession.[249]

Ullman focused attention not on *the theories of government* that were shared by rather small numbers of upper-class people, but on *the actual practices and functioning institutional arrangements* by which most people ordered their lives. After the collapse of the Roman imperium, European political orders splintered and military defense had to be reorganized to fend off raids and invasions. Following the withdrawal of the Roman legions (or their replacement by Germanic mercenaries) and the greater vulnerability to invasion from the North (the Norsemen), the South (the "Saracens"), and the East (the Avars and Magyars), the old order could not be maintained. Military decentralization was followed by political and legal decentralization, as well.[250]

The institutions that emerged to solve problems of social co-ordination (including defense against aggression) helped to set the stage for liberal individualism and modernity.

> If one wishes to understand why and how it came about that from the late thirteenth century the individual gradually emerged as a full-fledged citizen, it would seem profitable to look at two rather practical facets of medieval society: on the one hand, the manner in which those far away from the gaze of official governments conducted their own affairs and, on the other hand, the feudal form of government which was practiced all over Europe.[251]

Both of the facets of medieval society that Ullman identified were matters of practice and trial-and-error, rather than theoretical speculation. Merely intellectual history without attention to the emergence of practice is unable to explain what happened, for without attention to the actual legal practices of the people, "it would seem well-nigh impossible to explain why there was the somewhat radical change toward the end of the thirteenth century, a change that in more than one respect ushered in the period which we like to call modern."[252] The fracturing of kingly power through the system of political contract that came to be known as "feudalism,"[253] and the emergence of a multitude of legal systems with competing and overlapping jurisdictions[254] all contributed to an ever-wider space for individual action and more restrictions on the power of rulers.

The growth of cities was especially important; it was from the cities that the key institutions of "civil society" were to emerge. The legal order of the cities, or "communes," was focused on peace and freedom. As Henri Pirenne described the citizens ("burghers"),

> The burghers were essentially a group of *homines pacis*—men of peace. The peace of the city (*pax villae*) was at the same time the law of the city (*lex villae*).[255]

The city was a place of peace (certainly relative to the countryside outside its walls) and the citizens enjoyed liberty, at least relative to the peasants who resided outside their walls: "just as agrarian civilization had made of the peasant a man whose normal state was servitude, trade made of the merchant a man whose normal condition was liberty."[256] If you could get into a city and stay for a year and a day, you became a free person: "City Air Makes One Free" was a distinguishing feature of the cities of Europe.[257]

The replacement of war and subjugation with peaceful commerce and contractual relationships corresponded to, indeed, demanded, increases in rational self-control, notably the ability to ignore or control harmful impulses, especially aggression, and to delay gratification. As Benjamin Constant noted, "A man who was always the stronger would never conceive the idea of commerce. It is experience, by proving to him that war, that is the use of his strength against the strength of others, exposes him to a variety of obstacles and defeats, that leads him to resort to commerce, that is to a milder and surer means of engaging the interest of others to agree to what suits his own. War is all impulse, commerce, calculation."[258] The gradual replacement of war by commerce went hand in hand with the replacement of impulse by calculation, zero-sum games by positive-sum games, short-term by long-term thinking, and subjection to power by personal responsibility and liberty.[259] The gradual replacement of violence and repression has been facilitated by commerce.[260]

According to Siedentop, authority and legal order descended from above in accordance with theories set out in books, but the historical record suggests that the legal orders of modernity emerged from forms of association generated through practice and trial and error, in other words, from the bottom up. In Ullman's words,

[T]here were throughout the Middle Ages numerous associations, unions, fraternities, guilds, and communities which in one way or another considered the individual a full member. What these truly numberless associations exhibit is the urge of individuals to combine into larger groups: partly for reasons of self-protection, partly for reasons of mutual insurance, partly for reasons of pursuing sectional interests, these unions were to all intents and purposes communities, which provided for the individual the security which he would otherwise have lacked. . . . In the village potteries, smithies, tileries, quarries et cetera, working conditions were laid down by the village community itself. In other words, we have here a "system" at work which shows all the characteristic features of the ascending theme of government and law, according to which original power resided in the members of the community, in the individuals themselves.[261]

A major element in the decentralization of power (military, political, and legal) was the rivalry between the church and the empire and other political authorities, which set the stage for a competition that distinguished Western Europe from the other political systems of the Eurasian landmass in a way that religious texts did not (as both Latin and Orthodox churches accepted the Pauline Epistles that Siedentop considers so important). Harold Berman terms the change the "Papal Revolution" and it set in motion changes that are still playing out.[262] Notable among them was the formulation of the idea of the supremacy of law (the "rule of law") and of what has come to be known as "constitutionalism." Magna Carta, which doesn't merit a mention in Siedentop's book, looms large in the history of nations deriving their political institutions from English law; it was itself strongly influenced by the Papal Revolution.[263] That raises a problem similar to that raised by Siedentop's account. Focusing exclusively on Magna Carta reveals the danger of a different kind of essentialism, which asserts that "only the English" understand liberty, because Magna Carta, some assert, was unique.[264] But as important as Magna Carta is, it was not the only such charter of liberties; it was an important part of a movement that was European in character, and not merely English.[265] One could mention its many precedents, including Henry I's "Charter of Liberties" issued in 1100, which made various concessions to the English barons and knights;[266] the Assizes of Ariano, promulgated in 1140 by King Roger II of Sicily;[267] and shortly after 1215 the Golden Bull of Hungary of 1222, signed by King András, which instituted a long period of constitutionalism in central Europe;[268] the Constitutions of Melfi issued by Emperor Frederick II in 1231;[269] and numerous others. Even the important terms regarding "the law of the land" and "trial by one's peers," which later reappeared in the US Constitution, predated Magna Carta, for example, in a constitution agreed to by Emperor Conrad II in 1037, which declared that no vassal should be deprived of an imperial or ecclesiastical fief "except in accordance with the law of our predecessors and the judgment of his peers."[270]

Not only was law important, including limitations on arbitrary power of the sort instituted in the items just listed, but also important was the decline of hierarchy and the emergence of a more fluid social order, that is, a civil society. Recognition of individuality is not sufficient by itself for a liberal society, nor even is a system of predictable laws, although both are necessary conditions. A third necessary condition is a society in which even the poorest and most humble is allowed "to pursue his own interest his own way, upon the liberal plan of equality, liberty, and justice," as Adam Smith put it when contrasting the liberal approach with the "extraordinary privileges" and "extraordinary restraints" of the "mercantile system."[271] The liberal plan of equality, liberty, and justice had to replace the extraordinary privileges and extraordinary restraints to make possible the modern world and the enormous "great enrichment" and personal freedom it has ushered in. As Deirdre McCloskey notes, "A society can be individualistic in a thoroughgoing way but still honor only noblemen, not letting ordinary people have a go at spinning jennies and desktop computers."[272]

It was not inevitable that liberal individualism would emerge among European Christians (and Jews), nor were the ideas of Paul (or "Christian intuitions") sufficient to germinate liberal individualism among the countries in which Orthodoxy held sway. To identify the processes that gave rise to liberal individualism entails identifying those that could have produced it elsewhere, as well. We should remember that ideas do not have to be created or germinated independently by each person or group for them to be shared commonly; having once been produced, ideas may be communicated in poems, songs, and books, through art and science, in blog posts and Tweets, and they may be understood, embraced, or followed by people whose ancestors did not themselves produce the ideas. In the case of the moral, legal, and political principles of liberalism, that's especially obvious; refugees from tyrannies often embrace the norms of the freer societies in which they find refuge, including the expectation of respect for their rights and willingness to respect the rights of others, even if their societies of origin had had little tradition of such respect.

Once learned and embraced, principles and ideas can be forgotten; their transmission may require certain ongoing experiences. Habits and practices generally require repetition for them to be sustained and transmitted to new generations. At least some of the conditions that made liberalism possible may be necessary for its maintenance, as well, such as free exit from legal and political orders and competition among political and legal authorities to attract taxpayers and capital. (Thus, federalism, when combined with freedom of movement for person and goods, recommends itself to classical liberals as a political structure that tends to sustain liberty.) Much as some sciences require laboratory experiments to be learned, some moral, legal, and political principles require continuous manifestations of the institutional conditions under which they emerged for their maintenance.

## Conclusion

Self-control, individual freedom, and limits on state power have their particular intertwined histories, but like other concepts and practices, that does not preclude universal application. The history of self-control is one of increasingly voluntary association for liberty, a process whereby individuals secured their liberty and respect for their own choices as individuals by creating rule-governed relationships with others. As Antony Black put it of the guilds and communes of Europe,

> The crucial point about both guilds and communes was that here individuation and association went hand in hand. One achieved liberty by belonging to this kind of group. Citizens, merchants, and artisans pursued their own individual goals by banding together under oath.[273]

A society is not an entity separate from the members of society; it is not a big person like the persons who constitute it, or even a great body of which the "members" are like the "members"—the hands, feet, kidneys, head—of a human body. Groups, associations, churches, clubs, societies, and governments are made up of individuals *and* their complex and multifarious relationships. There is no individual who is completely unrelated to any others who joins similarly unrelated individuals to form human society, but within the context of their inherited relationships humans do, in fact, form myriad associations, connections, and relationships. The more complex the social order, the greater the need for its members to exercise self-control.

The right to self-control is not limited only to inheritors of one or another tribe or culture, or to practitioners of only one or another religion, or to speakers of one or another language. It is the right of all human beings as such, regardless of religion, color, language, nationality, or other features. It offers the choice to live one's life as one chooses in association with others in communities one chooses. Some exercise their self-control to live in highly structured voluntary communities (monasteries and convents are the obvious examples), others in fluid urban neighborhoods; some like to live in stable and rooted communities and others prefer to roam the world and experience many ways of life. Free and self-controlling persons make such choices for themselves. They are not dictated to by others. The self-controlling individual is neither atomistic nor anomic, but creates or accepts relations based on choice and voluntary agreement.

The legal historian Sir Henry Sumner Maine described well "the movement of the progressive societies" as "a movement from Status to Contract."[274] Creating contracts, rather than merely acquiescing in what is assigned to one by birth, means acquiring the habit of self-control. The philosopher Robert Nozick called it a "framework for utopia," meaning not one perfect and blissful utopia, but a framework of choices from within which people may choose their own preferred arrangements.[275] It's not perfection, but it is far better for the vast majority of human beings than being subjected to controls imposed on them by others who are generally no wiser, no smarter, no more moral, and no better informed about the life situations of those others whom they control.

Self-controlling individuals pursue happiness by using their own knowledge to achieve their own ends. Those who pursue happiness may not always achieve it, but when someone does, it is *his or her* achievement, which is something that slaves, serfs, subordinates, subjects, and those subjected to the coercive will of others cannot say.

# 10

# Philosophical Issues of Freedom and Responsibility

*By Tom G. Palmer*

*For what am I responsible? Can there be freedom without responsibility or responsibility without freedom? How is freedom of choice possible in a world governed by causation? What kind of self is free and responsible—an individual self or a collective self? Many philosophers have sought to understand the relationship between freedom and responsibility—from Aristotle to Immanuel Kant to Martin Heidegger, Harry Frankfurt, and Daniel Dennett. Their contributions and others are examined in the search for a coherent philosophy of freedom.*

> *"Liberty not only means that the individual has both the opportunity and the burden of choice; it also means that he must bear the consequences of his actions and will receive praise or blame for them. Liberty and responsibility are inseparable."*[276]
>
> —F. A. Hayek

The discussion of self-control has a long history, and many difficult questions have engaged thinkers over the millennia, including what constitutes a self, the nature of freedom, whether freedom is a necessary or sufficient condition for responsibility (and vice versa), whether freedom and responsibility are even possible in a world governed by scientific laws or God's will, and how a set of principles that have a distinct history can be said to be universally true or valid. There is no way I could hope to cover all such topics, especially in a short essay, but I introduce and address some of the important issues that are relevant to the choice between state control and self-control in the hope that others will be induced to take up those issues and to provide new insights into the relationship between individual freedom and responsibility.

The alternative to controlling oneself is to be controlled by others. By control I don't mean persuasion or example, such as may be provided by friends and family, or moral suasion and inspiration, such as may be provided by philosophies and religions, but the use of force to override one's own choices.[277] Many persons and groups, from patriarchs to tribal councils to warlords to parliamentary majorities to generals (and many others), have systematically exercised force against others. In the past, those who used force to control others were usually slave masters, tribal chieftains, and warlords, but in the modern age, the main alternative to self-control is control by "the state," or by government, as Americans tend to say. We face a choice of state control or self-control.

The "self," as it is used in common language, is also known as the "I"—when we speak in the first person, we say "I," whether the one speaking is you, me, or the person walking down the street. Each of us, while sharing things in common, has a unique identity.

Fiction provides a means to imagine the world differently. A number of works have explored a world in which states animated by collectivist ideologies attempt to eradicate individuality. Yevgeny Zamyatin's *We* was first published in English in 1924 (he wrote it in Russian, but it was suppressed in the USSR). In *We*, the mathematician D-503 records his thoughts in a world in which individuals are reduced to mere numbers. The slogan of the OneState is "Long live OneState! Long live the numbers! Long live the Benefactor!"[278] In 1937 the Russian émigré writer Ayn Rand theorized an even more radical vision of collectivism in which the pronoun "I" had been abolished. She published a short novel, *Anthem*, about the rediscovery of individuality in a world governed by a state dedicated to a simple creed:

> We are one in all and all in one.
> There are no men but only the great WE,
> One, indivisible and forever.[279]

In her novel, everyone refers to himself or herself as "We," for "I" is unknown. In a key turn in the story, the main characters discover their love for one another.

> Today, the Golden One stopped suddenly and said:
> "We love you."
> But then they frowned and shook their head and looked at us helplessly.
> "No," they whispered, "that is not what we wished to say."
> They were silent, then they spoke slowly, and their words were halting, like the words of a child learning to speak for the first time:
> "We are one . . . alone . . . and only . . . and we love you who are one . . . alone . . . and only."[280]

George Orwell's novels articulated the incoherence and futility of attempts to abolish the self, which inevitably degenerated not into harmonious collectivist egalitarianism, but into brutal oppression by small groups of people. In *Animal Farm* (1945) he showed how the attempt to suppress individuality led merely to another form of domination of the majority by a minority, as the "Seven Commandments" of the revolution, including "All animals are equal," were compressed to the more accurate "All animals are equal, but some are more equal than others." In *1984* (written in 1948 and originally titled "The Last Man in Europe"), Orwell artfully laid bare the colossal and unending efforts necessary to crush the human spirit under the system of "Oligarchical Collectivism" (officially titled "Obliteration of the Self" in one of the three competing, but otherwise identical, collectivist states). It is possible to kill, oppress, imprison, and psychologically cripple millions or billions of people, but it is ultimately impossible to suppress the reality of the individual self.[281]

The individual is real and cannot be eradicated. The state, on the other hand, is an abstraction, not a materially individuated person like you and me. The state is "real," but not "material." "State" is the term we use to refer to "that human community which (successfully) lays claim to the monopoly of legitimate physical violence within a certain territory, this 'territory' being another of the defining characteristics of the state," to use the canonical definition of the sociologist Max Weber.[282] State entities are made up of individual persons exercising power through violence *and* their complex relationships amongst themselves and with others. It turns out that when the state decides for us, a big person we refer to as "We" doesn't end up deciding for "Us," but instead some—the most manipulative, articulate, powerful, wealthy, numerous, or intimidating—decide for others. That is always the case. In most contemporary political orders those who decide then typically insist that it was the others—the ones on whom decisions were imposed—who really were making the decisions. It is a myth, at best one of Plato's "noble lies," that serves to keep most people in line.

A free person makes her own choices and manages her own life; an unfree person's life is managed by someone else. The free person bears responsibility for her acts and the unfree person does not. If we want to be free, it's not enough merely to demand freedom: we must also demand the responsibility for our own actions and our own lives. And if we wish to be moral and upstanding people, we must embrace the freedom to make our own choices and to take the praise or the blame—that is, the responsibility—for them.

## Levels of Freedom and Responsibility

The relationship between freedom and responsibility is manifested on many levels, from the most abstract and metaphysical to the most practical and everyday. We are free persons, rather than mere material objects, because we can be held accountable for our acts. We are distinguished as individuals by what we do—the very things for which we are responsible. Responsibility for our actions and the freedom to choose for ourselves foster social cooperation, coordination, and harmony, and when our freedom and responsibility are overridden, social order is disrupted and conflict replaces harmony. When others, most notably, but not exclusively, those who are organized as "the state," force others to do this or not do that, the responsibility for what was done or not done shifts to those who used the force. If your money was transferred to another person because it was taken by taxes, you weren't being "generous." If you abstain from what may be a "vice" merely because of fear of arrest by the vice squad and imprisonment, you're not being virtuous. If you do something dangerous because you were drugged without your consent, you're not responsible for the harm you caused while under the influence of the drug.

The sign of morality, according to one influential and deep thinker, is praise and blame. His language may be somewhat dense, but it's worth quoting Aristotle at length.

> It is clear that all the acts of which man is the principle and controller may either happen or not happen, and that their happening or not happening—those at least of whose existence or non-existence he has the control—depends on him. But of what it depends on him to do or not to do, he is himself the cause; and what he is the cause of depends on him. And since excellence and badness and the acts that spring from them are respectively praised or blamed—for we do not give praise or blame for what is due to necessity, or chance, or nature, but for what we ourselves are causes of; for what another is the cause of, for that he bears the blame or praise—it is clear that excellence and badness have to do with matters where the man himself is the cause and source of his acts. We must then ascertain of what actions he is himself the source and cause. Now, we all admit that of acts that are voluntary and done from the choice of each man he is the cause, but of involuntary acts he is not himself the cause; and all that he does from choice he clearly does voluntarily. It is clear then that excellence and badness have to do with voluntary acts.[283]

When voluntary choices are overridden by force, neither the excellence nor the badness of the outcome can be morally attributed to the person who was forced. One is not fully responsible for what one was forced to do. If we want to be credited either way, voluntary choice is necessary.[284]

## Can There Be Moral Responsibility without Freedom?

Many thinkers have tested Aristotle's description of responsibility, some by suggesting that nothing is truly voluntary, others by suggesting that there may be very odd cases in which we may still be responsible for choices despite not being able to change the outcome. Some of those challenges raise interesting questions for logicians and may help to test our intuitions by raising odd, bizarre, or marginal cases, but none of them successfully uncouple freedom and responsibility.

Aristotle noted that while we may investigate many things, we only *deliberate* about those things that "are in our power and may be done,"[285] that is, we only deliberate about and make choices regarding what is, in popular language, "up to us." An especially influential critic has denied that whether something is "up to us" is a necessary condition for moral responsibility; it may help to understand moral responsibility and freedom by considering that objection. Harry Frankfurt rejects the criterion of moral responsibility according to which "a person is morally responsible for what he has done only if he could have done otherwise"; he calls that "the principle of alternate possibilities."[286]

Frankfurt argues that "A person may well be morally responsible for what he has done even though he could not have done otherwise."[287] He poses a problem about a hypothetical person, Jones:

> Jones decides for reasons of his own to do something, then someone threatens him with a very harsh penalty (so harsh that any reasonable person would submit to the threat) unless he does precisely that, and Jones does it. Will we hold Jones morally responsible for what he has done? I think this will depend on the roles we think were played in leading him to act, by his original decision and by the threat.[288]

If Jones "acted on the basis of his own decision and not because of the threat . . . I think we would be justified in regarding his moral responsibility for what he did as unaffected by the threat even though, since he would in any case have submitted to the threat, he could not have avoided doing what he did."[289] Thus, whether the act is "up to us" is, for Frankfurt, irrelevant to whether we should be held responsible.

The central problem in Frankfurt's account is that it merely displaces, outside the arbitrarily demarcated boundaries of the problem he has set, the point at which one "could have done otherwise."[290] Let's examine two cases:

A) At t1 Bill decided to steal $10 (and was then threatened with death by a master criminal if he were not to steal the $10, meaning that Bill could not have done otherwise than steal the $10) and at t2 Bill does steal the $10; Bill is held responsible for stealing the $10.

B) At t1 Mary decided *not* to steal $10 (and was then threatened with death by a master criminal if she were not to steal the $10, meaning that Mary could not have done otherwise than steal the $10) and at t2 Mary does steal the $10; Mary is *not* held responsible for stealing the $10.

Besides the obvious practical problem with such scenarios—which is acknowledged by Frankfurt—i.e., that it may be very difficult to untangle the various motives from which a person acted (e.g., an undocumented decision to take $10 or a desire to avoid being killed),[291] Frankfurt has not denied moral responsibility, but at most merely suggested that the condition of being "up to us"—namely, whether we acted freely—is not a necessary condition for moral responsibility. He concludes that "When a fact is in this way irrelevant to the problem of accounting for a person's action it seems quite gratuitous to assign it any weight in the assessment of his moral responsibility. Why should the fact be considered in reaching a moral judgment concerning the person when it does not help in any way to understand either what made him act as he did or what, in other circumstances, he might have done?"[292]

But, assuming that the ascriptions of responsibility above are correct (Bill is responsible, and Mary is not), whatever it is that distinguishes cases A and B (and there must be *some* factor that would lead us to different conclusions in the two cases), it still must depend on there being some earlier point at which Bill or Mary "could have done otherwise." There must have been something that Bill "could have done" that would have allowed Bill to join Mary in avoiding moral responsibility, and following that alternate course of action would be to have done otherwise. He could have decided earlier (at t1) *not* to steal the $10, before the threat was revealed to him, and in that case, i.e., had he done otherwise, he would not have been held responsible at t2 for stealing the $10. Bill's moral responsibility would still hinge, as Aristotle and a long tradition have maintained, on an act being up to him.[293]

Intentions are central elements in the ascription of moral responsibility for acts, but Frankfurt has raised another objection regarding common understandings of the relationship between freedom and responsibility. He distinguishes between desires as normally understood (e.g., "I desire to eat an apple") and "second-order desires" or "desires of the second order," e.g., the desire "to have (or not to have) certain desires and motives."[294] Frankfurt argues against commonsense notions of moral responsibility by claiming that "It is not true that a person is morally responsible for what he has done only if his will was free when he did it. He may be morally responsible for having done it even though his will was not free at all."[295] That is so, he argues, because:

> A person's will is free only if he is free to have the will he wants. This means that, with regard to any of his first-order desires, he is free either to make that desire his will or to make some other first-order desire his will instead. Whatever his will, then, the will of the person whose will is free could have been otherwise; he could have done otherwise than to constitute his will as he did. It is a vexed question just how "he could have done otherwise" is to be understood in contexts such as this one. But although this question is important to the theory of freedom, it has no bearing on the theory of moral responsibility. For the assumption that a person is morally responsible for what he has done does not entail that the person was in a position to have whatever will he wanted.[296]

Frankfurt does not seek directly to undermine moral responsibility, but to disconnect it from freedom. He claims that "it is irrelevant to the evaluation of his moral responsibility to inquire whether the alternatives that he opted against were actually available to him,"[297] a claim in line with his rejection of the "principle of alternative possibilities" as a criterion of moral responsibility. The key move that Frankfurt makes and others have taken up suggests that, say, a cigarette smoker who smokes but who at the same time wishes that she did *not* have the desire to smoke is *not* choosing freely when choosing to smoke. Frankfurt does not deny the moral responsibility of the smoker, but he does deny the freedom he or she exercises in choosing to smoke. That approach has been deployed by others to undermine both the freedom of the chooser and the moral responsibility for the choices he or she makes and, as a consequence, has provided support for interventionist "nanny states." A disjunction between freedom and responsibility undermines both; if there is no moral responsibility, why should freedom of choice be important (and thus protected in law), and if there is no freedom of choice, why worry about ascribing moral responsibility? It is hardly self-evident that the presence of an unwanted desire makes the will unfree. People choose regularly to ignore unwanted desires; the fact that some choices are more difficult than others does not by itself reduce or increase the freedom exercised in making choices to follow or to ignore them.

### Freedom and Responsibility in Society

Freedom and responsibility are unavoidable in a world in which we recognize other people as other "I's" and not merely as machines or pieces of meat. Other people are not mere objects. They are participants with us in a wide variety of interactions. To see other people as "other I's" is to see them as beings capable of owning their acts and of being held accountable for them, as we are held accountable for ours.

We inevitably see other agents in what P. F. Strawson refers to as the "participant" attitude, in contrast to the "objective" attitude.[298] Seeing other agents in the participant attitude entails such attitudes as "gratitude, resentment, forgiveness, love, and hurt feelings."[299] The objective attitude entails seeing others, "as something certainly to be taken account, perhaps precautionary account, of," but without "resentment, gratitude, forgiveness, anger, or the sort of love which two adults can sometimes be said to feel reciprocally, for each other."[300] We are capable of holding both attitudes toward the same people, but the objective attitude is not sustainable and represents an aberration or a temporary suspension of the participant attitude:

> The human commitment to participation in ordinary inter-personal relationships is, I think, too thoroughgoing and deeply rooted for us to take seriously the thought that a general theoretical conviction might so change our world that, in it, there were no longer any such things as interpersonal relationships as we normally understand them; and being involved in inter-personal relationships as we normally understand them precisely is being exposed to the range of reactive attitudes and feelings that is in question.[301]

Strawson's point is that, regardless of what theories we may hold about freedom or determinism, under normal circumstances if someone were to punch me in the nose, I would resent it, and I would expect to hold the person responsible, unless there were some mitigating factor: perhaps she was suffering from a brain tumor that impaired her judgment or eliminated her impulse control, or she was threatened with a horrible punishment if she did not punch me, or her arm was moved forcefully by another, in which last two cases I would resent the person who threatened her or moved her arm. In the absence of mitigating factors, we *do* hold people responsible for their behavior; we *do* evaluate the acts of others on the basis of whether they could have done otherwise. Our acts and their consequences can, at least under normal circumstances, be traced back to us. Even the most convinced behaviorist would be unlikely to respond to a personal insult or assault from another person in the same way as she would respond to a bacterial infection or a stumble over a stone that she had not seen on the path before her.

Regardless of the complexities of which moral and legal responsibility may admit, the fact is that interacting with other human beings means, in almost all cases, recognizing that they can be held responsible for their acts when they are free to act otherwise.[302] Were someone to assert otherwise, possibly on the basis of an idiosyncratic philosophical theory, she should be invited to imagine her reaction if another human were to slowly and evidently deliberately grind a spiked shoe into her hand; resentment seems quite impossible to avoid—it is a natural reaction—and the implication of such resentment is that the other agent is held responsible for the act. The presence of an unwanted desire to harm another would not reduce the freedom of the one doing the harming, nor the resentment of the one being harmed.

## Is There Freedom in a World of Causes and Effects?

Responsibility and freedom are principles that are applied in contexts. Not everything that involves one's own body is one's own responsibility. Even in cases in which it *looks like* a person is acting, and not merely being pushed, there may be other causes to which responsibility should be attributed. For example, a brain lesion may lead someone to act impulsively or violently and, once it's removed, the person becomes his or her old peaceful self. Accidental ingestion of a drug may lead to impulsive behavior or cause hallucinations that lead someone to think that others can fly unaided, after which the victim of the drugging pushes people out of the window, perhaps even laughing while doing so. In such cases we don't hold the person responsible for the actions, but instead "blame" the identifiable cause.[303]

Some have suggested that all human behavior has causes that can, at least in principle, be identified and that if modern science has proven that reality is governed deterministically, then so are our actions, so that it could never be the case that we could do otherwise and thus, we could never be free.[304] And without such freedom, then how could we ever be held accountable for our acts? Moreover, if we're not free and responsible, why treat other people as if they are moral beings at all, rather than just things to be manipulated as we desire? It's an old debate and it's unlikely that I could introduce a completely new approach here, but I will argue that it may, in fact, not be relevant to the practical issues of freedom and responsibility in human interactions in the way that many people fear it would. Even in a fully deterministic world, both freedom and responsibility would be characteristics of human interaction.

Many of those who have wrestled with the problem have been inspired by Immanuel Kant's distinction between experience, which is conditioned by the category of causality, and things as they are in themselves, prior to being understood as structured by categories. Empirically understood (that is, as a part of our experience), everything is caused, but understood "transcendentally," that is, through reason alone and thus shorn of the categories that provide structure to experience, at least some things can be understood to be uncaused: our choices, which proceed from a free will, are the causes of our acts but are not themselves caused by anything antecedent to them. According to Kant, it is this "transcendental idea of freedom on which the practical concept of freedom is grounded."[305] The practical freedom we enjoy as moral agents lies in the fact that our moral choices cause our moral acts, but are not themselves caused by anything we can perceive. To follow reason is to act freely. The immediate problem is that it would seem to follow that only choices that are morally right are free, a position also upheld by some theologians. But if that were the case, it would seem to follow that immoral choices would not be freely made and, if not free, they would not be choices for which we might be held responsible.[306] But the free and responsible person is held accountable for his or her choices, whether good or bad, moral or immoral. If one can only be praised for the right choices, but never blamed for the wrong choices, "praise and blame" cease to have any function. Freedom and responsibility are linked not only through the freedom to make the right choices and be praised for them, but through the freedom to make the wrong choices and to be blamed for them, as well. As the philosopher Daniel Dennett puts it, "Blame is the price we pay for credit, and we pay it gladly under most circumstances."[307]

Some deny the principle of causal predictability altogether, or appeal to quantum indeterminism as a way to allay the fear that a deterministic world would void moral freedom and responsibility. The problem with that approach, in a nutshell, is that if our choices are determined randomly, in what way could we be said to be responsible for them?

Perhaps someone has a truly brilliant and original new approach to the issue of freedom of the will and determinism and if so, he or she is welcome to add it to the discussion. A more modest, but still helpful, approach is to acknowledge that science does indeed rest on the search for causes and that, indeed, in some cases we can identify physical causes (brain lesions and accidental drug interactions, for examples) on the basis of which we do not hold people responsible for their actions (because they weren't "their" chosen actions at all), but that that need not undermine our general belief in each others' freedom to make choices and our responsibility for them. We may live in a deterministic universe, and the state of that universe includes the states of our brains, but that by itself need not undermine our freedom or our responsibility. There may be at this instant only one physically possible future, but it does not follow from that that the past states of the world were necessary conditions for the present or the future.[308]

More directly relevant to the issue, we can ask the question "Why" of our fellow humans and of ourselves: "Why did you do X and not Y?" We can also provide answers that involve choices we made, choices that could have been otherwise. Human beings (and perhaps other moral agents, if there are any) are distinctive in our ability to give accounts of what we are doing. That sets us apart from machines, which "do" things when we manipulate them in the right way, and even from other animals, who may respond to requests, but who can't explain to each other or to us why they do so.[309]

Unlike machines or even other animals, humans do not always require extensive training to learn to do things, much less conditioning by painful or pleasurable stimuli, as behaviorists suggest. We can speak, meaning that we can tell each other how to do things. As Daniel Dennett points out,

> We human beings not only can do things when requested to do them; we can answer inquiries about what we are doing and why. We can engage in the practice of asking, and giving, reasons.[310]

Speech—logos—is a key to human freedom. Aristotle in his treatise on *Politics* observed that

> man alone among the animals has speech. The voice indeed indicates the painful or pleasant, and hence is present in other animals as well; for their nature has come this far, that they have a perception of the painful and pleasant and signal these things to each other. But speech serves to reveal the advantageous and the harmful, and hence also the just and the unjust. For it is peculiar to man as compared to the other animals that he alone has a perception of good and bad and just and unjust and the other things of this sort; and community in these things is what makes a household and a city.[311]

Human beings have an evolved capability that the other evolved things we encounter and engage with don't seem to have; we can talk to each other and give reasons. And that is sufficient to hold us accountable; we can tell why we did something and thus, what else we could have done. In short, when we explain our choices, we acknowledge that we could have done otherwise, that our choice is "up to us." Even in a causally determined world, we still ask and give accounts of our behavior. It is for that reason that humans have been able to transform the world and themselves in so short a period of time. It is because we have freedom and the capacity to coordinate our acts for common purposes that we are able to live together in large numbers, cooperate through the division of labor, and hold one another responsible for our acts.[312] Asking and giving accounts of our behavior is the foundational act of moral responsibility and it is the inescapable foundation of social life. Creatures incapable of controlling their impulses or justifying their behavior to their fellows are incapable of achieving substantial levels of social coordination; speech and the freedom and responsibility it makes possible are the evolutionary secrets of human success.

People flourish when they are free and responsible. The awareness of responsibility is a powerful boost to social cooperation. Conversely, convincing people that they are not free and not responsible reduces cooperative behavior and makes people less successful in life. Experimental psychology is helping us to understand how a world in which people embrace their freedom and responsibility is a far better, more cooperative and social, more honest, less violent, and more peaceful world.[313]

The idea that one could have done otherwise is not the same as saying that what he or she does is contrary to the laws of cause and effect that govern the universe. When we assert the freedom and responsibility of ourselves and of our fellow humans, we are doing so in a moral and social context, not in a laboratory study of physical interactions.[314]

As empirical psychologist Roy Baumeister notes, "Perhaps ironically, free will is necessary to enable people to follow rules."[315]

### Responsibility to Others

One could write at great length about the relationship between freedom and responsibility and many writers have done just that. The upshot of a lot of complicated philosophical arguments is an insight that was reached long ago in a variety of languages and traditions.

> Zigong asked, "Is there one expression that can be acted upon until the end of one's days?"
>
> The Master [Confucius] replied, "There is *shu* 恕: do not impose on others what you yourself do not want."[316]

And

> When a heathen who wished to become a Jew asked him for a summary of the Jewish religion in the most concise terms, Hillel said: "What is hateful to thee, do not unto thy fellow man: this is the whole Law; the rest is mere commentary" (Shab. 31a).[317]

Both Confucius and Hillel were expressing the very cornerstone of civility. It's sometimes called the "Silver Rule," to distinguish it from the more exacting "Golden Rule," as expressed by Jesus of Nazareth in the Book of Matthew: "So whatever you wish that men would do to you, do so to them; for this is the law and the prophets."[318] The Silver Rule is less demanding than the Golden Rule, but all the more a *necessary* condition for humans to live together peacefully.

We move among our fellow humans not as we move among machines, but in a context that presupposes mutual recognition. Rational agents share not only a common nature, as do lobsters with other lobsters and cabbages with other cabbages, but in addition we make possible for one another an apprehension of the world as objective reality. That is an apprehension of the world that is not similarly facilitated by interaction with inanimate or non-rational entities.

We interact with other humans in the knowledge that they are moral agents, in the awareness that, for example, they have values and can engage in strategic behavior. Even the slave masters did not treat slaves simply as automata, as Descartes was said to have treated a dog crying in pain (as he casually dissected it) as no different from a machine that needed oil. The philosopher Edmund Husserl sought in the fifth of his *Cartesian Meditations* to understand the relations of humans and to "discover in what intentionalities, syntheses, motivations, the sense 'other ego' becomes fashioned in me and, under the title, harmonious experience of someone else, becomes verified as existing and even as itself there in its own manner."[319] Our "transcendental clue," or clue to what makes such an appreciation possible, is that we don't see other people as just "things" in the world, but as other agents who also experience the world:

> In changeable harmonious multiplicities of experience I experience others as actually existing and, on the one hand, as world Objects—not as mere physical things belonging to Nature, though indeed as such things in respect of one side of them. They are in fact experienced also as *governing psychically* in their respective natural organisms. Thus peculiarly involved with animate organisms, as "psychophysical" Objects, they are *"in" the world*. On the other hand, I experience them at the same time as *subjects for this world*, as experiencing it (this same world that I experience) and, in so doing, experiencing me too, even as I experience the world and others in it.[320]

For individuals the identity (or sameness) of an object is achieved only within a manifold of different views, perceptions, and so forth; the identity of an object is that which remains the same as the percepts change, and that identity is not just *another* perception or impression, as David Hume assumed (he despaired of finding that impression of the identity of an object). When we first meet, I see the front of your head, but not the back; I see the back after you turn around. The identity of your head is not one of those impressions—not one impression among many—but the pole of sameness within that changing manifold of impressions. The identity of an object can only be understood through a "transcendental move" of consciousness, in which we appreciate the interplay of sameness and otherness through which identity is achieved. The identity of an object is the immanent pole of the "same" within a manifold of differing perceptions; I cannot achieve something as an identity until I experience it in two or more "slants" or views, and the identity of the object is not just another impression among those views.

The appreciation of others as being "subjects for this world" has implications for each ego, specifically, for her capacity to experience the world itself. *We make possible for each other the experience of objectivity.* A completely isolated individual, besides suffering from a lack of human cooperation (and thus extreme deprivation), would also lack the ability to experience the objectivity of the world; she would on her own achieve the identity of objects in their manifold impressions, but not in the inter-subjective mode made possible by interactions with other minds who also apprehend the world. She would lack access to views and perspectives on the world that were not hers, but through which she would be able to achieve an objective view.

Just as identity is achieved only as the pole of sameness within a multiplicity of views of an object, achieving the objectivity of the world requires an appreciation of the interplay of sameness and otherness made possible by a multitude of perceptions and appreciations, not only within one "transcendental subjectivity," but within "transcendental *intersubjectivity*," i.e., within a *community* of experiencing egos. As Husserl pointed out in his essay "Phenomenology and Anthropology,"

In the course of these studies a fundamental distinction comes to light, within the ego's transcendental sphere of cognition, between that which belongs, so to speak, to his own person and that which is alien to him. Starting out from myself as ego constituting existential meaning, I reach the transcendental others, who are my peers, and at the same time the entire open, infinite transcendental intersubjective realm. In this transcendental community the world as "objective" and as the same for everybody is constituted.[321]

This community of experiencing egos "is an essentially *unique connectedness*, an actual community and precisely the one that makes transcendentally possible the being of a world, a world of men and things."[322]

What is significant for our purposes is that the necessity of other humans for the achievement of an objective world rests on an apprehension of the importance of other egos: "there is implicit a *mutual being for one another*, which entails an *Objectivating equalization* of my existence with that of all others—consequently: I or anyone else, as a man among other men."[323] If I apprehend each as not merely an object in the world, but as a "subject for this world," and a necessary partner in my own achievement of the world as an identity and an objectivity, I realize that each other person *has a life to lead*.[324] Although one might *want* or *prefer* that others submit to one's dominion, they remain unavoidably sources of self-direction, capable of being held accountable for their choices and of making their own claims. There is an "objectivating equalization" of my existence with that of all other rational beings; each has a life to lead. As the condemned old leveller Richard Rumbold proclaimed from the scaffold before his execution in 1685,

I am sure there was no man born marked of God above another; for no man comes into the world with a saddle on his back, neither any booted and spurred to ride him.[325]

The phrase was repeated by Thomas Jefferson in his last letter, regretfully declining the opportunity to celebrate the fiftieth

American Independence Day on July 4, 1826: "All eyes are opened, or opening, to the rights of man. The general spread of the light of science has already laid open to every view the palpable truth, that the mass of mankind has not been born with saddles on their backs, nor a favored few booted and spurred, ready to ride them legitimately, by the grace of God. These are grounds of hope for others. For ourselves, let the annual return of this day forever refresh our recollections of these rights, and an undiminished devotion to them."[326] (Jefferson died on that fiftieth anniversary.)

Each person is an autonomous being, i.e., a being who is self-ruled, in the sense that she is capable of choosing, of acting one way or another, and of being held responsible for her actions. The great human rights pioneer Francisco de Vitoria founded his defense of the indigenous people of the Americas on the realization that "a person is master of his own actions insofar as he is able to make choices between one course or another."[327] It is that ability to choose from among courses of action, the possibility that we could have acted otherwise, that makes us responsible beings. In Husserl's terms, persons "are in fact experienced also as *governing psychically* in their respective natural organisms."

Despite many interesting and subtle complications, the basic issue is rather straightforward: We hold each other accountable because we recognize moral agents. Freedom and responsibility are inescapably bound up with our social interaction. They may be suppressed or violated or denied, but they are always there.

## Responsibilities for Outcomes

Without responsibility freedom is, at best, fragmentary and unstable. Without freedom people are discouraged from claiming their responsibility. Freedom and responsibility wax and wane together.

Some have argued that what we are responsible for is not only our own lives, over which we exercise our free choices, but overall social outcomes and thus, for making choices for others. One outspoken advocate for responsibility for aggregate outcomes is Robert Goodin, who has argued that any claims about what individuals should do are relevant neither to what collectives should undertake, nor to the powers that they should exercise over individuals:

> [S]tatements about your personal responsibilities are first and foremost statements about what *you* should do. Nothing necessarily follows from those propositions as to what others should do, if you fail to do what you should have done. Sometimes others should make you do it; other times it seems better for them simply to do it for you or do something else altogether in the place of what you were supposed to have done; still other times it seems better for them to do something that will put you in a better position to do it for yourself subsequently. It is simply impossible to read off of statements about what *you* should do any automatic conclusions about what, failing that, *we* should do.[328]

Thus, the point is that regardless of whether individuals should be responsible for their own spheres of action, "we" are responsible for the behavior of others and for the overall or aggregate outcome of all of those behaviors together. Indeed, Goodin insists that it's our inordinate attention to our own affairs that is the greatest cause of injustice: "Working within the constraints set by natural scarcity, the greatest practical obstacle to achieving as much justice as resources permit is, and always has been, the supposition that each of us should 'cultivate his own garden.' . . . It is our particular obligations that all too often blind us to our larger social responsibilities. Whatever claim the world at large may have upon us, it inevitably takes second place behind the claims of particular others: our families, friends, colleagues, clients, compatriots, and so on."[329] Collective responsibility is what matters, not individual responsibility, although notably it is individuals who are jailed by the state for not obeying, and not "us" in the sense of the entire collective. (Who would be the jailer and who the jailed in the case of authentic collective responsibility? Collectivists apotheosize collective action, but it is individuals whom they punish for failing to obey their commands.)

Many thinkers and students of social relations have turned their attention to the reason why such collective assumption of responsibility fails, but few have added substantially to the insights of Thomas Aquinas, who argued for a system of justiciable individual rights and responsibilities on the following grounds:

> First because every man is more careful to procure what is for himself alone than that which is common to many or to all: since each would shirk the labor and leave to another that which concerns the community, as happens where there is a great number of servants. Secondly, because human affairs are conducted in more orderly fashion if each man is charged with taking care of some particular thing himself, whereas there would be confusion if everyone had to look after any one thing indeterminately. Thirdly, because a more peaceful state is ensured to man if each one is contented with his own. Hence it is to be observed that quarrels arise more frequently where there is no division of the things possessed.[330]

There is a crucial difference between one being dependent on the support of one's friends, family, association, or community and being dependent on the decisions of "us." Just as things possessed must be divided ("several property," as it used to be called), there must be apportionment of responsibilities, such that "externalities" are "internalized." David Schmidtz, with whom Goodin debated in their book *Social Welfare and Individual Responsibility*, clarified that what mattered for material progress "has less to do with responsibility and more to do with internalized responsibility,"[331] that is, that we not create messes for others. The responsibility may be internalized individually (I create a mess in the kitchen and I clean it up) or through any of the collective enterprises and associations through which people realize common objectives, whether families, or firms, or temples, or Scout troops, or any of the myriad other ways in which people voluntarily cooperate. Goodin phrases his concerns in terms of "once X has happened" then "we" must do something; Schmidtz phrases his in terms of how we should expect people to behave when their responsibilities are known to them.[332]

When "we" are responsible for all of "us," then responsibility is diluted to the point where it is hard to know who among "us" deserves credit for success or blame for failure. Moreover, opportunities are also created for the politically well connected and the astute to benefit.[333] Collectivist and statist ascriptions of rights and responsibilities frequently merely open the door to unscrupulous cronyism. Evading individual and voluntarily assumed responsibility in the name of collective, i.e., state responsibility, doesn't generally have a very happy ending.

## Empirical Freedom vs. Higher, Truer, Authentic Freedom

Some identify submission to state control with real or true or higher freedom. They sometimes even opine that true freedom is not the freedom of the person you experience yourself to be, the mere "empirical self," because true freedom is the realization of the "real" or "higher" or "rational" self. Those motivated by the ideology of Karl Marx, for example, insist that those who disagree with them suffer from "false consciousness," which is what causes them to resist the attempts by followers of Marx to "liberate" them. Others condemn individual freedom as "inauthentic" or as a threat to the "unity" of the nation, or the class, or the race, or the masses, or the faithful, or the people, or some other collective.

It is frequently argued that true freedom means only doing what we ought to do; not what we in fact choose to do, but what reason, morality, religion, racial or class consciousness, or our betters tell us we should do. To the extent that we deviate from those standards, they argue, we are not acting freely. The standard of freedom for the philosopher Jean-Jacques Rousseau was the "general will," which is "always rightful."[334] Given that, "whoever refuses to obey the general will shall be constrained to do so by the whole body, which means nothing other than that he shall be forced to be free."[335]

Those who believe one or another version of that thesis are convinced that when people are subjected to state control (of the right sort) they are in fact being liberated. They are being forced to be free. As Isaiah Berlin, one of the most important intellectual opponents of dictatorship in the last century, pointed out,

> Once I take this view, I am in a position to ignore the actual wishes of men or societies, to bully, oppress, torture them in

the name, and on behalf of, their "real" selves, in the secure knowledge that whatever is the true goal of man (happiness, performance of duty, wisdom, a just society, self-fulfillment) must be identical with his freedom—the free choice of his "true," albeit often submerged and inarticulate, self.[336]

As a general matter, that story does not end well. That is true not only in murderous dictatorship of the far "left" and the far "right," but in less collectively dramatic (although individually catastrophic) ways in generally freer societies, as well. Various forms of political "paternalism" and "maternalism," victimless crime laws, vice squads, welfare statism, censorship, nanny statism, labor conscription, and other substitutions of state control for self-control generate systematically negative consequences: prohibition of intoxicating or mind-altering substances generates violence, lawless black markets, organized crime, numerous deaths from overdosing and impurities, and anti-social behavior; welfare states tax to provide (frequently monopolistically) through political means what could be provided and chosen voluntarily—from retirement income, to medical care, to housing, to education—and in the process induce people to reduce their savings, engage in riskier behavior, abandon voluntary mutual aid organizations, and pay less attention to securing their own well being and that of their families and communities; nanny states suppress both personal freedom and the development of good habits; censorship to "protect us" from bad or impure or untrue thoughts quashes critical thinking and the search for truth. Replacing self-control with state control rarely generates any of the benefits claimed by its enthusiasts and always generates other, unintended, consequences.[337]

## From "Higher Freedom" to "Collective Self"

Frequently combined with the claims of protecting "true" or "higher" freedom are assertions that freedom is necessarily collective, the freedom of the collective against other collectivities and over the individual. As such, freedom is not really a property of individuals, but of collective entities, whether the nation, the country, the people, the state, the class, the race, or some other abstract entity. Michael Sandel promotes a kind of philosophically soft collectivism (although the coercion is quite real and hard when visited on people) and has suggested that to the extent that our identities are constituted by shared "aspirations and attachments," "our constitutive self-understandings comprehend a wider subject than the individual alone, whether a family or tribe or city or class or nation or people."[338]

The greater or more encompassing "subject" (or self) that is apotheosized by such thinkers is then treated as if it had the attributes of a natural person, like you or me. The freedom of the group is then seen not as the freedom *among* its members, but as the freedom of the group as such, as if it were a person who had the right and the expectation of respect and autonomy, which it most decidedly is not. One hears such language repeatedly from spokespeople for various tyrannical governments, who insist that any person, whether a "domestic" private individual, a global religious leader, or a "foreign" individual, who dares to criticize the violent or oppressive acts of those governments, is thereby infringing on the freedom of the nation over which that government rules. Thus, merely issuing a statement in support of dissidents is "interfering" in the affairs of the other country, as if the dissidents being harassed, imprisoned, beaten, tortured, or executed were of no account, and their treatment something like my treatment of my hair, which I cut periodically.

The fact is that a family, nation, tribe, state, firm, association, club, etc., etc., is not a person like the persons who constitute it; it is made up of those persons and all of their complex relationships.[339] In fact, treating a group, whether a state or a chess club, as a big person merely blinds us to the complex relationships that make up the subject matter of journalism, political science, and the search for truth generally.[340] It obscures who is deciding for whom, which is the interesting question.

Some philosophers have argued that individual freedom is an illusion, personal responsibility a delusion, and the individual herself a mere fiction, the intersection of social "forces" that are more real than the ephemeral flesh-and-blood organism we call a human being.

Indeed, some have argued that only the nation, the race, the class, or the state is real, is the true self, and that the individual human being is less a self than a single cell of an organism. Karl Marx insisted that man is a "species being," that is, that he exists as such only in and through a community and that individual rights subvert human existence by separating humans from each other. For Marx,

> Human emancipation will only be complete when the real, individual man has absorbed into himself the abstract citizen; when as an individual man, in his everyday life, in his work, and in his relationships, he has become a *species-being*; and when he has recognized and organized his own powers (*forces propres*) as *social* powers so that he no longer separates this social power from himself as a political power.[341]

The claims of classical liberals on behalf of individual liberty were dismissed by Marx in his famous tract on the Jews[342] as "the liberty of man regarded as an isolated monad, withdrawn into himself": moreover, classical liberal arguments for political equality were disposed of as having "no political significance. It is only the equal right of liberty as defined above; namely that every man is equally regarded as a self-sufficient monad."[343] Unsurprisingly, Marx called for making such individuals "impossible,"

> by "individual" you mean no other person than the bourgeois, than the middle-class owner of property. This person must, indeed, be swept out of the way, and made impossible.[344]

It remains a wonder that so many were so surprised when followers of his ideas, who proclaimed themselves "Marxists," proceeded in the twentieth century to carry out that vision of making individuals impossible: they marched millions of individual human beings into slave labor camps and "liquidated" tens of millions in the name of "liberating" an abstract "species being."[345]

All such theories lead, in the end, not to the realization of some higher and greater being, call it the nation or the people or the race or the state, but to the domination of some flesh-and-blood individual humans by others.

Martin Heidegger was one of the most influential of all twentieth-century philosophers; his anti-individualist ideas have infused and motivated the far right, the far left, radical and violent "Islamism,"[346] and other collectivist movements. He was at the same time one of the least understood of philosophers because he was, on the one hand, so efficient at concealing his ideas behind clouds of impenetrable prose, and, on the other, quite successful in falsifying after the war his record of support for National Socialism from 1933 to 1945.[347] Decades of post–World War II writers puzzled over his writings about "existence" ("*Dasein*" in German) and thought that Heidegger was writing about what it means to "be" a human or to exist as a human and that that question provided the access to the question of being. In fact, as he made more clear during the period of National Socialism (Nazism), when he could speak more openly about his ideas, Dasein is something of which one can speak only in the collective "we," and specifically, the Dasein of a particular people, the German *Volk*. As Heidegger declared in his lectures after the National Socialist seizure of power,

> The German people is now passing through a moment of historical greatness: the youth of the academy knows this greatness. What is happening, then? The German people as a whole is coming to itself, that is, it is finding its leadership. In this leadership, the people that has come to itself is creating a state.[348]

That is to say, in "finding its leadership," the leader ("der Führer") will decide for all of the people. And, indeed, that collective Dasein, by finding its leadership, will be infused with power: "Only when we are what we are coming to be, from the greatness of the inception of the Dasein of our spirit and people, only then do we remain fit for the power of the goal toward which our history is striving."[349] René Descartes, famous for his "Cogito ergo sum" formulation ("I think, therefore I am") was denounced by Heidegger because, for Descartes (in Heidegger's words), "The *I* of the thinking human being thus moves into the center of what can truly be humanly known."[350] Heidegger wished

175

to displace the "I" with the "We" of a collective. As he stated in a very strange lecture course on logic delivered under the National Socialist regime, which had little to do with what is normally understood as logic and much to do with Heidegger's enthusiastic racism and National Socialism, "we have . . . the advantage that the question of who *we* ourselves are is timely, as distinguished from the time of liberalism, the I-time. Now is the We-time."[351]

The "We" was not merely this or that "nameless crowd" or "revolting mass," but the *Volk.* As for Marx, for Heidegger, Dasein, or existence, was not the existence of an "isolated" and "self-forlorn" individual, nor of mere collections of them, but of a self-conscious collective, in Marx's case the class and state, and in Heidegger's case the *Volk* and state: "it becomes clear why the character of the self does not consist in the reflexivity of the I, of the subject; for it is precisely the blasting of I-ness and of subjectivity by temporality, which delivers Dasein, as it were, away from itself to being and thus compels it toward self-being."[352] The entire performance is mired in *non sequiturs*, opaque language, unjustified leaps of inference (often justified by whether words sound similar), and other moves, but Heidegger considered it one of his most important works, although not published until many years after his death, as his explicitly Nazi convictions started to re-emerge from the archives.

Heidegger set the stage for the rejection of individual freedom and responsibility among intellectuals of both the far "left" and the far "right" (which have more in common than the "left-right" spectrum suggests) in recent decades by insisting that the center stage should be occupied by a *We*, in his own case the We of the German People (*Volk*), which he considered a historical people with a historical mission. Heidegger's elevation of the concept of "authenticity" as the test of true existence set the stage for a wide range of anti-individualist movements: nationalist, racist, socialist, ethnic, and even the recent surge of "politically correct" identities. Others have merely substituted for the German *Volk* other collectivities, consistently with Heidegger's polylogism (the idea that there are different truths for different groups) and rejection of universal truths.[353] In each case, it is an authentic existence that is asserted to be collective, as distinguished from the mere

"I" in the company of other individuals that characterizes classical liberalism. Metaphysical collectivism, the assertion that existence itself is inherently collective, was eagerly taken up by aggressive anti-individualist extremists of left and right, all of whom assert that their ideological submersion of the individual into the greater whole represents the embrace of "authentic" Dasein, and all of whom are united in their rejection of the idea of individual freedom and responsibility. Of course, such absorption of the individual into the "We" always means subordination of some individuals, usually the majority, to other individuals, usually a small and well-organized clique of people who have seized power for themselves in the name of the collective. (That was one of Orwell's insights in *1984*: the doctrine of "Oligarchical Collectivism" refers precisely to that inevitability.)

Collectivism invariably means the destruction of both freedom and responsibility. The freedom of the individual is shattered by coercion and violence and, ultimately, responsibility is dissipated. The people, the race, the party, the community, the masses, the nation, or some other collective entity is held to be the agent of action. Displacing freedom and responsibility from the individual human being to some allegedly greater or higher entity merely evaporates both into nothing. The German novelist Robert Musil pondered the idea of the "Nation" in his essay " 'Nation' as Ideal and as Reality," which was written shortly after at least seventeen million people had been killed in the First World War. "Germany," as the defeated power, was blamed by the victors for the war. Musil asked who was really responsible for the horrors of the war.

How false the childish excuse, which is, unfortunately, often heard in Germany: We didn't do it! The Emperor, the generals, the diplomats did it! Of course we did it: we let it happen; it happened without our interfering. Here as in other countries. How false too the other excuse one often hears: We simply weren't firm enough, we let ourselves be fooled.... The individual . . . simply showed himself incapable of anything, and allowed it all to happen. In the complete illusion of his own free will, he followed without exercising his will. We did it, they did it; that is, no one did it, just "it" did it.[354]

Collectivism represents the extreme form of the denial of both freedom and responsibility. Indeed, collectivists insist that true freedom is the abandonment of individual responsibility and submission to the state. For Heidegger, that entailed that "Freedom is not the independence of doing and letting, but carrying through the inevitability of being, taking over the historical being in the knowing will, reforming of the inevitability of being into the dominance of a structured order of a *Volk*. Care of freedom of the historical being [*Seins*] is in itself empowering of the power of the State as the essential-jointure of an historical mission."[355] As Musil, a classical liberal critic of emergent collectivism, noted, in collectivist orders, the independent human being is absolved of responsibility, for no one really acts or is responsible for crimes; "it" does them. That's the conclusion of all forms of collectivism. And when their regimes come crashing down, the leaders who exercised power in the name of the collective do all they can to avoid any personal responsibility when their crimes are revealed. "It" did it, which means that no one is accountable at all.

Of course, individuals do act in coordination with others to achieve collective goals, whether good, bad, or indifferent. We speak of groups "acting," whether those groups are chess clubs, peace societies, trade unions, business enterprises, parliaments, universities, or states. But although it's meaningful to speak of such groups acting, those groups are not individuals like the members who make them up. They are, in fact, made up of individuals *and* all their relationships among themselves. Groups are not entities like the constituents that form them. Nor are they higher forms of consciousness; if anything, they may represent a degradation of human consciousness, as Musil noted; they are frequently the means by which people *evade* their own freedom and responsibility.

If we wish to locate the responsibility for actions, it is in the human beings who think, deliberate, plan, speak, move, and act. The individual human being is the locus of moral agency; the group is the network within which it may be exercised, but when misunderstood, it becomes the vaporous cloud within which it is dispersed, denied, disappeared.

At least outside of science fiction stories, very unusual cases of multiple personalities, hypothetical philosophy thought-experiments, and brain injury and other rare medical situations, each self is distinctly embodied, that is, each of us is associated with one materially individuated body. It is through our bodies that we interact with the material objects of the world and it is through our bodies that we learn to distinguish what is us from what is not us. Thomas Hodgskin, a journalist and radical free-trade and peace agitator who wrote for the *The Economist*, grounded personal identity in the fact that one's body belongs to oneself:

> Mr. Locke says, that every man has a property in his own person; in fact, individuality—which is signified by the word *own*—cannot be disjoined from the person. Each individual learns his own shape and form, and even the existence of his limbs and body, from seeing and feeling them. These constitute his notion of *personal* identity, both for himself and others; and it is impossible to conceive—it is in fact a contradiction to say—that a man's limbs and body do not belong to himself: for the words him, self, and his body, signify the same material thing.
>
> As we learn the existence of our own bodies from seeing and feeling them, and as we see and feel the bodies of others, we have precisely similar grounds for believing in the individuality or identity of other persons, as for believing in our own identity. The ideas expressed by the words mine and thine, as applied to the produce of labour, are simply then an extended form of the ideas of personal identity and individuality.[356]

The individual human being, the living form of a single organic body, is the natural foundation of responsibility and freedom. Even if I do, might, or should "identify" with some group, there is no way in which I could "identify" with the other members in quite the same way that I identify with myself, for I cannot feel and perceive, nor control, the motions of the bodies of others in the way that I do my own. I have control and possession of my body in a way that I can never have over another's. (One is free to speculate about artificial intelligences that may be loci of freedom and responsibility, alien beings with collective identities, and so on, but embodied agents are all we now encounter.)

"Bodily self-ascription" has the marked advantage of "immunity to error through misidentification."[357] As Gareth Evans notes,

> we have what might be described as a general capacity to perceive our own bodies, although this can be broken down into several distinguishable capacities: . . . . Each of these modes of perception appears to give rise to judgments which are immune to error through misidentification. None of the following utterances appears to make sense when the first component expresses knowledge gained in the appropriate way: "Someone's legs are crossed, but is it my legs that are crossed?"; "Someone is hot and sticky, but is it I who am hot and sticky?"; "Someone is being pushed, but is it I who am being pushed?" There just does not appear to be a gap between the subject's having information (or appearing to have information), in the appropriate way, that the property of being $F$ is instantiated, and his having information (or appearing to have information) that $he$ is $F$; for him to have, or to appear to have, the information that the property is instantiated just is for it to appear to him that $he$ is $F$.[358]

Epictetus considered such bodily self-ascription the most certain kind of knowledge. In his response to the skepticism of the Pyrrhonists and the Academic philosophers, Epictetus argued, "But that you and I are not the same persons, I know very certainly. Whence do I get this knowledge? When I want to swallow something, I never take the morsel to that place, but to this."[359]

Each person is identified with one and only one body, spatio-temporally distinct from all others. Each person is a source or principle of motion for one body. Each body provides demarcation of a sphere of "ownness." The values that one acts to attain or preserve are the values of materially individuated agents; they may be held in common with others, but they are "agent-relative." Each person is responsible for those acts in cases in which she "could have done otherwise." Each person is responsible for the acts of her own body, but not (excepting special cases, such as guardianship of minors and the mentally deficient) for the acts of the bodies of others, for these are the responsibility of other agents, i.e., those whose spheres of "ownness" are defined by these bodies.[360]

Responsibility and freedom ultimately are entwined together in the locus of human action, the individual human being. Attempts to undo the connection between freedom and responsibility have failed, while philosophers who conjure up and endow with personality mythical collective selves have had enough political success to cause enormous harm to individuals and to social relationships in the real world. The former have been murdered in the hundreds of millions in the last century alone, while the latter have been suppressed, disrupted, and generally displaced by organized states whose propagandists claim that they are really "us." A world of free and responsible individuals cooperating in voluntary association is a far better alternative to the suffering and the social atomization created by state control.

# 11

# Increasing and Improving Your Own Self-Control

*By Tom G. Palmer*

*What practical implications does embracing freedom and responsibility have for the conduct of one's own life? How can one improve one's self-control and effectively grasp one's freedom and responsibility? Research is providing not only answers to scientific questions, but techniques for achieving greater self-control, success, and happiness. Here is a short guide to some of the key techniques and guides to self-control.*

> "There is something magnificent about control directed upon oneself, resulting in an independently operating, intelligent, responsible, and persevering agent. The self-motivating person who takes no commands from others and needs no others to command comes close to the best the human race has produced. In such an individual, habits of independence are coupled with deep respect for the independence of others. The tendency to leave others alone is rooted not in indifference to the fate of people, but in the conviction that under normal circumstances we can benefit them most by letting them pursue their own ends without interference."[361]
>
> —John Lachs, Centennial Professor
> of Philosophy, Vanderbilt University

*"[P]eople and societies can cultivate the faculty of self-control over time and thereby drive down their rates of violence."*[362]
—Steven Pinker, Johnstone Family Professor
of Psychology, Harvard University

"Man wants liberty to become the man he wants to become. *He does so precisely because he does not know what man he will want to become in time. Let us remove once and for all the instrumental defense of liberty, the only one that can possibly be derived from orthodox economic analysis. Man does not want liberty in order to maximize his utility, or that of the society of which he is a part.* He wants liberty to become the man he wants to become."[363]
—James Buchanan, Nobel Laureate
in Economic Science

Self-control is attainable. It's not something one just has or doesn't have. It can be increased, cultivated, improved, and made a foundation for lives of freedom, compassion, achievement, earned self-respect, and happiness in community with others. For those who lament that we just are what we are and cannot change, there is very good news. We have the freedom to change ourselves, to replace harmful habits with useful ones, to achieve our purposes, to become less violent and more respectful of others, to become the people we want to become. We can grow in compassion and improve our lives and the lives of those around us. And there's a true silver lining: improvement in self-control and spiritual growth are possible not only for young people, but for old, as well.

Before looking into how we can improve our self-control, though, it might help to dispel some popular misunderstandings about what self-control is. Once that's done, we can look to the burgeoning science of self-control (sometimes also referred to as "willpower") to draw some practical lessons that we can use to improve our self-control, serve our enlightened self-interests, and secure our liberty.

For some people the term "self-control" evokes the image of a steely-eyed person staring down some temptation, with perhaps a bead of sweat slowly trickling down his or her face and shaking hands hidden under the table, or an incredibly brave hero refusing to betray the resistance—or even to cry out in pain—while enduring the most terrible of tortures. Those images are very misleading. Except in very unusual circumstances (and movies) self-control isn't about steely resolve and doesn't entail lots of pain and suffering. It's not about being "rugged" or unemotionally logical, either. It's about being mindful of what you hope to accomplish and how your goals fit together. It's about acquiring, sometimes slowly and over long periods of time, the habits that are conducive to reaching your goals. It's about being aware of those who are around you and of their interests, perceptions, and rights. People with self-control acquire the ability to avoid temptations without having to shake and sweat.

Thinking about self-control goes back a very long time and is found in many philosophical and religious traditions. It has long been understood that with effort we can make ourselves into the people that we want to be. We become the people we want to be by acting as we should. Aristotle noted that the word "ethics," which has come from ancient Greek to modern English, derives from ἦθος, or habit. He contrasted "those things in us by nature," such as our faculties of sight and hearing, which we use because we have them, with virtues, which we have because we use them: "the virtues we come to have by engaging in the activities first, as is the case with the arts as well. For as regards those things we must learn how to do, we learn by doing them—for example, by building houses, people become house builders, and by playing the cithara, they become cithara players. So too, then, by doing just things we become just; moderate things, moderate; and courageous things, courageous."[364]

Habituating ourselves to doing the right thing allows us to become the people we want to become. The habits we already have are, as it turns out, virtually impossible to simply eliminate; they have become integrated into the physical structures of our brains. We can, however, deliberately acquire habits we want and, even if we can't eliminate the bad habits we have, we can replace them with others that we prefer.[365] Modern neuroscience now explains better than Aristotle was able to do how those habits are incorporated into the structures of our brains. The brain is capable of change, and even of being consciously changed, throughout life. The modern term for that capacity for change is "neuroplasticity," and it refers to the ways in which brain structures that underlie our habits, our personalities, our perceptions, and more are alterable. The good news is that we can alter the physical substrate of our selves at our own initiative. The material substrate of our selves places limits on what we can do, but that materiality does not eliminate our freedom. We have the metaphysical freedom to shape our own lives, to become the people we want to become. Doing so takes work, even struggle. Achieving greater self-control yields benefits not only in better lives, but also in greater ability to struggle for our freedom as legal equals in free societies. Greater self-control is something we can acquire, something we can integrate into our lives, something we can learn.

- Learning to make better decisions helps us to avoid failure and secure our independence;
- Learning to be mindful of the interests of others helps us to become better at cooperating voluntarily to benefit ourselves, our families, our communities, and all of humanity;
- Learning to save more for the future helps us to avoid entrapment by and dependence on the welfare state;
- Learning to be mindful of the rights of others, including people with very different values or ways of life, helps us to respect them and with them to secure mutual liberty;
- Learning to control our impulses helps us to achieve our deeper and more rational purposes and to enjoy lives of meaning and dignity;
- Learning to plan and guide our own lives helps us to stand up against the nanny state and its prohibitions, controls, and behavioral mandates;
- Learning to be aware of our own dignity helps us to turn down bailouts and subsidies extracted by force from others and to reject the mentality of "rent-seeking," or "loot before you are looted," and to stand with our neighbors as free citizens of free countries;

- Learning to improve our self-control helps us not only to live, but to let live.

Achieving greater self-control helps us to assert our freedom, tell the politicians and bureaucrats that we can make our own choices, and take back both our freedom and our responsibility.

# APPENDIX

**Useful Guides and Tips for Increasing Self-Control**

It would be presumptuous of me to write a guidebook on how to improve one's self-control. As a work in progress, I'm better prepared to provide a guide to some important books on the topic, with a few lessons drawn from each. That both saves me from shameful immodesty and offers the reader a chance to explore the issues herself or himself. Most of the books I've selected are easy to read and contain very useful pointers. (I'll indicate some of the more useful in **bold text**.) They offer practical exercises, as well.

*If you were to acquire only one of the following works, I'd recommend one of the first two. (You might buy both, but then you might let them both sit on the shelf staring at you, so I'd recommend choosing one and being sure to read that one. Then you might want to buy the other.)*

**Training and Maintaining the Willpower Muscle**
*Willpower: Rediscovering the Greatest Human Strength*, by Roy Baumeister and John Tierney (New York: Penguin Books, 2011)

An experimental psychologist, Roy Baumeister, and a science writer for the *New York Times*, John Tierney (who contributed a chapter to the book you are reading now), teamed up to produce a book that is fascinating, grounded in empirical scientific study, delightfully written, and useful. They show that willpower, the capacity for self-control, is strongly related to our brain chemistry, in particular, to our available supply of glucose. They show that **willpower is in limited supply and that it can be depleted**. Every time you make a decision, you spend some of your scarce willpower, so **it's wise to avoid spending it on unimportant decisions that will leave you depleted when you face a really important decision**. Moreover, rather like a muscle, **willpower can be strengthened by practicing it, even with practicing small things such as sitting up straight**. (Your parents knew a thing or two when they admonished you not to slouch.)

Exercising your willpower can increase your supply of it overall. **Setting realistic goals and then revisiting them** (to see how unrealistic they were, so you can scale them down to achievable goals the next time around) is a key step to self-control. **Part of setting a goal is to establish a reward for yourself for meeting it**; merely using self-control to deny ourselves pleasures leads to failure, whereas the positive incentive of rewarding yourself is more likely to motivate you (that is, the desiring parts of your brain) to do what you want to do.

**Monitoring your own behavior can help you to achieve self-control**; financial software such as Mint.com helps me to control my finances (it shows me what I've spent, in detail and in the big picture, reminds me of bills, and strengthens my willpower to avoid impulse purchases), while **simply having (and regularly stepping on) a simple bathroom scale is one of the most powerful aids for dieters who are struggling to control their weight**.

Promising ourselves that we will indulge in something we want (such as food) later, rather than saying "Never!" turns out to help us to satisfy our craving; when we do try a bit later, we tend to indulge less, whereas when we say "Never!" we tend to indulge a lot more when the occasion presents itself; **delaying, rather than denying, gratification can be a more effective means of cutting back**. The authors describe the enormous scientific research of recent years into willpower and apply that science to understand why we fail and how we can succeed.

### The Power of "I Won't," "I Will," "I Want"

*The Willpower Instinct: How Self-Control Works, Why It Matters, and What You Can Do to Get More of It,* by Kelly McGonigal (New York: Avery/Penguin, 2012)

Stanford University psychology instructor Kelly McGonigal teaches courses on self-control and has written a user-friendly manual on how to manage our selves. She draws on recent discoveries in neuroscience and applies those lessons to the challenges we all face in managing our lives. McGonigal starts with **simple exercises to achieve greater self-knowledge**, asking you to focus (even if only briefly) on the times you wish you would say "no," the times when you wish you would say "yes," and, as a framework, what you want to achieve in life: **"I will," "I won't," and "I want."**

You can strengthen your "I will" power by **committing yourself to some small task, such as discarding daily one useless thing that is cluttering up your home or quietly sitting and breathing (meditating) for five minutes a day.** You can strengthen your "I won't" power by **committing yourself to not doing some small thing, such as using swear words or slumping in your chair.** You can strengthen your "I want" by **committing to regularly monitoring yourself**, either with a bathroom scale and a paper and pencil, or with Mint.com, or with some of the mechanisms available at QuantifiedSelf.com.

**Avoid traps that encourage behavior you want to avoid,** such as when you buy apparently virtuous "organic" or "green" products that turn out to be high in calories (trading off one virtue for another) or when you feel "licensed" after a workout to eat a high-calorie meal. **Reward yourself for difficult, but desirable, behavior by linking it with something you really like and anticipate.** Put the power of imagination to work for you by **imagining very clearly and visually your future self and how grateful he or she will be** to you ("present you") for being so helpful and nice to "future you."

## Changing Habits
*The Power of Habit: Why We Do What We Do in Life and Business,*
by Charles Duhigg (New York: Random House, 2014)

*New York Times* reporter Charles Duhigg started to notice the importance of habits when he was a war-zone reporter and saw how riots were avoided by police paying attention to habits (namely, the habit of eating; you can read the book to learn more). He started investigating the neuroscience of habit and in his book he shares what he learned and applies it to a number of historical and everyday occurrences.

There's one big takeaway from the book: **once you've acquired a habit, you really can't get rid of it.** It's "wired" into your brain, as it were, and when the right occasion (the "cue") comes, you'll slip back into it. The good news is that **you can lay down a new habit that will replace the habit you don't want**. To do so you need to **identify the elements of your habit: the routine into which you habitually slip (snacking or biting your nails or smoking or snapping back at your spouse or whatever it might be); what triggers it (the "cue"), and what reward you receive for doing it**.

Duhigg offers not only a clear explanation of the neuroscience behind habits, but very practical techniques for acquiring good habits and for replacing bad habits with better ones. As he explains, "to modify a habit, you must *decide* to change it. You must consciously accept the hard work of identifying the cues and rewards that drive the habits' routines, and find alternatives. You must know you have control and be self-conscious enough to use it."[366]

## Thinking Clearly . . . and Avoiding Mental Potholes
*The Art of Thinking Clearly,* by Rolf Dobelli (London: Sceptre, 2013)

Rolf Dobelli is a businessman, novelist, and writer and a careful reader of behavioral economics. He has drawn from such sources as Daniel Kahneman and Nassim Nicholas Taleb ninety-nine lessons, presented as very short and enjoyable chapters.[367] Dobelli alerts you to such common mental errors as the "**conjunction fallacy**," "**confirmation bias**," the "**law of small numbers**," and "**availability bias**." Once you're aware of how common and natural such mistakes are, you can take special care to avoid them in making your own decisions. You can read one short chapter per day for a little over three months and avoid a lot of mistakes in life.

## Meditate Your Way to Self-Control

*Buddha's Brain: The Practical Neuroscience of Happiness, Love, & Wisdom,* by Rick Hanson, with Richard Mendius (Oakland: New Harbinger Publications, 2009)

Many religions and spiritual communities have developed traditions of contemplation and activities that are intended to bring one closer to the divine. Buddhism has provided a foundation for contemplative practice (i.e., meditation) for thousands of years. Buddhist techniques of meditation emerged from a particular religious context,[368] but the techniques can be applied to achieve greater self-control even without the religious background within which Buddhist practitioners developed those techniques. Rick Hanson ties in Buddhist meditative practices with neuroscience to understand the "self-transforming brain." Buddhist practices can help us to achieve a state of calm and "mindfulness," to increase our compassion (starting with our compassion for the person who is often last on our list: our own self), to increase steadiness of purpose, and to create peace.[369]

## There's Always More to Read

For those who really want to dive into the literature on self-control, there is a wealth of interesting and useful works. The following I found especially interesting and helpful:

> *A Mind for Numbers: How to Excel at Math and Science* (*Even If You Flunked Algebra*), by Barbara Oakley (New York: Jeremy P. Tarcher/Penguin, 2014);

> and

*The Marshmallow Test: Understanding Self-Control and How to Master It*, by Walter Mischel (London: Corgi/Penguin, 2015).

The following two very useful books can help you to achieve a more organized—and thus purposeful and effective—life:

*Getting Things Done: The Art of Stress-Free Productivity*, by David Allen (New York: Penguin Books, 2001); and
*Never Too Busy to Cure Clutter*, by Erin Rooney Doland (New York: William Morrow, 2016).

(Clutter is a major problem for me, and Erin Rooney Doland's books have helped me; but as with all of the above—and as a peek into my office would show—I'm definitely just a work-in-progress.)

## Online
Finally, there's also a wealth of online resources. Lifehacker.com, Mint.com, QuantifiedSelf.com, and other sites offer tools that enable us to achieve greater self-control. At a much deeper level, *systems thinking* and *decision analysis* offer means whereby rational processes can be made explicit and even habitual. They were developed to help in logistics and business, but they are helpful in assisting anyone to make better decisions for his or her personal life, as well. Three integrated educational programs apply advanced business practices to life problems generally and translate tools developed for logistics and business into useful lessons that are packaged for young people. (They may be packaged for youth, but they're also used in the training programs and strategic planning processes of some of the largest and most successful business firms in the world.)[370]

**Systems Thinking in Schools**: Sponsored by the Waters Foundation, systems thinking draws on work done at MIT on systems dynamics and helps people to visualize and incorporate into their decision-making the consequences of their choices. The programs, including modules for personal and for classroom use, can be found at www.watersfoundation.org.

**Decision Analysis**: Decision analysis was pioneered at Stanford University and is applied to business decisions by such firms as the Strategic Decisions Group (www.sdg.com). Two educational foundations offer extensive programs to teach decision skills to students in elementary, middle, and high school; the programs are crafted for young people, but the contents are useful to anyone at any age or stage of life. The Decision Education Foundation offers their programs at www.DecisionEducation.org and How I Decide offers their programs at www.HowIDecide.org.

From the *Dhammapada*, one of the oldest texts of Buddhism:

> Others do not understand
> That we must control ourselves here;
> But for those who do understand this—
> Through it, their quarrels cease.[371]

> By self alone evil is done;
> By self one is defiled.
> By self evil is not done;
> By self one is purified.
> Purity and impurity are individual matters:
> No one can purify another.[372]

# Endnotes

## Preface

1. *The Meditations of Marcus Aurelius Antoninus,* A. S. L. Farquharson, trans. (Oxford: Oxford University Press, 1990), 5.

## Chapter 1: The Great Choice

2. Benjamin Constant, "The Liberty of the Ancients Compared with that of the Moderns" [1819], in Benjamin Constant, *Political Writings,* ed. Biancamaria Fontana (Cambridge: Cambridge University Press, 1988), 326
3. Adam Smith, *The Theory of Moral Sentiments* (Indianapolis: Liberty Press, 1982), 111, n. 3 (reproducing text from the third through fifth editions).
4. Ibid., 114.
5. Ibid., 114.
6. Ibid., 115.
7. Frederick Douglass, *Narrative of the Life of Frederick Douglass, an American Slave, Written by Himself* (1845; New York: Penguin Books, 1986), 115.
8. Ibid., 117.
9. Ibid., 83.
10. Ibid., 85.
11. Randy E. Barnett, "The Harmful Side Effects of Drug Prohibition," *Utah Law Review* (2009): 29–31
12. Jeffrey A. Miron and Jeffrey Zwiebel, "Alcohol Consumption during Prohibition." *American Economic Review* 81 (1991): 242–247.
13. See the historical accounts of the creation of government pension plans in *After the Welfare State,* Tom G. Palmer, ed., (Ottawa, Illinois: Jameson Books, 2012), available online at https://studentsforliberty.org/wp-content/uploads/2012/04/After-the-Welfare-State-PDF.pdf.
14. "Social Security Trust Fund Sits in West Virginia File Cabinet," *USA Today* (February 28, 2005): www.usatoday.com/news/washington/2005-02-28-trust-fund_x.htm.
15. Nick Eberstadt, *A Nation of Takers* (West Conshohocken, Pennsylvania: Templeton Press, 2012).
16. Diana Furchtgott-Roth and Jared Meyer, *Disinherited: How Washington Is Betraying America's Youth* (New York: Encounter Books, 2015).
17. "The Debt Fallout: How Social Security Went 'Cash Negative' Earlier Than Anyone Expected," *Washington Post* (October 29, 2011).
18. "The law will consist of purpose-independent rules which govern the conduct of individuals towards each other, are intended to apply to an unknown number of further instances, and by defining a protected domain of each, enable an order of actions to form itself wherein the individuals can make feasible plans." F. A. Hayek, *Law, Legislation, and Liberty: Volume I, Rules and Order* (Chicago: University of Chicago Press, 1973), 85–86.
19. See his 1947 essay "Planned Chaos," available online at http://fee.org/resources/planned-chaos-2 and his 1952 essays in *Planning for Freedom,* ed. Bettina Bien Greaves (Liberty Fund: Indianapolis, 2008), available online at http://oll.libertyfund.org/titles/mises-planning-for-freedom-let-the-market-system-work-a-collection-of-essays-and-addresses. Advocates of socialism and intervention always believe that what they are doing is imposing reason on the "anarchy" of society, but in fact the results

don't correspond to any rational thought, but are the mere accretions of one coercive intervention after another.

20. Sloan Frost, "The Tangled Dynamics of Interventionism: The Case of Health Care," in *Why Liberty*, ed. Tom G. Palmer (Ottawa, Illinois: Jameson Books, 2013), 83–95, at http://studentsforliberty.org/wp-content/uploads/2013/07/Why-Liberty-Final-Typeset-with-Cover.pdf.

21. "What is required if the separate actions of the individuals are to result in an overall order is that they not only do not unnecessarily interfere with one another, but also that in those respects in which the success of the action of the individuals depends on some matching action by others, there will be at least a good chance that this correspondence will actually occur." F. A. Hayek, *Law, Legislation, and Liberty: Volume I, Rules and Order*, 98–99.

22. F. A. Hayek. *The Road to Serfdom: Text and Documents—The Definitive Edition* (1944; Chicago: University of Chicago Press, 2007) (Kindle Locations 1442–1445). Kindle Edition.

23. John Locke, *Two Treatises of Government*, ed. Peter Laslett (Cambridge: Cambridge University Press, 1988); *Second Treatise of Government*, Chap. VI, §57, 306. Liberty, for Locke, "is *not a State of License*," ibid., 311. The distinction between liberty and license is clearly articulated in Randy E. Barnett, *The Structure of Liberty: Justice & the Rule of Law* (2nd ed.; Oxford: Oxford University Press, 2014), "Introduction: Liberty v. License," 1–40.

24. Richard Overton, "An Arrow against All Tyrants," in *The English Levellers*, ed. Andrew Sharp (Cambridge: Cambridge University Press, 1998), 55.

25. Frederick Douglass, "A Friendly Word to Maryland," an address delivered in Baltimore, Maryland, on November 17, 1864, cited in Nicholas Buccola, *The Political Thought of Frederick Douglass: In Pursuit of American Liberty* (New York: New York University Press, 2012), 23.

26. Plato, *The Republic*, trans. Alan Bloom (New York: Basic Books, 1968), 235, 557b.

27. Ibid., 241, 563b-c.

28. The seizure of power by such educated intellectuals as Khieu Samphan, Huo Yuon, Ta Mok, and Saloth Sar [Pol Pot] in Cambodia led to the horror of the "Killing Fields." The Khmer Rouge seizure of power is one of the worst cases, but not the only one; it should stand forever as a warning about the dangers of allowing intellectuals to seize power.

29. General rules, which are not intended to create any particular outcome, facilitate the emergence of complex systems of order that incorporate far more knowledge than could be the case were they created with specific ends in mind. See Lode Cossaer and Maarten Wegge, "How Do You Know? Knowledge and the Presumption of Liberty," in *Why Liberty*, ed. Tom G. Palmer, (Ottawa, Illinois: Jameson Books, 2013), 97–110. The book can be downloaded in its entirety at http://studentsforliberty.org/wp-content/uploads/2013/07/Why-Liberty-Final-Typeset-with-Cover.pdf. The English political theorist Norman Barry wrote a scholarly and comprehensive essay on the history of the idea: "The Tradition of Spontaneous Order," *Literature of Liberty*, Vol. V, No. 2 (Summer 1982): http://www.econlib.org/library/Essays/LtrLbrty/bryTSO.html.

30. Constant, "The Liberty of the Ancients Compared with that of the Moderns," 326.

## Chapter 2: How Brain Chemistry Explains Human Freedom and Helps Us to Realize It

31. W. Mischel, Y. Shoda, and P. Peake, "The Nature of Adolescent Competencies Predicted by Preschool Delay of Gratification," *Journal of Personality and Social Psychology* 54 (1988): 687–96.

32. J. P. Tangney, R. F. Baumeister, and A. L. Boone, "High Self-Control Predicts Good Adjustment, Less Pathology, Better Grades, and Interpersonal Success," *Journal of Personality* 72 (2004): 271–322.

33. R. N. Wolfe and S. D. Johnson, "Personality as a Predictor of College Performance," *Educational and Psychological Measurement* 55 (1995): 177–85. Also see A. L.

Duckworth and M. E. P. Seligman, "Self-Discipline Outdoes IQ in Predicting Academic Performance of Adolescents," *Psychological Science* 16 (2005): 939–44.

34. R. F. Baumeister et al., "Ego Depletion: Is the Active Self a Limited Resource?" *Journal of Personality and Social Psychology* 74 (1998): 1252–65.

35. R. F. Baumeister, K. D. Vohs, and D. M. Tice, "Strength Model of Self-Control," *Current Directions in Psychological Science* 16 (2007): 351–55. M. S. Hagger, C. Wood, C. Stiff, N. L. Chatzisarantis, "Ego depletion and the strength model of self-control: a meta-analysis," *Psychological Bulletin* 136 (2010): 495–525. Although this meta-analysis of eighty-three studies reported a confirmation of the ego-depletion effect, the strength of this effect has been questioned because of a subsequent study led by one of the authors, M. S. Hagger, that failed to find evidence of ego depletion after experimental subjects performed a reading task on a computer. Baumeister has criticized the methodology of the new study, arguing that the computerized task did not adequately deplete the subjects' willpower. As this book went to press, he and other researchers were preparing a new research protocol to test the effects of ego depletion.

36. W. Hofmann et al., "Everyday Temptations: An Experience Sampling Study of Desire, Conflict, and Self-control," *Journal of Personality and Social Psychology* 102 (2012): 1318–35.

37. K. D. Vohs et al., "Making Choices Impairs Subsequent Self-Control: A Limited Resource Account of Decision Making, Self-Regulation, and Active Initiative," *Journal of Personality and Social Psychology* 94 (2008): 883–98.

38. J. Levav et al., "Order of Product Customization Decisions: Evidence from Field Experiments," *Journal of Political Economics* 118 (2010): 274–99.

39. M. Gailliot et al., "Self-control Relies on Glucose as a Limited Energy Source: Willpower is More Than a Metaphor," *Journal of Personality and Social Psychology* 92 (2007): 325–336.

40. M. Muraven, R. F. Baumeister, and D. M. Tice, "Longitudinal Improvement of Self-Regulation through Practice: Building Self-Control through Repeated Exercise," *Journal of Social Psychology* 139 (1999): 446–57.

41. M. Oaten and K. Cheng, "Improved Self-Control: The Benefits of a Regular Program of Academic Study," *Basic and Applied Social Psychology* 28 (2006): 1–16; M. Oaten and K. Cheng, "Longitudinal Gains in Self-Regulation from Regular Physical Exercise," *British Journal of Health Psychology* 11 (2006): 717–33; M. Oaten and K. Cheng, "Improvements in Self-Control from Financial Monitoring," *Journal of Economic Psychology* 28 (2006): 487–501.

42. R. I. M. Dunbar, "The Social Brain Hypothesis," *Evolutionary Anthropology* 6 (1998): 178–90.

43. W. A. Roberts, "Are Animals Stuck in Time?" *Psychological Bulletin* 128 (2002): 473–89.

44. M. Donald, *A Mind So Rare: The Evolution of Human Consciousness* (New York: Norton, 2002).

45. G. Ainslie, *Breakdown of Will* (New York: Cambridge University Press, 2001).

46. J. Mathews et al., "Reliability and Validity of the Brief Self-Control Scale among Incarcerated Offenders" (poster presented at the annual meeting of the American Society of Criminology, Atlanta, Georgia, November 2007).

47. T. Moffitt et al., "A Gradient of Self-Control Predicts Health, Wealth, and Public Safety," *Proceedings of the National Academy of Sciences* (January 24, 2011), http://www.pnas.org/content/early/2011/01/20/1010076108.

48. A. S. Westman, J. Willink, and J. W. McHoskey, "On Perceived Conflicts between Religion and Science: The Role of Fundamentalism and Right-Wing Authoritarianism," *Psychological Reports* 86 (2000): 379–85; John T. Jost et al., "Political Conservatism as Motivated Social Cognition," *Psychological Bulletin* 129 (2003): 339–375.

49. Markus Kemmelmeier, Cherry Danielson, and Jay Basten, "What's In a Grade? Academic Success and Political Orientation," *Personality and Social Psychology Bulletin* 31 (2005): 1386–1399.

50. Joshua J. Clarkson et al., "The Self-control Consequences of Political Ideology," *PNAS* 112 (2015): 8250–3.

51. R. R. Wing et al., "'STOP Regain': Are There Negative Effects of Daily Weighing?" *Journal of Consulting and Clinical Psychology* 75 (2007): 652–56.

52. Hofmann et al., "Everyday Temptations," 1318–35.

53. C. N. DeWall et al., "Depletion Makes the Heart Grow Less Helpful: Helping as a Function of Self-regulatory Energy and Genetic Relatedness," *Personality and Social Psychology Bulletin* 34 (2008) 1663–76.

## Chapter 3: Life in the Nanny State: How Welfare Impacts Those Who Receive It

54. Romia Boccia, Allison Acosta Fraser, and Emily Goff, "Federal Spending by the Numbers 2013: Government Spending Trends in Graphics, Tables, and Key Points," *Heritage Foundation*, no. 140 (2013): 3.

55. Ibid.

56. Michael Harrington, *The Other America: Poverty in the United States* (New York: Macmillan Publishing Co., 1969).

57. Carmen DeNavas, Bernadette D. Proctor, and Jessica C. Smith, "Income, Poverty, and Health Insurance Coverage in the United States: 2009," US Census Bureau, Current Population Reports (2010): 3.

58. Robert Rector, Katherine Bradley, and Rachel Sheffield, "Obama to Spend $10.3 Trillion on Welfare: Uncovering the Full Cost of Means-Tested Welfare or Aid to the Poor," *Heritage Foundation*, SR-67 (2009): 20.

59. Ibid., 30.

60. Pam Fessler, "Both Parties Agree the Food Stamp Program Needs To Change. But How?" *National Public Radio*, last modified March 20, 2015, http://www.npr.org/sections/thesalt/2015/03/20/394149979/a-push-to-move-food-stamp-recipients-into-jobs.

61. Isabel V. Sawhill, "Poverty in America," *Library of Economics and Liberty* (2008). http://www.econlib.org/library/Enc/PovertyinAmerica.html

62. "Poverty Thresholds," US Census Bureau (2015), accessed here: https://www.census.gov/hhes/www/poverty/data/threshld/.

63. Ibid.

64. "The Uninsured: A Primer," *The Henry J. Kaiser Family Foundation*, #7451-07 (2011).

65. David J. Armor and Sonia Sousa, "Restoring a True Safety Net," *National Affairs*, Issue No. 13 (2012): 4.

66. Serena Lei, "The Unwaged War on Deep Poverty," *Urban Institute* (2015).

67. Ben Cosgrove, "War on Poverty: Portraits from an Appalachian Battleground, 1964," *Time*, last modified January 7, 2014, http://time.com/3878609/war-on-poverty-appalachia-portraits-1964/.

68. Michael Tanner, "The War on Poverty Turns 50: Are We Winning Yet?" Cato Institute, Number 761 (2014): 16.

69. "Drug Testing for Welfare Recipients and Public Assistance," National Conference of State Legislatures (2015).

70. "Editorial: Drug Testing Welfare Applicants Nets Little," *USA Today*, last modified March 18, 2012, http://usatoday30.usatoday.com/news/opinion/editorials/story/2012-03-18/drug-testing-welfare-applicants/53620604/1.

71. Julia Griggs and Robert Walker, "The Costs of Child Poverty for Individuals and Society," Joseph Rowntree Foundation (2008).

72. Ibid.

73. Ibid.

74. Eric Pianin, "20 Percent of Global Suicides Linked to Unemployment," *The Fiscal Times*, last modified February 23, 2015, http://www.thefiscaltimes.com/2015/02/23/20-Percent-Global-Suicides-Linked-Unemployment.

75. John Ifcher, "The Happiness of Single Mothers after Welfare Reform," *The B. E. Journal of Economic Analysis & Policy*, Vol. 11 Issue 1 (2011): 1–29.

76. Chris Herbst, "Welfare Reform and the Subjective Well-being of Single Mothers," *Journal of Population Economics*, Vol. 26 Issue 1 (2013): 203–238.

77. Ibid.

78. Ibid.
79. Ifcher, "The Happiness of Single Mothers after Welfare Reform," 1–29.
80. Franklin D. Roosevelt, "Annual Message to Congress," *The American Presidency Project* (1935), accessed here: http://www.presidency.ucsb.edu/ws/?pid=14890.
81. Warren Buffet, "Better Than Raising the Minimum Wage," *The Wall Street Journal*, last modified May 21, 2015, http://www.wsj.com/articles/better-than-raising-the-minimum-wage-1432249927.

## Chapter 4: Does Consumer Irrationality Justify the War on Drugs?

82. I take no stand on whether "non-rational" behavior is best described as irrational, myopic, behavioral, or just "less than fully rational." These concepts overlap but are not equivalent; the differences, however, are not important for the discussion here. For a recent review of these issues, see: Matthew Rabin, "Incorporating Limited Rationality into Economics," *Journal of Economic Literature* 51, no. 2 (2013): 528–543, http://dx.doi.org/10.1257/jel.51.2.528.
83. Jeffrey A. Miron, "The Economics of Drug Prohibition and Drug Legalization," *Social Research* (2001): 835–855.
84. Higher costs might partially cause lower profits, rather than just higher prices, if entry barriers (such as aversion to working in an illegal industry) have not already prevented profits (adjusted for risk, danger, and so on) from being driven to zero.
85. Jeffrey A. Miron, "The Effect of Drug Prohibition on Drug Prices: Evidence from the Markets for Cocaine and Heroin," *Review of Economics and Statistics*, 85, no. 3 (2003): 522–530.
86. Jeffrey A. Miron and Jeffrey Zwiebel, "Alcohol Consumption During Prohibition," *American Economic Review* 81 (1991): 242–247; Suren Basov, Jeffrey Miron, and Mireille Jacobson, "Prohibition and the Market for Illegal Drugs," *World Economics* 2, no. 4 (2001): 113–158; Angela K. Dills and Jeffrey A. Miron, "Alcohol Prohibition and Cirrhosis," *American Law and Economics Review* 6, no. 2 (2004): 285–318; Angela K. Dills, Mireille Jacobson, and Jeffrey A. Miron, "The Effect of Alcohol Prohibition on Alcohol Consumption: Evidence from Drunkenness Arrests," *Economics Letters* 86, no. 2 (2005): 279–284; Chris Feige and Jeffrey A. Miron, "The Opium Wars, Opium Legalization, and Opium Consumption in China," *Applied Economics Letters* 15, no. 12 (2008): 911–913; Jeffrey A. Miron, *Marijuana Policy in Colorado* (Cato Institute, October 23, 2014).
87. Jeffrey A. Miron, "Violence, Guns, and Drugs: A Cross-Country Analysis," *Journal of Law and Economics* 44, no. S2; "Guns, Crime, and Safety: A Conference Sponsored by the American Enterprise Institute and the Center for Law, Economics, and Public Policy at Yale Law School" (October 2001): 615–633.
88. Milton Friedman, "The War We Are Losing," in *Searching for Alternatives: Drug-Control Policy in the United States*, ed. Melvyn B. Krauss and Edward P. Lazear (Stanford, California: Hoover Institution Press, 1991): 53–67; Jeffrey A. Miron, "Violence and the US Prohibitions of Drugs and Alcohol," *American Law and Economics Review* 1, no. 1–2 (Fall 1999): 78–114. Figure 1 is reproduced from Figure 8.17 of Angela S. Dills and Jeffrey A. Miron, "What Do Economists Know About Crime?" in *The Economics of Crime: Lessons for and from Latin America,* eds. Sebastian Edwards, Rafael Di Tella, and Ernesto Schargrodsky (Chicago: University of Chicago Press, 2010).
89. Miron, "Violence, Guns, and Drugs: A Cross-Country Analysis," *Journal of Law and Economics* (2001).
90. Miron, "The Effect of Drug Prohibition on Drug Prices," (2003) argues that prohibition's impact on drug prices is probably smaller than estimated in earlier work, but still substantial.
91. Bruce L. Benson and David W. Rasmussen, "Relationship between Illicit Drug Enforcement Policy and Property Crimes," *Contemporary Policy Issues* IX (October 1991): 106–115; Bruce L. Benson et al., "Is Property Crime Caused by Drug Use or by Drug Enforcement Policy?" *Applied Economics* 24 (1992): 679–692.
92. Steven B. Duke and Albert C. Gross, *America's Longest War: Rethinking Our Tragic*

*Crusade against Drugs* (New York: G. P. Putnam's Sons, 1993): 37–42, 53–54, 64–66, 73–74; US Department of Justice, *Drugs, Crime, and the Justice System: A National Report for the Bureau of Justice Statistics* (Washington DC, 1992): 5.

93. Steven B. Duke, "Drug Prohibition: An Unnatural Disaster," *Connecticut Law Review* 27 (1994): 571. See also http://www.independent.co.uk/news/world/europe/portugal-decriminalised-drugs-14-years-ago--and-now-hardly-anyone-dies-from-over-dosing-10301780.html.

94. John P. Morgan, "The Jamaica Ginger Paralysis," *Journal of the American Medical Association* 245, no. 15 (October 15, 1982): 1864–1867. Figure 2 is reproduced from Figure 1 in Jeffrey A. Miron and Jeffrey Zwiebel, "Alcohol Consumption during Prohibition," *American Economic Review* (1991): 242–247.

95. Duke and Gross. *America's Longest War: Rethinking Our Tragic Crusade against Drugs.*

96. William J. Chambliss, "Another Lost War: The Costs and Consequences of Drug Prohibition," *Social Justice* (1995): 108–111; Randy E. Barnett, "The Harmful Side Effects of Drug Prohibition," *Utah Law Review* (2009): 29–31; Jeffrey A. Miron and Jeffrey Zwiebel, "The Economic Case against Drug Prohibition," *The Journal of Economic Perspectives* (1995): 175–192.

97. Jeffrey A. Miron and Katherine Waldock, "The Budgetary Impact of Ending Drug Prohibition," (The Cato Institute, September 2010), http://ssrn.com/abstract=1710812.

98. Eric Schlosser, "Reefer Madness," *Atlantic Monthly* (August 1994): 45–63.

99. Andy Greenberg, "Two Charts Show How the Drug War Drives Domestic Spying," *Wired* (July 17, 2015), http://www.wired.com/2015/07/drug-war-driving-us-domestic-spying.

100. Samuel R. Friedman, Theresa Perlis, and Don C. Des Jarlais, "Laws Prohibiting Over-the-Counter Syringe Sales to Injection Drug Users: Relations to Population Density, HIV Prevalence, and HIV Incidence," *American Journal of Public Health* 91, no. 5 (2001): 791.

101. Lester Grinspoon and James B. Bakalar, *Marijuana: The Forbidden Medicine* (New Haven: Yale University Press, 1993).

102. James Zacny et al., "College on Problems of Drug Dependence Taskforce on Prescription Opioid Non-medical Use and Abuse: Position Statement," *Drug and Alcohol Dependence* 69, no. 3 (2003): 215–232.

103. Robert J. Barro, "To Avoid Repeats of Peru, Legalize Drugs," *Wall Street Journal* (April 27, 1992).

104. Miron and Waldock (2010).

105. This statement ignores the possibility of externalities from drug use, which might occur even if consumers were rational. Many goods cause externalities, however, and the appropriate policy response targets the externality generating behavior (e.g., driving under the influence) rather than banning the good entirely. Thus, externalities aside, all of prohibition's effects are negative if consumers are rational.

106. Gary S. Becker and Kevin M. Murphy, "A Theory of Rational Addiction," *Journal of Political Economy* 96 (1988): 675–700; Donald S. Kenkel, Robert R. Reed III, and Ping Wang, *Rational Addiction, Peer Externalities, and Long Run Effects of Public Policy,* no. w9249 (National Bureau of Economic Research, 2002); Michael Grossman and Frank J. Chaloupka, "The Demand for Cocaine by Young Adults: A Rational Addiction Approach." *Journal of Health Economics* 17, no. 4 (1998): 427–474.

107. Miron and Zwiebel, *The Journal of Economic Perspectives*; Jeffrey A Miron, "Drug Prohibition" in *The New Palgrave Dictionary of Economics and the Law*, ed. Peter Newman (London: The Macmillan Press, 1998): 648–652.

108. The possibility of addiction does not, by itself, create special concerns for policy. Caffeine, for example, is addictive, yet few people want to ban coffee, tea, and cola drinks. The risk—for irrational consumers—comes from addictive goods that have serious side effects, especially if those materialize only after long-term use.

109. See footnote 84 above on whether higher costs imply higher prices or lower profits.

## Chapter 5: How Property Rights Undergird Environmental Responsibility

110. Hawk Mountain Sanctuary, History, n.d. Available at http://www.hawkmountain.org/who-we-are/history/page.aspx?id=387. Accessed September 4, 2015.
111. Ecotopia, "Rosalie Edge: A Brief Biography," n.d. Available at http://ecotopia.org/ecology-hall-of-fame/rosalie-edge/biography. Accessed September 4, 2015.
112. David Hume, *Treatise on Human Nature*, (1738, Oxford: Oxford University Press, 1978), 501–525
113. Garrett Hardin, "The tragedy of the commons," *Science* 162, no. 3859 (1968): 1243–1248.
114. Ronald Coase, "The Problem of Social Cost," *Journal of Law and Economics* 3 (1960): 1–62.
115. Elinor Ostrom, *Governing the Commons* (Cambridge: Cambridge University Press, 1990).
116. Denny Ellerman et al., *Markets for Clean Air: The US Acid Rain Program* (New York: Cambridge University Press, 2000) in Terry Anderson and Donald Leal, *Free Market Environmentalism for the Next Generation* (London: Palsgrave Macmillan, 2015), 43.
117. Anderson and Leal, *Free Market Environmentalism for the Next Generation*, 105.
118. Ibid., 109.
119. Michael 't. Sas-Rolfes, *Saving African Rhinos: A Market Success Story,* Property and Environment Research Center, PERC Case Study series (n.d.). Available at http://www.perc.org/sites/default/files/Saving%20African%20Rhinos%20final.pdf. Accessed September 10, 2015; Timothy Taylor, "Property Rights and Saving the Rhino," *Conversable Economist,* August 25, 2014. Available at http://conversableeconomist.blogspot.com/2014/08/property-rights-and-saving-rhino.html. Accessed September 10, 2015.

## Chapter 6: First Person Singular: Literature and Individual Resistance

120. "The Art of War," in Tom G. Palmer, ed., *Peace, Love, & Liberty* (Ottawa, Illinois: Jameson Books, 2014), 126–131

## Chapter 7: Rules and Order without the State

121. For an extended treatment of this, see Lon L. Fuller, *Principles of Social Order: Selected Essays of Lon L. Fuller*, Kenneth I. Winston ed. (North Carolina: Duke University Press, 1982)
122. Elinor Ostrom, *Governing the Commons: The Evolution of Institutions for Collective Action* (Cambridge: CUP, 2015).
123. Catholic Church, *Catechism of the Catholic Church* (London: Geoffrey Chapman, 1994), no. 2431.
124. Kevin Dowd and Martin Hutchinson, "How Should Financial Markets Be Regulated?" *Cato Journal* 34(2) (2014): 353–388.
125. Andrew G. Haldane, "The Dog and the Frisbee," speech given to Federal Reserve Bank of Kansas City's 36th economic policy symposium, "The Changing Policy Landscape." Jackson Hole, Wyoming, USA (2012).
126. http://www.conservativehome.com/thecolumnists/2014/10/lord-flight-regulation-the-collectivist-wolf-in-sheeps-clothing.html. The US also saw substantial increases in the enforcement powers of, and the number of regulations issued by, state regulatory agencies, Mark A. Calabria, "Did Deregulation Cause the Financial Crisis," *Cato Policy Report* (July/August 2009), http://www.cato.org/policy-report/julyaugust-2009/did-deregulation-cause-financial-crisis.
127. Jeffrey Friedman, "A Crisis of Politics, Not Economics: Complexity, Ignorance, and Policy Failure," *Critical Review*, Vol. 21, Nos. 2–3 (2009): 127–183.

128. Philip Booth, *Verdict on the Crash—Causes and Policy Implications,* Hobart Paperback 37 (London: Institute of Economic Affairs, 2009).

129. See www.bankofengland.co.uk/publications/Documents/quarterlybulletin/qb070211.pdf.

130. This would include people such as one of the authors who is a Fellow of the Institute of Actuaries, has a PhD in finance, and has been an Institute of Actuaries' examiner for twenty-three years.

131. William Ashworth, *The Genesis of Modern British Town Planning* (London: Routledge and Kegan Paul, 1954).

132. James Howard Kunstler, *The Geography of Nowhere: The Rise and Decline of America's Man-Made Landscape* (New York: Free Press, 1994).

133. C. W. Chalklin, *The Provincial Towns of Georgian England: A Study of the Building Process 1780–1820* (London: Edward Arnold, 1974).

134. Stephen J. Davies, "Laissez-Faire Urban Planning," in David T. Beito, Peter Gordon, and Alexander Tabarrok, eds, *The Voluntary City: Choice, Community and Civil Society* (Ann Arbor, Mich.: Michigan University Press, 2002), 18–46.

135. Richard Dennis, "The Geography of Victorian Values: Philanthropic Housing in London, 1840–1900," *Journal of Historical Geography* 15(1)(1989): 40–54.

136. In the case of banking, the issue is more complex because the central bank could often regulate banks in rather subtle ways. However, there was no regulation of the amount of spare capital that banks had to hold, which is the important issue for the purposes of this discussion.

137. A buffer of assets over liabilities.

138. Forrest Capie and Geoffrey Wood, *Do We Need Regulation of Bank Capital? Some Evidence from the UK,* IEA Current Controversies 40 (London: Institute of Economic Affairs, 2013).

139. Renee Haltom and Jeffrey M. Lacker, "Should the Fed Have a Financial Stability Mandate? Lessons from the Fed's First 100 Years," *Federal Reserve Bank of Richmond Annual Report* (Richmond, Virginia, USA, 2013).

140. Booth, *Verdict on the Crash*, 2009; and Roger Koppl, *From Crisis to Confidence: Macroeconomics after the Crash*, Hobart Paperback 175 (London: Institute of Economic Affairs, 2014).

141. Philip Booth, "Freedom with Publicity—The Actuarial Profession and Insurance Regulation from 1844 to 1945," *Annals of Actuarial Science*, 2(1) (2007): 115–146.

142. Most obviously, the actuarial profession.

143. They find it more difficult to access capital and it is more difficult for owners (customers) to discipline managers than in the case of shareholder-owned companies—in other words, principal-agent problems are greater.

144. Because the owners are the customers.

145. See, for example, John Nicoll and J. Chisholm, "The Relation of the Actuarial Profession to the State," *Journal of the Institute of Actuaries,* Vol. 34, (1898): 158–251.

146. Booth, "Freedom with Publicity," 2007.

147. See: http://www2.isda.org/about-isda/

148. For a more detailed history, see Philip Booth, "Stock Exchanges as Lighthouses," *Man and the Economy*, 1(2)(2014): 171–188 (memorial issue for Prof. Ronald Coase); Terry Arthur and Philip Booth, *Does Britain Need a Financial Regulator? Statutory Regulation, Private Regulation and Financial Markets* (London: Institute of Economic Affairs, 2010), 168; and the excellent book by Edward Stringham, *Private Governance: Creating Order in Economic and Social Life* (Oxford: Oxford University Press, 2015).

149. Philip Booth, *Thatcher: the Myth of Deregulation,* Discussion Paper 60 (London: Institute of Economic Affairs, 2015).

150. Royal Commission on the London Stock Exchange, 1878, 5; see Edward Stringham, "The Unseen Beauty that Underpins Markets," in *Private Governance: Creating Order in Economic and Social Life,* 226–236.

151. Kenneth Durr and Robert Colby, *The Institution of Experience: Self-Regulatory Organizations in the Securities Industry, 1792–2010,* Securities and Exchange Commission Historical Society (Washington DC, 2010).

# Chapter 8: The Welfare State and Erosion of Responsibility

152. Franklin D. Roosevelt, Annual Message to Congress, January 4, 1935 (The American Presidency Project), accessed June 10, 2015, www.presidency.ucsb.edu/ws/?pid=14890.

153. Friedrich Heinemann, "Is the Welfare State Self-Destructive? A Study of Government Benefit Morale," *Kyklos* 61 (2008): 237–257.

154. Erns Fehr and Urs Fischbacher, "Social norms and human cooperation," *Trends in Cognitive Sciences* 4 (2004): 185–190, esp. 186.

155. Heinemann, "Is the Welfare State Self-Destructive?" 240.

156. Tom G. Palmer, "Bismarck's Legacy," *After the Welfare State*, ed. Tom G. Palmer (Ottawa, Illinois: Jameson Books, 2012), 42–45, available at https://studentsforliberty.org/wp-content/uploads/2012/04/After-the-Welfare-State-PDF.pdf

157. Ronald Reagan, Radio Address to the Nation on Welfare Reform, February 15, 1986 (The American Presidency Project), accessed June 10, 2015, www.presidency.ucsb.edu/ws/?pid=36875.

158. Ibid.

159. Bill Clinton, "How We Ended Welfare, Together," *New York Times*, August 22, 2006.

160. Paul Krugman, "Socialist Hellhole Blogging," *New York Times*, August 19, 2011. The text appeared in Krugman's blog, The Conscience of a Liberal. Accessed June 10, 2015, http://krugman.blogs.nytimes.com/2011/08/19/socialist-hellhole-blogging.

161. The term "moral hazard" is used to describe situations in which two or more parties have incomplete and asymmetric information about the intentions of the other. Examples include situations in which one party makes decisions and the other bears the costs; situations in which a party insures against risk and, because he or she is now insured, may be more likely to engage in risky behavior; and situations in which people who are provided public benefits to shield them from the effects of joblessness or low incomes reduce their productive efforts in order to qualify for the benefits.

162. Robert H. Nelson, "Max Weber Revisited," in *Religion, Economy and Cooperation*, ed. Ilkka Pyysiäinen (Berlin and New York: Walter de Gruyter GmbH & Co., 2010).

163. Assar Lindbeck, "Hazardous Welfare-State Dynamics," *American Economic Review*, Papers and Proceedings 85 (1995): 9–15; and Assar Lindbeck, "An Essay on Welfare State Dynamics," CESifo Working Paper Series No. 976 (2003).

164. Niclas Berggren, Mikael Elinder, and Henrik Jordahl, "Trust and Growth: A Shaky Relationship," *Empirical Economics* 35 (2008): 251–274.

165. In this study, Iceland, the small Nordic-cousin which has a more limited welfare state, is also included.

166. Jan Delhy and Kenneth Newton, "Predicting Cross-National Levels of Social Trust: Global Patterns or Nordic Exceptionalism?" *European Sociological Review* 21 (2005): 311–27.

167. Nima Sanandaji, *Scandinavian Unexceptionalism—Culture, Markets, and the Failure of Third-Way Socialism*, (London: Institute of Economic Affairs, 2015). I explore welfare-norms and norm erosion in Scandinavia.

168. Daniel Arnold, "Benefit Morale and Cross-Country Diversity in Sick Pay Entitlement," *Kyklos* 66 (2013): 27–45.

169. OECD tax database. Norway and Finland did have somewhat higher tax rates, at 28 and 27 percent of GDP respectively. Even these two countries however had lower taxes than the United Kingdom, which at the time had a 30 percent rate.

170. Sanandaji, *Scandinavian Unexceptionalism* (2015).

171. Andreas Bergh and Christian Bjørnskov, "Historical Trust Levels Predict the Current Size of the Welfare State," *Kyklos* (2011): 1–19.

172. Eric M. Uslaner, "Where you stand depends upon where your grandparents sat—The inheritability of generalized trust," *Public Opinion Quarterly* (2008): 725–740; Tino Sanandaji, "Proving Bo Rothstein wrong: Why do Swedes trust more? Culture, not welfare state policy," blog post October 2, 2010, accessed March 28, 2016, http://www.tino.us/2010/10/proving-bo-rothstein-wrong-why-do-swedes-trust-more-culture-not-welfare-state-policy/.

173. Bergh and Bjørnskov, "Historical Trust Levels," 1.
174. The American Community Survey (ACS) from 2013 shows that the poverty rate amongst Scandinavian Americans, Swedish Americans and Finnish Americans was 5.1 percent. Amongst Norwegian Americans it was 4.7 percent and amongst Danish Americans 4.2 percent. This can be compared to the national average of 11.7 percent. Economists Geranda Notten and Chris de Neubourg have in a paper from 2011 calculated the poverty rates in European countries and the United States using the same way of measuring poverty. They show the rates to be 6.7 percent in Denmark, 9.3 percent in Sweden, and 15 percent in Finland.
175. Sanandaji, *Scandinavian Unexceptionalism* (2015).
176. Philipp Doerrenberg et al., "Nice Guys Finish Last: Do Honest Taxpayers Face Higher Tax Rates?" *Kyklos* 1 (2014): 29–53.
177. Heinemann, "Is the Welfare State Self-Destructive?" 237.
178. World Value Survey data for question V198, "Justifiable: claiming government benefits": http://www.worldvaluessurvey.org/WVSDocumentationWV5.jsp (select WV6_Results_v_2015_04_18.pdf)
179. Jean-Baptiste Michau, "Unemployment Insurance and Cultural Transmission: Theory and Application to European Unemployment," CEP Discussion Paper No. 936, Centre for Economic Performance (London: London School of Economics and Political Science, 2009): 2.
180. Martin Halla, Mario Lackner, and Friedrich G. Schneider, "An Empirical Analysis of the Dynamics of the Welfare State: The Case of Benefit Morale," *Kyklos* 1 (2010): 55–74, esp. 56 and 71.
181. Lindbeck, "Hazardous Welfare-State Dynamics"; Assar Lindbeck, "Prospects for the Welfare State," Seminar paper No. 755 (Stockholm: Institute for International Economic Studies, Stockholm University, 2008).
182. Lindbeck, "Prospects for the Welfare State." It is worth noting that Scandinavian countries have relatively large shadow economies compared with countries such as the United States. Scandinavian shadow economies have reduced as a share of total GDP over time, coinciding with a shift towards greater economic freedom. For estimations of the size of shadow economies, see Friedrich Schneider and Colin C. Williams, "The Shadow Economy," Hobart Paper 172 (London: Institute of Economic Affairs, 2013).
183. Arne Modig and Kristina Broberg, "Är det OK att sjukskriva sig om man inte är sjuk?" memo T22785 (Stockholm: TEMO, 2002).
184. Peter Skogman Thoursie, "Reporting Sick: Are Sporting Events Contagious?" *Journal of Applied Econometrics* 19 (2004): 809–823.
185. Malin Persson, "Korta sjukskrivningar under fotbolls-VM 2002—en empirisk studie," mimeo (Uppsala: Department of Economics, Uppsala University, 2005). In both cases, the sickness rate amongst women is used as a control for other variations.
186. Martin Ljunge, "Yngre generationers högre sjukskrivningstal—ett mått på hur snabbt välfärdsstaten förändrar normer," Ekonomisk Debatt 5 (2013): 56–61. Translated from Swedish.
187. Casper Hunnerup Dahl, "Velfærdsstat og Arbejdsmoral," (Copenhagen: CEPOS, 2013): 2. Translated from Danish. See also *New York Times*, "Danes Rethink a Welfare State Ample to a Fault," April 10, 2013.
188. *Politiken*, "Corydon: Konkurrencestat er ny velfærdsstat," August 23, 2013.
189. Økonomi og indenrigsministeriet, "Økonomisk redegørelse August 2013," August 2013.
190. See more in Nima Sanandaji, "The Dutch rethink the welfare system," *New Geography*, February 11, 2013, accessed June 10, 2015, at www.newgeography.com/content/004028-the-dutch-rethink-welfare-state.
191. In the 2015 election the British conservatives, which during their previous term in government had limited welfare programs extensively, won re-election. To the surprise of the world, the conservatives increased their seats so that they were able to form a majority government, instead of the coalition government that they had previously formed together with the centrist Liberal Democrats.
192. *Financial Times*, "Norway: Cruise Control," February 6, 2014.

193. Dagens Möjligheter, "Svensk arbetsmoral utklassar norrmännens," November 14, 2012.

194. Bjørgulf Claussen, Lisbeth Smeby, and Dag Bruusgaard, "Disability pension rates among immigrants in Norway," *Journal of Immigrant and Minority Health* 14 (2012): 259–263.

195. *Dagbladet*, "En «trygdesnylters» bekjennelser," March 31, 2012.

196. Gordon B Dahl, Andreas Ravndal Kostøl, and Magne Mogstad, "Family Welfare Cultures," *The Quarterly Journal of Economics* 129 (2014): 1711–52.

197. R. Fogel, "Catching Up with the Economy," January 4, 1999. Speech during meeting arranged by American Economic Association in New York. Accessed June 10, 2015, www.die-gdi.de/fileadmin/user_upload/pdfs/messner/Fogel_Catching_up_with_the_economy.pdf.

## Chapter 9: The Self-Controlling Individual in Society and Community

198. "The groups with which the individual is affiliated constitute a system of co-ordinates, as it were, such that each new group with which he becomes affiliated circumscribes him more exactly and more unambiguously. To belong to any one of these groups leaves the individual considerable leeway. But the larger number of groups to which an individual belongs, the more improbable it is that other persons will exhibit the same combination of group-affiliations, that these particular groups will 'intersect' once again [in a second individual]." Georg Simmel, "The Web of Group Affiliations" in *Conflict & The Web of Group Affiliations*, trans. Kurt H. Wolff and Reinhard Bendix (respectively) (New York: The Free Press, 1955), 140.

199. John Locke, *An Essay Concerning Human Understanding*, Peter H. Nidditch, ed. (1684; Oxford: Clarendon Press, 1975), Book II, chapter XXVII, § 26, 346.

200. Georg Simmel, "Group expansion and the Development of Individuality," in Georg Simmel, *On Individuality and Social Forms*, ed. Donald N. Levine (Chicago: University of Chicago Press, 1971), p. 271. See also Karl Joachim Weintraub, *The Value of the Individual: Self & Circumstance in Autobiography* (Chicago: University of Chicago, 1978), xvii.

201. "Atomism" refers to the theory of the "ἄτομον" ("uncuttable") primary elements (atoms) whose motions in a void ancient philosophers believed were the real elements that explained the physical world as we experience it. The philosopher Charles Taylor has tried to appropriate the term and affix it to liberal individualism—noting in passing that liberal individualists reject the term, which "seems to be used almost exclusively by its [liberalism's] enemies"—and argues that to believe in individual rights requires a belief in an atomistic social theory, which "affirms the self-sufficiency of man alone or, if you prefer, of the individual." For Taylor one "belongs" to a state if that state (a "political society") is the context within which one acquired one's intellectual and moral capacities and became a moral agent. [Charles Taylor, "Atomism," in Charles Taylor, *Philosophical Papers, Vol. 2: Philosophy and the Human Sciences* (Cambridge: Cambridge University Press, 1985), 187–210]. Yet, if individuals are "atoms," as Taylor asserts individualists believe, then, as one wag put it, they are invariably found in molecules. A more accurate and less question-begging description of the liberal individualist understanding of the relationship of individuals and groups is provided by the anthropologist Ernest Gellner, who suggested modularity as a descriptive term, for modules can be combined with others in a variety of manners: "There are firms which produce, advertise, and market modular furniture. The point about such furniture is that it comes in bits which are agglutinative: you can buy one bit which will function on its own, but when your needs, income, or space available augment, you can buy another bit. It will fit in with the one acquired previously, and the whole thing will still have a coherence, aesthetically and technically. You can combine and recombine the bits at will. . . . What genuine Civil Society really requires is not modular furniture, but modular man." Ernest Gellner, *Conditions of Liberty: Civil Society and Its Rivals* (New York: Penguin Books, 1994), 97. (The "agglutinative" furniture to which Gellner refers is what one buys in IKEA stores.)

202. John Benson combines them in this statement of individualism: "each individual has within herself or himself something worthy of respect; that each individual has the possibility of making a positive contribution to society, and (if one accepts a religious viewpoint) the possibility of achieving some form of salvation; and, finally, that there exists a positive responsibility to respect the choices and peculiar characteristics of others, even when they differ from the positions of other individuals of the majority of a given society." John Benson, "Individualism and Conformity in Medieval Western Europe," in *Individualism and Conformity in Classical Islam*, ed. Amin Banani and Speros Vryonis Jr. (Wiesbaden: Otto Harrassowitz, 1977), 148.

203. The sociologist Norbert Elias put it neatly: "the special shaping and differentiation of mental functions that we refer to as 'individuality' is only possible for a person who grows up in a group, a society." "With the growing specialization of societies, the individual's path on the way to becoming a self-reliant, self-determining person grows longer and more complicated. The demands on his or her conscious and unconscious self-control increase." Norbert Elias, *The Society of Individuals* (New York: Continuum, 2001), 22, 124

204. Norbert Elias, *The Civilizing Process* (Oxford: Blackwell Publishing, 2000), esp. 47–182.

205. See the treatment of the horrific violence of the past, partially inspired by his reading of Elias, in Steven Pinker, *The Better Angels of Our Nature: A History of Violence and Humanity* (London: Penguin Books, 2011), esp. 1–82.

206. Norbert Elias, *The Civilizing Process*, 117.

207. John Locke, *Two Treatises of Government*, ed. Peter Laslett (Cambridge: Cambridge University Press, 1988), Second Treatise, Chap. VI, §57, 306. As the historian R. W. Southern points out, the worst part of serfdom was not the subordination to others, but having to live under arbitrary power. "What men feared and resented in serfdom was not its subordination, but its arbitrariness. The hatred of that which was governed, not by rule, but by will, went very deep in the Middle Ages. . . . When the thirteenth-century lawyer Bracton wanted a single phrase to sum up the attributes of serfdom, he said that the serf did not know today what he would have to do tomorrow—he was at the will of another. As a practical test this definition would have been quite worthless: most serfs knew very well what they would have to do tomorrow, probably better than their masters; but the idea of living according to the will of another struck the imagination—it expressed better than anything else the degradation of serfdom. The higher one rose towards liberty, the more the area of action was covered by law, the less it was subject to will." R. W. Southern, *The Making of the Middle Ages* (New Haven: Yale University Press, 1953), 107–108.

208. "[T]he development of society towards a higher level of individualization in its members opens the way to specific forms of fulfillment and specific forms of dissatisfaction, specific chances of happiness and contentment for individuals and specific forms of unhappiness and discomfort that are no less society-specific. The opportunity individuals now have to seek the fulfillment of personal wishes on their own and largely on the basis of their own decisions, carries with it a particular kind of risk. It demands not only a considerable amount of persistence and foresight; it also constantly requires the individual to pass by momentary chances of happiness that present themselves in favour of long-term goals that promise more lasting satisfaction, or to juxtapose these to short-term impulses. Sometimes they can be reconciled, sometimes not. One can take a risk. One has the choice. More freedom of choice and more risk go together." Norbert Elias, *The Society of Individuals*, 129. Elias notes that the process is reversible: "because the development in this direction was not a biological one, was not, as often seems to be believed, rooted in human nature, it can also be reversed. The long chains of actions with their division of functions can shrink again. The social and psychological control of behaviour can be reduced—not just here and there, but over the whole of humanity," 134.

209. Advocates of state control often assert that all products of state action are by definition public goods and infer that public goods can only be produced through coercion, thus necessitating state action. That is simply an abuse of language. Goods with the characteristics of "publicness" have two characteristics: consumption of them is "non-rivalrous," meaning that, unlike an apple, if you listen to and thus consume a

radio broadcast, it does not diminish my ability to listen to the same broadcast; and exclusion costs, meaning that resources must be used to exclude from consuming the good those who do not pay for it. It is demonstrably not the case that publicness requires coercion, as is immediately obvious in the case of radio and television [or more broadly audio and video content], which in many countries is financed through advertising, cable access subscription fees, online streaming access, etc. See for some case studies Tyer Cowen, ed., *The Theory of Market Failure* (Fairfax, Va.: George Mason University Press, 1988). I also review the literature on public goods and its applicability to transportation infrastructure in "Infrastructure: Public or Private," in Tom G. Palmer, *Realizing Freedom: Libertarian Theory, History, and Practice* (2nd ed.: Washington DC: Cato Institute, 2009), 485–494.

210. An individual can only make choices if he or she has a mind and even the emergence of mind requires social interaction. Minds are themselves products of evolution and that evolution takes place through social interaction. "Mind is as much the product of the social environment in which it has grown up and which it has not made as something that has in turn acted upon and altered these institutions. It is the result of man having developed in society and having acquired those habits and practices that increased the chances of persistence of the group in which he lived. The conception of an already fully developed mind designing the institutions which made life in society possible is contrary to all we know about the evolution of man." F. A. Hayek, *Law, Legislation, and Liberty: Vol. I, Rules and Order* (Chicago: University of Chicago Press, 1973), 17.

211. Norbert Elias, *The Society of Individuals*, 14–16. Jean Hampton distinguishes "state contractarianism" from "moral contractarianism" in her essay "Two Faces of Contractarian Thought," in Peter Vallentyne, ed., *Contractarianism and Rational Choice* (Cambridge, 1991), 31–55. Moral contractarianism, agreement on the fundamental rules and norms, is incoherent, because it requires norms to structure agreements; contractarianism is historically implausible when applied to actual states, but its general form is plausible in the formation of voluntary law-generating and law-enforcing organizations, which can be, have been, and are created contractually, including condominium associations, adjudication associations, cattlemen's associations, mining camps, stock exchanges, bank clearing houses, neighborhood associations, gardening clubs, and many other institutions that provide and enforce rules of order. Much contemporary law emerged not from commands or edicts of princes or presidents, but from people peacefully settling disputes and creating order. See for a globally relevant example Leon Trakman, *The Law Merchant: The Evolution of Commercial Law* (Littleton, Colorado: Fred B. Rothman & Co., 1983). For recent examples from American history, see Robert Ellickson, *Order Without Law: How Neighbors Settle Disputes* (Cambridge, Mass.: Harvard University Press, 1994) and Terry Anderson and P. J. Hill, *The Not So Wild, Wild West: Property Rights on the Frontier* (Stanford: Stanford University Press, 2004).

212. "Individualism: True and False," in F. A. Hayek, *Individualism and Economic Order* (Chicago: University of Chicago Press, 1948), 8–9.

213. See F. A. Hayek, "The Use of Knowledge in Society," *American Economic Review*, XXXV, No. 4; September, 1945, 519–30; available online at http://www.econlib.org/library/Essays/hykKnw1.html.

214. "From the awareness of the limitations of individual knowledge and from the fact that no person or small group of persons can know all that is known to somebody, individualism also derives its main practical conclusion: its demand for a strict limitation of all coercive or exclusive power. Its opposition, however, is directed only against the use of coercion to bring about organization or association, and not against association as such. Far from being opposed to voluntary association, the case of the individualist rests, on the contrary, on the contention that much of what in the opinion of many can be brought about only by conscious direction, can be better achieved by the voluntary and spontaneous collaboration of individuals." F. A. Hayek, "Individualism: True and False," 16.

215. Jonathan Haidt, *The Righteous Mind: Why Good People Are Divided by Politics and Religion* (New York: Penguin Books, 2012), 105.

216. F. A. Hayek, "Individualism: True and False," 12. James Madison argued against

reliance on "enlightened statesmen" in the design of institutions, "It is in vain to say, that enlightened statesmen will be able to adjust these clashing interests, and render them all subservient to the public good. Enlightened statesmen will not always be at the helm: nor, in many cases, can such an adjustment be made at all, without taking into view indirect and remote considerations, which will rarely prevail over the immediate interest which one party may find in disregarding the rights of another, or the good of the whole." "Federalist Number 10," *The Federalist: The Gideon Edition,* by Alexander Hamilton, John Jay, and James Madison (Indianapolis: Liberty Fund, 2001), 45.

217. For an enlightening treatment of the crimes carried out by "progressives" who were implementing the ideology of expertise *par excellence,* see Thomas C. Leonard, *Illiberal Reformers: Race, Eugenics, and American Economics in the Progressive Era* (Princeton: Princeton University Press, 2016).

218. For a short and very readable introduction to the topic, see Eamonn Butler, *Public Choice—A Primer* (London: Institute of Economic Affairs, 2012), available online for free at http://www.iea.org.uk/publications/research/public-choice-a-primer.

219. A very useful and readable treatment of liberalism is George H. Smith, *The System of Liberty: Themes in the History of Classical Liberalism* (Cambridge: Cambridge University Press, 2013).

220. Merely having power does not justify its exercise, but neither is it a corollary of the lack of justification for tyranny that other, more liberal, states should be presumed to be justified in waging war to eliminate tyrannies; in any case, the track record of such "humanitarian" wars is not promising.

221. "Reciprocal cooperation can be stable with a larger range of individuals if discrimination can cover a wide variety of others with less reliance on supplementary cues such as location. In humans this ability is well developed, and is largely based on the recognition of faces. The extent to which this function has become specialized is revealed by a brain disorder called prosopagnosia. A normal person can name someone from facial features alone, even if the features have changed substantially over the years. People with prosopagnosia are not able to make this association, but have few other neurological symptoms other than a loss of some part of the visual field. The lesions responsible for the disorder occur in an identifiable part of the brain: the underside of both occipital lobes, extending forward to the inner surface of the temporal lobes. This localization of cause, and specificity of effect, indicates that the recognition of individual faces has been an important enough task for a significant portion of the brain's resources to be devoted to it. Just as the ability to recognize the other player is invaluable in extending the range of stable cooperation, the ability to monitor cues for the likelihood of continued interaction is helpful as an indication of when reciprocal cooperation is or is not stable." Robert Axelrod, *The Evolution of Cooperation* (rev. ed., New York: Basic Books, 2006), 102–103.

222. The classic account of the formation of feudal society as a response to invasion can be found in Marc Bloch, *Feudal Society* (1940; New York: Routledge, 2014), 5–61.

223. See the chapter on "The Origin of the Western Legal Tradition in the Papal Revolution," in Harold Berman, *Law and Revolution: the Formation of the Western Legal Tradition* (Cambridge, Mass.: Harvard University Press, 1983), 85–119.

224. See Eric Jones, *The European Miracle: Environments, Economies, and Geopolitics in the History of Europe and Asia* (Cambridge: Cambridge University Press, 2003); Nathan Rosenberg and L. E. Birdzell Jr., *How the West Grew Rich: The Economic Transformation of the Industrial World* (New York: Basic Books, 1987); Robert S. Lopez, *The Commercial Revolution of the Middle Ages, 950–1350* (Cambridge: Cambridge University Press, 1976).

225. Of special significance was the rediscovery of the codification of the Roman law that was supervised by the lawyer Tribonian (and sponsored by the Emperor Justinian; the texts are thus popularly known as the *Digest of Justinian* and the *Institutes of Justinian*) and which provided a sophisticated legal framework for an emerging commercial society. Also important were the copying and circulation of texts by Aristotle, Cicero (notably his *On Duties*), and other thinkers from the ancient world.

226. The growth and development of libertarian thought has been told many times; for a short introduction, including citations for further study, see my "The History and Structure of Libertarian Thought" in *Why Liberty*, ed. Tom G. Palmer (Ottawa, Illinois: Jameson Books, 2013), available for downloading in PDF form at http://studentsforliberty.org/wp-content/uploads/2013/07/Why-Liberty-Final-Typeset-with-Cover.pdf.

227. The scholar Lin Yutang, writing of twentieth-century reinterpretation of the policies of Wang Anshih from the eleventh century, refers to "Western ideas of collectivism." See Lin Yutang, *The Gay Genius: The Life and Times of Su Tungpo* (New York: The John Day Company, 1947), 96.

228. Consider the lament of Helen in Euripides's play *Helen*: "For the deity hates violence, and biddeth all men get lawful gains without plundering others. Wealth unjustly gotten, though it bring some power, is to be eschewed. The breath of heaven and the earth are man's common heritage, wherein to store his home, without taking the goods of others, or wresting them away by force." Euripides (2012-04-30). *Helen*, trans. by E. P. Coleridge (Kindle Locations 809–811). Neeland Media LLC. Kindle Edition.

229. S. D. Goitein explores the rich tradition of individualistic depictions in Arabic literature in "Individualism and Conformity in Classical Islam," in *Individualism and Conformity in Classical Islam*, ed. Amin Banani and Speros Vryonis Jr., 3–17. Liberalism in the Islamic tradition is discussed in detail, from a libertarian perspective, in Mustafa Akyol, *Islam Without Extremes: A Muslim Case for Liberty* (New York: W. W. North & Co., 2011); Antony Black, *The History of Islamic Political Thought: From the Prophet to the Present* (2nd ed.; Edinburgh: Edinburgh University Press, 2011), discusses liberal ideals in the Ottoman Empire (281–299); especially interesting is his treatment of Khayr Al-Din Al-Tunisi, reformer and author of *The Surest Path to Know the Conditions of the State* (290–293). Khayr Al-Din Al-Tunisi explained the prosperity of Europe by their policies, and wrote that the rise of Europe "is solely because they have implemented laws providing the basic requirements of liberty (as already explained) for preserving the rights of the individual in his person, honor and wealth, and of consensus on how to foster the public interest and ward off corruption by giving careful consideration to the prevailing customs, circumstances and the times with various rulings of the type our own shari'a makes allowances for." It was "For the sake of these and like advantages, kings and ministers endure the original bitterness of being restricted in order to enjoy the authority and civilization which will follow." Kahry al-Din al-Tunisi, *The Surest Path: The Political Treatise of a Nineteenth Century Muslim Statesman*, Leon Carl Brown, trans. (Cambridge, Mass.: Harvard University Press, 1967), 175. See also the discussion among Muslim philosophers of the question of whether the human soul is one for all of humanity or individuated for all humans in Lenn E. Goodman, *Avicenna*, updated edition (Cornell: Cornell University Press, 2006), 127–128. Ibn Rushd (Averroes) argued that we all share in the same soul, whereas Avicenna (Ibn Sīnā) maintained "that the intellectual soul that is subject to immortality is thought or consciousness, and thought must be focused and individuated: focused objectively, individuated subjectively" (Goodman, 128). The debate also took place among Christian thinkers, pitting the "Latin Averroists," notably Siger of Brabant, against St. Thomas Aquinas over whether there is one "intellective soul" for all of mankind. The Latin Averroists argued that for two individuals to know the same thing, they have to have the same form impressed by the agent intellect into the same material (or possible) intellect; to know the same form, they must share the same material intellect. (See Siger of Brabant, "On the Intellective Soul," in *Medieval Philosophy: From St. Augustine to Nicholas of Cusa*, ed. John F. Wippel and Allan B. Wolter, O. F. M. [London: Collier Macmillan Publishers, 1969], 358–65.) The implications for personal responsibility were clear: if you and I have the same soul and you lead a good life and achieve salvation, then I will, too, regardless of what sins I commit. St. Thomas argued that the idea of one soul for all of mankind, a deep form of metaphysical collectivism, was absurd on its face: "If . . . the intellect does not belong to this man in such a way that it is truly one with him, but is united to him only through phantasms or as a mover, the will will not be in this

man, but in the separate intellect. And so this man will not be the master of his act, nor will any act of his be praiseworthy or blameworthy. That is to destroy the principles of moral philosophy. Since this is absurd and contrary to human life (for it would not be necessary to take counsel or to make laws), it follows that the intellect is united to us in such a way that it and we constitute what is truly one being." Thomas Aquinas, *On the Unity of the Intellect Against the Averroists* (Milwaukee: Marquette University Press, 1968), chap. II, par. 82, p. 57. According to Thomas, the impressed intelligible species is not literally the very form of the thing itself raised to a higher level of intelligibility but rather that by which we know the thing: "It is . . . one thing which is understood both by me and by you. But it is understood by me in one way and by you in another, that is, by another intelligible species. And my understanding is one thing, and yours, another; and my intellect is one thing, and yours another." Thomas Aquinas, *On the Unity of the Intellect Against the Averroists,* chap. V, par. 112, p. 70. The issue is canvassed in Herbert Davidson, *Alfarabi, Avicenna, and Averroes on Intellect* (Oxford: Oxford University Press, 1994).

230. Classical Chinese writers such as Lao Tzu, Confucius, Mencius, and Su Tung-p'o are sources for much contemporary Chinese libertarian thought. For a treatment of classical themes of liberty and responsibility in a modern context, see Liu Junning, *Tao of Liberty: Dialogue in Heaven between Laozi and Kongzi* (Potsdam: Friedrich Naumann Foundation, 2014), available for download in PDF at http://www.fnfasia. org/wp-content/uploads/2015/03/Tao-of-Liberty-Dialogue-in-Heaven-between-Laozi-and-Kongzi-e-book.pdf. See also the discussions of "statism" and "non-action" (*wu wei*) found throughout Kung-chuan Hsiao, *A History of Chinese Political Thought, Vol. I: From the Beginning to the Sixth Century A.D.* (Princeton: Princeton University Press, 1979), F. W. Mote, trans. For a treatment of individualism in the Neo-Confucian tradition during the Sung and Ming dynasties, including "learning for the sake of one's self," "getting it oneself," "finding [the Way in] oneself," "taking responsibility [for the Way] oneself," see Wm. Theodore de Bary, *The Liberal Tradition in China* (Hong Kong and New York: The Chinese University Press and Columbia University Press, 1983). For a sympathetic treatment of Su Tung-p'o from a broadly liberal perspective, see Lin Yutang, *The Gay Genius: The Life and Times of Su Tungpo.*

231. The Mahabharata and other key texts of Indian civilization are suffused with important concepts, such as dharma (virtue, "doing the right thing") and ahimsa (non-violence). Gurcharan Das's *On the Difficulty of Being Good: On the Subtle Art of Dharma* (Oxford: Oxford University Press, 2009) presents ethical problems, with great stress on responsibility, through the stories and lessons of the Mahabharata and Das's own experience in business. See also his "The Dharma of Capitalism," preface to Indian edition of Tom G. Palmer, ed., The *Morality of Capitalism* (New Delhi: Centre for Civil Society, 2011). The Mahabharata story of the lizard who, when about to be crushed by Prince Ruru, turns to him and says "ahimsa paramo dharma"— "nonviolence is the highest dharma"—thus convincing the Prince not to harm him, offers a very memorable image by which to visualize libertarian nonviolence.

232. Colin Morris, *The Discovery of the Individual, 1050–1200* (New York: Harper & Row, 1972), 7

233. "The discovery of the individual was one of the most important cultural developments in the years between 1050 and 1200. It was not confined to any one group of thinkers. Its central features may be found in many different circles: a concern with self-discovery; an interest in the relations between people, and in the role of the individual within society; an assessment of people by their inner intentions rather than by their external acts." Morris, *The Discovery of the Individual, 1050–1200,* 158.

234. See John F. Benson, "Consciousness of Self and Perceptions of Individuality," in Robert L. Benson and Giles Contable, with Carol D. Lanham, eds., *Renaissance and Renewal in the Twelfth Century* (Cambridge, Mass.: Harvard University Press, 1982), 263–295.

235. Innocent IV, "On Decretales, 3.34.8, Quod Super, Commentaria (c. 1250), fol. 429-30," in *The Crisis of Church and State, 1050–1300,* ed. Brian Tierney (Toronto: University of Toronto Press, 1988), 153. The primary passage from the book of Matthew cited by Innocent deserves greater attention: "You have heard that it was

said, 'You shall love your neighbor and hate your enemy.' But I say to you, Love your enemies and pray for those who persecute you, so that you may be sons of your Father who is in heaven; for he makes his sun rise on the evil and on the good, and sends rain on the just and on the unjust. For if you love those who love you, what reward have you? Do not even the tax collectors do the same?" (Matthew 5:43–46, Revised Standard Version). The book of Matthew also contains a statement of a principle found in other cultures and traditions, as well: the Golden Rule. "So whatever you wish that men would do to you, do so to them; for this is the law and the prophets" (Matthew 7:12, Revised Standard Version).

236. Larry Siedentop, *Inventing the Individual: The Origins of Western Liberalism* (Cambridge, Mass.: Harvard University Press, 2014), 63. For a radically different evaluation of Paul's writings and their impact, see Charles Freeman, *The Closing of the Western Mind: The Rise of Faith and the Fall of Reason* (New York: Vintage, 2005), esp. 107–127.

237. Colin Morris notes, "It is at once obvious that the Western view of the value of the individual owes a great deal to Christianity. A sense of individual identity and value is implicit in belief in a God who has called each man by name, who has sought him out as a shepherd seeks his lost sheep. Self-awareness and a serious concern with inner character is encouraged by the conviction that the believer must lay himself open to God, and be remade by the Holy Spirit . . . Ultimately a Christian origin can be found for many of the elements in the European concept of the self." *The Discovery of the Individual, 1050–1200,* 10–11. That passage is followed immediately by "Yet, if we turn to the Fathers and the writers of the New Testament, we find that their concept of personality qualified its stress upon the individual by the inclusion of some very important corporate elements. Jesus Christ was regarded not as another human being, separate from (although better and greater than) the believer. Saint Paul expresses his own experience in a quite different way: 'I have been crucified with Christ; it is no longer I who live, but Christ who lives in me; and the life I now live in the flesh I live by faith in the Son of God, who loved me and gave himself for me' (Gal. 2:20). The boundaries have been broken between Christ and Paul. It is not the relationship of two personalities, but the indwelling of one in the other. Since the believer is identified with Christ, he is therefore identified also with all other believers: 'There is neither Jew nor Greek, there is neither slave nor free, there is neither male nor female; for you are all one in Christ Jesus' (Gal. 3:28). The way was thus open for the community-language which is so characteristic of the New Testament. The Church is the body of Christ, each member a limb in it. All believers share in the one Spirit, all are stones in the living Temple. This element in early Christian thinking severely modified the strong individualism which we have also seen to be present, but it has received relatively little attention in the Western Church" (11–12). Morris suggests that an almost completely Christian social order, as medieval Europe was, would not stress the corporate element as much as the early church, which was made up of believers situated in a wider order in which they were often subject to terrible and cruel persecution. In any case, Paul's understanding of the relationship of the believers to each other was analogized with the parts of a single human body.

238. Siedentop, *Inventing the Individual: The Origins of Western Liberalism*, 35, 245. Reason is usually considered a universal feature of human beings, but Siedentop associates it instead exclusively with hierarchy, privilege, and inequality. In contrast, he associates experiences of faith, which are not so obviously universal, with equality. For support he turns to an insightful inquiry into the history of Greek and Roman institutions that was published in 1864, *The Ancient City*, by Numa Denis Fustel de Coulanges (New York: Doubleday Anchor, 1956). Fustel de Coulanges, who also wrote a refutation of the doctrines of primeval German communism on which Karl Marx had drawn (*The Origin of Property in Land,* trans. Margaret Ashley [London: Swan Sonnenschein & Co., 1891]) and a six-volume *History of the Political Institutions of Old France,* uncovered the key role of the family in the institutions of the ancient world, and specifically of the family religion, a form of ancestor worship. Siedentop seems, however, to read far more into Fustel de Coulanges than is warranted, even assuming that the role of family religion persisted well into the Christian era. For a sympathetic criticism of *The Ancient City*, see Alfred Zimmerman, *The Greek*

*Commonwealth: Politics and Economics in Fifth Century Athens* (New York: The Modern Library, 1956): "A full account of this patriarchal system is given in Fustel de Coulanges's *La Cité Antique*. This well-known book was written in 1864, but the first half of it is still the best general account, not of the City-State in itself but of the lesser loyalties out of which it grew. It may be worthwhile briefly suggesting some of the defects which time has revealed. (1) It is, like many French books, too tidy and logical; it simplifies the Old World and its beliefs too much. (2) It tries to deal with Greece and Rome at the same time—an impossible design which survives from the days when people believed in a parent Aryan civilization; hence its generalizations sometimes fall between two stools and fit neither. . . . (3) It greatly exaggerates the influence of the Conservative as opposed to the Radical elements in Greek life. So far as Athens is concerned its story admittedly ends with Cleisthenes (see p. 337, ed. 1906). It is, for instance, a gross exaggeration, or misuse of words, to say, as on p. 269, that ancient man never possessed liberty or even 'the idea of it.'" 75.

239. Siedentop, *Inventing the Individual: The Origins of Western Liberalism*, 77.

240. Ibid., 114.

241. Ibid., 206.

242. The long history of the persecution of heretics and the emergence of ideas of toleration among European Christians is recounted very ably by Perez Zagorin in his *How the Idea of Religious Toleration Came to the West* (Princeton: Princeton University Press, 2003). Zagorin rebuts those who claim that it was a decline in religious attachment that accounted for the rise of toleration and concludes that "In the battles over religious toleration that were so bitterly and widely waged in the sixteenth and seventeenth centuries, the idea of toleration was itself very largely inspired by religious values and was fundamentally religious in character" (289). The historical record, however, provides little or no support for Siedentop's claim that it was about drawing out intuitions from the writings of Paul.

243. Francis Dvornik provided a careful description of Byzantine theories of church-state relations and their impact on later Eastern European politics in "Byzantine Political Ideas in Kievan Russia," Dumbarton Oaks Papers, nos. 9 and 10 (Cambridge, Mass.: Harvard University Press, 1956), 73–121 and *The Slavs in European History and Civilization* (New Brunswick, New Jersey: Rutgers University Press, 1962), 369–76. The Byzantine tradition stressed subordination to power. The hard-won independence of the church from the state, which characterized Latin Christianity, but which receives little attention from Siedentop, never occurred in the East, where the Emperor (later Tsar) controlled the church. As one influential document described the proper attitude recommended by religion among Orthodox believers, "Incline thy head to everybody superior to thee. . . . Fear the prince with all thy strength. . . . Learn from him how to fear God. . . . He who does not fear the earthy lord, how will he fear Him whom he does not see?" Cited in "Byzantine Political Ideas in Kievan Russia," 91–92. It is understandable how such a tradition would not be very favorable to liberal individualism; in that context, Paul's writings would be invoked as powerful support for absolutism, rather than for liberal constitutionalism. Christian moral intuitions in Russia seem not to have generated what Siedentop expects of them. The historian Richard Pipes notes, "There is no evidence in medieval Russia of mutual obligations binding prince and his servitor, and, therefore, also nothing resembling legal and moral 'rights' of subjects, and little need for law and courts." Richard Pipes, *Russia Under the Old Regime*, 2nd ed. (London: Penguin Books, 1995), 51.

244. Brian Tierney, *The Idea of Natural Rights* (Atlanta: Scholars Press, 1997), 8. Siedentop also misconstrues the significance of nominalism and even seems to confuse Plato's metaphysics with Aristotle's. Ockham was advancing an understanding of the nature of science, for science concerns the establishment of the truth or falsity of propositions, not intuitions of universal forms or essences. According to Ockham, "[W]e must take note that natural science, just as any other science, is about universals and concepts, not about things. The proof for this is as follows: if it were about things, then it would be about universal or particular things. It is not about universal things, for there are no such things, as Aristotle proves in Book VII of the Metaphysics. Nor is it about singular things, as is also shown in the Metaphysics, Book VII, and frequently demonstrated elsewhere. Therefore, it is about concepts."

*Ockham on Aristotle's Physics: A Translation of Ockham's Brevis Summa Libri Physicorum*, trans. Julian Davies, OFM (St. Bonaventure, New York: The Franciscan Institute, 1989), 2. As Armand Maurer put it, "As for sciences of reality, Aristotle showed that they have for their primary objects universals and not individuals, but the universals in question are terms and propositions, not common realities. Indeed, according to Ockham, 'every science, whether it be a science of reality or rational science [i.e., logic], is concerned only with propositions as with what is known, for propositions alone are known.' He is not denying that we know individuals; they are the first objects of the intuitive cognition of the senses and intellect. Neither is he denying that science treats of individuals. The point he is making is that universal propositions are the immediate and direct object of scientific knowledge. Science deals with individuals insofar as the terms of propositions stand for them. In a science of reality (*scientia realis*) the terms of its propositions have personal supposition; that is, they stand for the things they signify, namely, individual realities outside the mind." Armand A. Maurer, "William of Ockham," in Jorge J. E. Gracia, ed., *Individuation in Scholasticism: The Later Middle Ages and the Counter-Reformation, 1150–1650* (Albany: State University of New York Press, 1994), 373–396, 376.

245. Annabel S. Brett also provides convincing textual grounds for dismissing the claim that Ockham's nominalism played a role in his development of the idea of individual rights. See Annabel S. Brett, *Liberty, Right, and Nature: Individual Rights in Later Scholastic Thought* (Cambridge: Cambridge University Press, 1997), 49–68.

246. John F. Benson warns, when "evaluating the role of religion" against "the un-warranted assumption that Christian religion was uniquely capable of fostering the development of consciousness and increased psychological awareness. If by some chance the Jewish Khazars or the Moslem Moors instead of the Catholic Franks had created an empire in early medieval Europe, interest in the examination of the subjective self might have recovered at the same rate, or perhaps even faster. This conclusion is based on the existence of a form of 'control group,' the small Jewish communities which shared much of the same cultural, economic, and even political environment as their Christian neighbors, though they differed both through the effects of exile, hostility, and persecution and in a greater devotion to learning, which one of Abelard's students observed with envy." John F. Benson, "Consciousness of Self and Perceptions of Individuality," 291.

247. Siedentop, *Inventing the Individual*, 362. Siedentop reveals his quite superficial understanding of contemporary religion when he casually remarks that in the United States "the rapid growth of Christian fundamentalism" is "in part, no doubt, a reaction to the threat of radical Islam." There is no warrant for that claim; "Christian fundamentalism" in America has roots that predate by many decades the Islamist attacks of September 11, 2011, and there is little reason to believe that the growth of Christian fundamentalism was driven by "the threat of radical Islam." Like so much in his book, it is a mere assertion.

248. Walter Ullman, *The Individual and Society in the Middle Ages* (Baltimore: The Johns Hopkins Press, 1966), 10.

249. Ibid., 18–19. As Ullman continues, "It was Paul who used the human body as a model in order to demonstrate the various functions within the *unum corpus Christi*. This organological or anthropomorphic thesis meant that each part of the human body functioned for the sake of the whole body, not for its own sake. If we translate this into terms of the corporate public body, we are here presented with the theory that the individual did not exist for his own sake, but for the sake of the whole society. This organological thesis was to lead in time to the full-fledged integration theory of the corporate body politic, in which the individual is wholly submerged in society for the sake of the well-being of society itself. This thesis also led without undue effort to the allegory of the head's directing the other parts of the human body, thus metaphorically expressing the superior function of the *caput*—be this king or pope—and the inferior position of the subject individual," 42–43.

250. There is a Chinese proverb, "The mountain is high and the emperor is far away" [ 山高皇帝遠], which expresses the basic idea, namely, that distance from the imperial power means that local affairs are run by local people.

251. Ullman, *The Individual and Society in the Middle Ages*, 54.

252. Ibid.

253. See Marc Bloch, "European Feudalism," in Talcott Parsons, Edward Shils, Kaspar D. Naegle, and Jesse R. Pitts, eds., *Theories of Society: Foundations of Modern Sociological Thought* (New York: The Free Press, 1965), 385–392. Bloch focused on the centrality of reciprocal obligation and accountability, as embodied in Europe's feudal history, as central to the emergence of modern political institutions: "The clearest legacy of feudalism to modern societies is the emphasis placed upon the notion of political contract. The reciprocity of obligations which united lord and vassal and caused with every grave dereliction by the superior the release of the inferior in the eyes of the law was transferred in the thirteenth century to the state. Practically everywhere, but with particular clearness in England and Aragon, the idea was expressed that the subject was bound to the king only so long as the latter remains a loyal protector. This sentiment counterbalanced the tradition of royal sanctity and finally triumphed over it," 392. The importance of reciprocal duties is emphasized by Anthony Black: "There were rights and duties on both sides: the lord had rights and duties against the vassal, and the vassal had rights and duties against the lord. It is essential to bear in mind this quite simple legal relationship involving the two individuals, for the contractual nature of feudalism became in course of time the very substratum from which some highly pregnant themes grew. Feudalism operated by forging first strong individual ties which in themselves created, in course of time, equally strong social bonds." Antony Black, *Guilds and Civil Society in European Political Thought from the Twelfth Century to the Present* (Ithaca, New York: Cornell University Press, 1984), 63. Sidney Painter claims that the relative independence of the feudal vassals, or nobles, set the model for the liberties to which the other elements of society aspired: "[T]he medieval nobleman enjoyed extremely extensive freedom to act as an individual. The feudal corporation to which he belonged imposed little restraint on him. The church could control him far less than it could other men. Even the state recognized him as especially privileged. Naturally the status of the noble was the envy of the other classes. Essentially the rights and liberties for which the middle and lower classes struggled throughout the seventeenth, eighteenth, and nineteenth centuries were those enjoyed by the nobles of the middle ages. Obviously the conception of individual freedom and the desire to possess it came from many sources and arose in many different legal environments, but the legal and political institutions which secured this freedom in western Europe and America were those forged by the feudal aristocracy. During the period when most men were closely controlled by corporate organizations the nobles retained and nurtured the concept of individual liberty." Sidney Painter, "Individualism in the Middle Ages," in Sidney Painter, *Feudalism and Liberty: Articles and Addresses*, ed. Fred A. Cazel Jr. (Baltimore: The Johns Hopkins University Press, 1961), 259.

254. The most synoptic and thorough description of the complex legal systems that emerged in Europe and that improved each other through competition is found in Harold Berman, *Law and Revolution: The Formation of the Western Legal Tradition* (Cambridge, Mass.: Harvard University Press, 1983). According to Berman, "Perhaps the most distinctive characteristic of the Western legal tradition is the coexistence and competition within the same community of diverse jurisdictions and diverse legal systems. It is this plurality of jurisdictions and legal systems that makes the supremacy of law both necessary and possible. Legal pluralism originated in the differentiation of the ecclesiastical polity from secular polities. The church declared its freedom from secular control, its exclusive jurisdiction in some matters, and its concurrent jurisdiction in other matters. Laymen, though governed generally by secular law, were subject to ecclesiastical law, and to the jurisdiction of ecclesiastical courts, in matters of marriage and family relations, inheritance, spiritual crimes, contract relations where faith was pledged, and a number of other matters as well. Conversely, the clergy, though governed generally by canon law, were subject to secular law, and to the jurisdiction of secular courts, with respect to certain types of crimes, certain types of property disputes, and the like. Secular law itself was divided into various competing types, including royal law, feudal law, manorial law, urban law, and mercantile law. The same person might be subject to the ecclesiastical courts in one type of case, the king's court in another, his lord's court in a third, the manorial court in a fourth,

a town court in a fifth, a merchants' court in a sixth. The very complexity of a common legal order containing diverse legal systems contributed to legal sophistication. Which court has jurisdiction? Which law is applicable? How are legal differences to be reconciled? Behind the technical questions lay important political and economic considerations: church versus crown, crown versus town, town versus lord, lord versus merchant, and so on. Law was a way of resolving the political and economic conflicts. Yet law could also serve to exacerbate them. The pluralism of Western law, which has both reflected and reinforced the pluralism of Western political and economic life, has been, or once was, a source of development, or growth—legal growth as well as political and economic growth. It also has been, or once was, a source of freedom. A serf might run to the town court for protection against his master. A vassal might run to the king's court for protection against his lord. A cleric might run to the ecclesiastical court for protection against the king," 10.

255. Henri Pirenne, *Medieval Cities: Their Origins and the Growth of Trade* (Princeton: Princeton University Press, 1937), 200.

256. Ibid., 50. Merchants were guaranteed personal protection, not merely as corporations, but as individuals, in both goods and body, while at the fairs or traveling to or from them. See Félix Bourquelot, *Études sur les foires de Champagne, sur la nature, l'étendue et les règles du commerce qui s'y faisaient, aux XIIe, XIIIe et XIVe siècles* (Paris: L'Imprimerie Impériale, 1865) 24, 77.

257. Hans Planitz, *Die Deutsche Stadt im Mittelalter: Von der Römerzeit bis zu den Zunftkämpfen* (Graz-Köln: Böhlau Verlag, 1954), 117–118. In the "Customs of Newcastle-Upon-Tyne in the Time of Henry I, 1068–1135" we find stated, "If a villein come to reside in the borough, and shall remain as a burgess in the borough for a year and a day, he shall thereafter remain there, unless there was a previous agreement between him and lord for him to remain there for a certain time." In John H. Mundy and Peter Riesenberg, *The Medieval Town* (Princeton, New Jersey: D. Van Nostrand, 1958), 138.

258. Benjamin Constant, "The Liberty of the Ancients Compared with that of the Moderns," in Constant, *Political Writings*, ed. Biancamaria Fontana, (Cambridge: Cambridge University Press, 1988), 313. Constant followed that statement with a claim that was far, far too bold: "Hence it follows that an age must come in which commerce replaces war. We have reached this age." Yet, as Steven Pinker documents in his study of the history and causes of violence, *The Better Angels of Our Nature: A History of Violence and Humanity*, violence of all sorts, including war, has fallen—dramatically so—since Constant's time and commerce was a very important part of that process.

259. "War costs a nation more than its actual expense; it costs besides, all that would have been gained, but for its occurrence." Jean-Baptiste Say, *A Treatise on Political Economy* (Philadelphia: Lippincot, Grambo & Co.), Book III, chapter 6, §. 51. Accessed online: http://www.econlib.org/library/Say/sayT39.html#Bk.III,Ch.VI.

260. As Spinoza wrote of the city that offered its citizens toleration, "The city of Amsterdam reaps the fruit of this freedom in its own great prosperity and in the admiration of all other people. For in this most flourishing state, and most splendid city, men of every nation and religion live together in the greatest harmony, and ask no questions before trusting their goods to a fellow-citizen, save whether he be rich or poor, and whether he generally act honestly, or the reverse. His religion and sect are considered of no importance; for it has no effect before the judges in gaining or losing a cause, and there is no sect so despised that its followers, provided that they harm no one, pay every man his due, and live uprightly, are deprived of the protection of the magisterial authority." Benedict de Spinoza, *A Theologico-Political Treatise*, trans. R. H. M. Elwes (New York: Dover Publications, 1951), 264. Merchants were pioneers of religious toleration; mutually beneficial voluntary exchange with others encourages one to put oneself in their shoes, not to mention that burning your customers alive ruled out repeat business. When the Spanish king offered to reorganize the bishoprics of the Netherlands and, in the process, to appoint resident inquisitors: "There was violent opposition to this measure from the magistrates of Antwerp (Antwerp was to be one of the new sees) on the grounds that the inquisition was contrary to the privileges of Brabant and that, more specifically, so many heretics came to Antwerp

to trade that its prosperity would be ruined if a resident inquisition were introduced."
Geoffrey Parker, *The Dutch Revolt* (New York: Penguin Books, 1988), 47. And, of
course, Voltaire's observations of the London Stock Exchange summarized the cal-
culating—and thus rational and tolerant—attitude of businesspeople: "Go into the
Exchange in London, that place more venerable than many a court, and you will see
representatives of all the nations assembled there for the profit of mankind, There the
Jew, the Mahometan, and the Christian deal with one another as if they were of the
same religion, and reserve the name of infidel for those who go bankrupt." Voltaire,
"On the Presbyterians," in *"Candide" and Philosophical Letters* (New York: Modern
Library, 1992), 141.

261. Ullman, *The Individual and Society in the Middle Ages*, 56.

262. "One may date the Papal Revolution from 1075—when Gregory proclaimed
papal supremacy over the entire church and ecclesiastical independence from,
and superiority over, the secular power—to 1122—when a final compromise was
reached between the papal and the imperial authority." Harold H. Berman, *Law and
Revolution, The Formation of the Western Legal Tradition*, 23.

263. Richard H. Helmholz, "Magna Carta and the ius commune," *University of Chicago
Law Review, Vol. 66,* (Spring 1999), 297–371.

264. An elegant statement of that thesis is found in Daniel Hannan, *Inventing
Freedom: How the English Speaking Peoples Made the Modern World* (New York:
Broadside Books, 2013).

265. In his classic study of Magna Carta, Holt noted that the appeal to tradition that
was central to Magna Carta "was also widespread on the continent" and gave examples of similar charters in France and Hungary. J. C. Holt, *Magna Carta* (Cambridge:
Cambridge University Press, 1992), 114.

266. "A.D. 1100. Aug. 5. Charter of Liberties issued by Henry I," *Select Charters and
Other Illustrations of English Constitutional History from the Earliest Times to the
Reign of Edward the First*, arranged and edited by William Stubbs, ninth ed. revised
by H. W. C. Davis (1870; Oxford: Clarendon Press, 1960), 116–119. Translated into
English as "Charter of Liberties of Henry I. 1100," in *Source Problems in English
History*, by Albert Beebe White and Wallace Notestein (New York: Harper &
Brothers Publishers, 1915), 367–369.

267. Berman, *Law and Revolution: The Formation of the Western Legal Tradition*,
419–421.

268. Ibid., 294.

269. Ibid., 425–434.

270. Ibid., 308.

271. Adam Smith, *An Inquiry into the Nature and Causes of the Wealth of Nations*
(1776; Oxford: Oxford University Press, 1976), Vol II, Book IV, Chapter IX, 664.

272. Deirdre McCloskey, *Bourgeois Equality: How Ideas, Not Capital or Institutions,
Enriched the World* (Chicago: University of Chicago Press, 2016), 296.

273. Black, *Guilds and Civil Society in European Political Thought from the Twelfth
Century to the Present*, 65.

274. Henry Sumner Maine, *Ancient Law* (1861; Brunswick, New Jersey: Transaction
Publishers, 2003), 170.

275. Robert Nozick, *Anarchy, State, and Utopia* (New York: Basic Books, 1974).

## Chapter 10: Philosophical Issues of Freedom and Responsibility

276. F. A. Hayek, *The Constitution of Liberty: The Definitive Edition,* ed. Ronald
Hamowy (1960; Chicago: University of Chicago Press, 2011), 133.

277. There are many ways to influence the behavior of others, and it is the height of
absurdity to characterize all of them as coercive or forcible. Persuasion, moral example, reciprocity, reputation, and many other forms of interaction can induce people
to change their behavior and can even encourage them to achieve greater self-control. See for examples David Schwab and Elinor Ostrom, "The Vital Role of Norms
and Rules in Maintaining Open Public and Private Economies," in *Moral Markets:*

*The Critical Role of Values in the Economy*, ed. Paul J. Zak (Princeton: Princeton University Press, 2008), 204–27; Deirdre McCloskey, *Bourgeois Dignity: Why Economics Can't Explain the Modern World* (Chicago: University of Chicago Press, 2010); and the empirical studies of institutions that rely on reputation, rather than force, to elicit good behavior collected in Daniel Klein, ed., *Reputation: Studies in the Voluntary Elicitation of Good Conduct* (Ann Arbor: University of Michigan Press, 1997).

278. Yevgeny Zamyatin, *We,* trans. Clarence Brown (New York: Penguin Books, 1993), 4.

279. Ayn Rand, *Anthem* (1937; Caldwell, Id.: The Caxton Printers, 1969), 19.

280. Ibid., 86–7.

281. Fiction offers the possibility of exploring many fascinating issues of individuality, continuity of the person, responsibility, and more. Fiction can help us to test intuitions and the applicability of concepts we take for granted to new situations. Contemporary author David Brin addresses issues of personal identity in many of his writings, notably in *Kiln People* (2002) and *Existence* (2012).

282. Max Weber, "The Profession and Vocation of Politics," in Max Weber, *Political Writings*, ed. Peter Lassman and Ronald Speirs (Cambridge: Cambridge University Press, 1994): 310–11.

283. Aristotle, *Eudemian Ethics*, 1223a4–20, trans. J. Solomon, in *The Complete Works of Aristotle, The Revised Oxford Translation*, ed. Jonathan Barnes, Vol. 2 (Princeton: Princeton University Press, 1995), 1936–37.

284. Of course, small degrees of force do not fully absolve one from all responsibility for one's acts; if someone were merely pinched or slapped until she had agreed to rob a bank, she could not claim to bear no responsibility because she was "forced." (Still, the pincher or slapper might bear some responsibility, but most likely not enough to absolve the robber from primary responsibility.) Sorting out just how much force was enough to reduce responsibility is a tricky matter and one that jurists ponder regularly.

285. Aristotle, *Nicomachean Ethics*, 1112a31, trans. W. D. Ross, revised by J. O. Urman, in *The Complete Works of Aristotle: The Revised Oxford Translation*, 1756.

286. Harry Frankfurt, "Alternate Possibilities and Moral Responsibility," in Gary Watson, ed., *Free Will* (Oxford: Oxford University Press, 2003).

287. Frankfurt, "Alternate Possibilities and Moral Responsibility," 167.

288. Ibid., 169.

289. Ibid., 170.

290. I have benefited from conversations and correspondence with Terry Price regarding this issue.

291. Frankfurt, "Alternate Possibilities and Moral Responsibility," 170: "No doubt it will be very difficult for anyone to know, in a case like this one, exactly what happened . . . It is not impossible, however, that the situation should be clearer than situations of this kind usually are."

292. Ibid., 174.

293. In a response to Frankfurt, David Widerker concluded that Frankfurt's conclusion regarding the necessity of the condition of "could have done otherwise" "is unwarranted, because it does not hold for decisions, forming of intentions, etc.—mental acts that for the libertarian constitute the primary *loci* of moral responsibility." David Widerker, "Libertarianism and Frankfurt's Attack on the Principle of Alternative Possibilities," *Philosophical Review* (1995), 104, in Gary Watson, *Free Will,* 188. Furthermore, all that Frankfurt's arguments would show, were one to accept them, is that the condition "could have done otherwise" is not necessary for moral responsibility for an action to be ascribed to an agent. He would not have shown, however, that "could have done otherwise" is not a *sufficient* condition for moral responsibility. It could still be the case that, if one "could have done otherwise," that would be a sufficient condition for ascribing moral responsibility for the act, and that would certainly account for almost all acts regarding which moral responsibility is important. (Note: The term "libertarian" is used by Widerker in its technical philosophical meaning that denotes a belief in freedom of the will, and not in its political meaning that denotes a belief in primacy of the presumption of individual liberty as a political value.)

294. Harry Frankfurt, "Freedom of the Will and the Concept of a Person," in John Christman, ed., *The Inner Citadel: Essays on Individual Autonomy* (Oxford: Oxford University Press, 1989), 64.

295. Ibid., 73.

296. Ibid.

297. Ibid.

298. P. F. Strawson, "Freedom and Resentment," in *Perspectives on Moral Responsibility*, John Martin Fischer and Mark Ravizza, eds. (Ithaca, New York: Cornell University Press, 1993): 45–66.

299. Strawson, "Freedom and Resentment," 48. Compare with Adam Smith in *The Theory of Moral Sentiments*: "the violation of justice is injury: it does real and positive hurt to some particular persons, from motives which are naturally disapproved of. It is, therefore, the proper object of resentment, and of punishment, which is the natural consequence of resentment." *The Theory of Moral Sentiments*, A. L. Macfie and D. D. Raphael, eds. (Indianapolis; Liberty Classics, 1982), 79.

300. Strawson, "Freedom and Resentment," 52.

301. Strawson, "Freedom and Resentment," 54.

302. H. L. A. Hart and Tony Honoré, in their *Causation in the Law* (2nd ed., Oxford: Oxford University Press, 1985), note that "causing harm of a legally recognized sort or being connected with such harm in any of the ways that justify moral blame, though vitally important and perhaps basic in a legal system, is not and should not be either always necessary or always sufficient for legal responsibility," 67. Hart and Honoré emphasize the centrality of personal responsibility to a legal system, but are not committed to the view that one may be held responsible only for what one caused, for there may be other "policy" issues to be considered by legislators and judges. Even that caveat is still compatible with the ascription of responsibility to individuals for their acts, for some determinations of responsibility may of necessity be purely conventional (and hence may vary from place to place or time to time), but such principles, e.g., which party shall yield at a crossroads, once having been established, allow us to ascribe responsibility for acts to persons. If, on the other hand, responsibility were simply to be ascribed arbitrarily, on the basis of whim or in some other way such that *no* act of the party to whom responsibility is ascribed could ever have allowed her to avoid bearing responsibility, then we have not law and order but mere power and chaos. In addition, Hart and Honoré include insurance and surety contracts within the sphere of grounds for holding a party (who is not, for example, a tortfeasor) legally responsible. Such contracts certainly do depend on the voluntary acts, including contractual agreements, of the parties. Even though the parties held responsible are not themselves responsible for the harm for which they have agreed to be held responsible, their acts of consent are the ground of their legal responsibility, in the sense of "being accountable for or answerable to." See Hart and Honoré, *Causation in the Law*, 65. Personal responsibility is so much a part of our human being that even those who deny the freedom of others find themselves acknowledging their freedom of action and their responsibility. Consider the Roman law of noxal actions governing the acts of slaves: "Noxal actions lie when slaves commit delicts—theft, robbery, loss, or contempt. The actions give the condemned owner an option to pay the damages as assessed in money or to make noxal surrender of the slave." *The Digest of Justinian*, Alan Watson, ed. (Philadelphia: University of Pennsylvania Press, 1998), Book IX, 4.8. According to the jurist Ulpian, responsibility was not undermined by one's enslavement, although the liability shifted to the master if the slave killed someone with the master's knowledge and thus under his direction: "If a slave has killed with his owner's knowledge, the owner is liable in full; for he himself is deemed to have done the killing, but if he did not know, the action is noxal; for he should not be held liable for his slave's misdeed beyond handing him over noxally." *The Digest of Justinian*, Book IX, 4.2. The Roman law scholar Barry Nichols explains that "The liability was that of the wrongdoer, and the injured person could take vengeance on him.... The true character of this noxal liability is plain from the rule that it followed the wrongdoer (noxa caput sequitur). This meant that if the slave was, for example, manumitted before the action was brought, he himself was liable to an ordinary action; or if he were sold, the noxal

action lay against his new owner." Barry Nichols, *An Introduction to Roman Law* (Oxford: Clarendon Press, 1991), 223.

303. Michael Shermer describes a number of such situations, but concludes that, those cases notwithstanding, we should not completely abandon "free will and moral responsibility." Michael Shermer, *The Moral Arc: How Science and Reason Lead Humanity toward Truth, Justice, and Freedom* (New York: Henry Holt & Co., 2015), 338. Even a thorough reductionist such as brain researcher Dick Swaab, who argues that "we are our brains," and characterizes "free will" as "a pleasant illusion," cannot bring himself to eliminate freedom of choice entirely. In his stimulating work *We Are Our Brains* (London: Penguin Books, 2014), he denies merely that choices are "*entirely* free" (326); refers to how "*our last little bit of freedom* is further curtailed by the obligations and prohibitions that society imposes on us" (328); claims that "the existence of free will, which—at least as far as *most of our actions* are concerned—simply doesn't exist" (331), thus indicating that it may "exist" for at least some of our actions; and asks us to "accept that *complete* freedom of will is illusory" (338). (Emphasis added.) Swaab cannot bring himself to eliminate freedom of choice altogether, but contents himself with dismissing claims about being "entirely free" and cannot eliminate "our last little bit of freedom."

304. Or, alternatively, that God's perfect foreknowledge of the world precludes any human freedom; as St. Augustine posed the problem, "how can the following two propositions, that [1] God has foreknowledge of all future events, and that [2] we do not sin by necessity but by free will, be made consistent with each other?" Saint Augustine, *On Free Choice of the Will*, trans. Anna S. Benjamin and L. H. Hackstaff (Indianapolis: Bobbs-Merrill, 1981), Book Three, Section III, "God's foreknowledge does not preclude man's freedom in sinning," 90. Augustine's answer is that if God knows his own acts in the future, then his acts would also be necessitated, but that would contradict the power of God, so that God's will must be free in determining what he will do tomorrow, which entails that, although God knows what you will do tomorrow, you are similarly free in doing what God knows you will do. The issue is a thorny one in theology.

305. Immanuel Kant, *Critique of Pure Reason*, trans. and ed. Paul Guyer and Allen W. Wood (Cambridge: Cambridge University Press, 1998) (A533/B561) (Kindle Locations 13032-13033). Cambridge University Press. Kindle Edition. "Freedom in this signification is a pure transcendental idea, which, first, contains nothing borrowed from experience, and second, the object of which also cannot be given determinately in any experience, because it is a universal law—even of the possibility of all experience—that everything that happens must have a cause, and hence that the causality of the cause, as itself having happened or arisen, must in turn have a cause; through this law, then, the entire field of experience, however far it may reach, is transformed into the sum total of mere nature," ibid. (A533/B561) (Kindle Locations 13025-13029).

306. The issue is a most complex one. Kant himself insisted that immoral actions are freely chosen, but it is hard to see how that position can be consistently maintained within the philosophy he articulated. Writing of the "final end" (or "goal," *telos* in Greek) in his *Critique of Judgment* [trans. James C. Meredith (Oxford: Clarendon Press, 1952), §26 (87), 116], Kant argued "if there is to be a final *end*, which reason must assign *a priori*, then it can only be *man*—or any rational being in the world— *subject to moral laws*." In the footnote to that passage, he distinguishes between being "under moral laws" and being "in accordance with such laws." He goes on in the footnote to explain that "According to our conceptions of free causality, good or bad conduct depends on ourselves." H. J. Paton in his study of Kant's moral philosophy, *The Categorical Imperative* (Philadelphia: University of Pennsylvania Press, 1971), identified the problem, quoted Kant's assertion of freedom, identified several concepts Kant introduced to deal with the problem, and then concluded that "the power of choosing to act against the law is not a *necessary* characteristic of freedom. He [Kant] apparently thinks that such a power in a rational being is unintelligible, as indeed it is; and he even declares it not a power, but rather an incapacity. Freedom in relation to the inner law-making of reason is alone properly called a power. All this is highly abstract and difficult, and it may be confused: but it all serves to show that

for Kant we are free so far as we are capable of obeying the moral law and this on his view is a characteristic not merely of saints, but of all men, and indeed of all rational agents; for apart from this there could be no recognition of duty and no moral responsibility for failure," 214. That strikes me as circular reasoning. In any case, the entire effort is a puzzle for more scholarship than is suitable for this essay. Brand Blanshard's examination of the issue concluded that "Kant was mistaken in supposing that when we were determined by reason we were not determined at all. This supposition seems to me wholly unwarranted. The determination is still there, but, since it is a determination by the moral necessities of the case, it is just what the moral man wants and thus is the equivalent of freedom. For the moral man, like the logician and the artist, is really seeking self-surrender. Through him as through the others an impersonal ideal is working, and to the extent that this ideal takes possession of him and molds him according to its pattern, he feels free and is free." "The Case for Determinism," in Sidney Hook, ed. *Determinism and Freedom in the Age of Science* (New York: Collier Books, 1958): 19–30, 29.

307. Daniel C. Dennett, *Freedom Evolves* (New York: Penguin Books, 2004), 292. Hayek, *The Constitution of Liberty*, 142–43: "The fact that a free society will function successfully only if the individuals are in some measure guided by common values is perhaps the reason why philosophers have sometimes defined freedom as action in conformity with moral rules. But this definition of freedom is a denial of that freedom with which we are concerned. The freedom of action that is the condition of moral merit includes the freedom to act wrongly; we praise or blame only when a person has the opportunity to choose, only when his observance of a rule is not enforced but merely enjoined."

308. Daniel Dennett defines determinism, following Peter Van Inwagen (*An Essay on Free Will* [Oxford: Clarendon Press, 1983], 3) as "the thesis that 'there is at any instant exactly one physically possible future.'" (*Freedom Evolves*, 25) He then proceeds to show that three popular claims about determinism are false: that it implies inevitability; that its denial would "give us agents some freedom, some maneuverability, some elbow room, that we just couldn't have in a deterministic universe"; and that "in a deterministic world, there are no *real* options, only apparent options." The argument is involved and complicated, but well worth reading. Notably, he shows that if determinism is true and thus at any instant there is one physically possible future, it is also true that the past is not similarly determined, for many different pasts might have led to the present. Thus, with many possible pasts, determinism does not uniquely prescribe the necessary conditions for the present: "Determinism is a doctrine about sufficiency: If $S_0$ is a (mind-bogglingly complex) sentence that specifies in complete detail the state description of the universe at $t_0$, and $S_1$ similarly specifies the state description at a later time $t_1$, then determinism dictates that $S_0$ is sufficient for $S_1$ in all physically possible worlds. But determinism tells us nothing about what earlier conditions are *necessary* to produce $S_1$ or any other sentence for that matter. Hence, since causation generally presupposes necessity, the truth of determinism would have little, if any, bearing on the validity of our causal judgments," 83–84.

309. See Dennett, *Freedom Evolves*, 250–255.

310. Dennett, *Freedom Evolves*, 251.

311. *Aristotle's Politics*, trans. Carnes Lord (2nd ed.; Chicago: University of Chicago Press, 2013), 1253a, p. 4 (Kindle Edition).

312. Robert Nozick very helpfully explores the issues of voluntary action and ethics in his essay on "The Genealogy of Ethics" in Robert Nozick, *Invariances: The Structure of the Objective World* (Cambridge, Mass.: Harvard University Press, 2001): 236–301. He considers the norm of "*voluntary cooperation*, the norm of unforced cooperation" as "the *core principle of ethics*," 263.

313. See Kathleen D. Vohs and Jonathan W. Schooler, "The Value of Believing in Free Will: Encouraging a Belief in Determinism Increases Cheating," *Psychological Science*, Vol. 19, No. 1 (2008), 49–54; and Roy F. Baumeister, E. J. Masicampo, and C. Nathan DeWall, "Prosocial Benefits of Feeling Free: Disbelief in Free Will Increases Aggression and Reduces Helpfulness," *Personality and Social Psychology Bulletin*, Vol. 35, No. 2, February 2009, 260–268.

314. "If we say that a person is responsible of the consequences of an action, this is not

a statement of fact or an assertion about causation. The statement would, of course, not be justified if nothing he 'might' have done or omitted could have altered the result. But when we use words like 'might' or 'could' in this connection, we do not mean that at the moment of his decision something in him acted otherwise than was the necessary effect of causal laws in the given circumstances. Rather, the statement that a person is responsible for what he does aims at making his actions different from what they would be if he did not believe it to be true. We assign responsibility to a man, not in order to say that as he was he might have acted differently, but in order to make him act differently." Hayek, *The Constitution of Liberty*, 138.

315. Roy F. Baumeister, "Free Will in Scientific Psychology," *Perspectives on Psychological Science*, Vol. 3, No. 1 (2008), 14–19, 16.

316. *The Analects of Confucius: A Philosophical Translation*, trans. Roger T. Ames and Henry Rosement Jr. (Ballantine Books: New York, 1998), 15.24, p. 189. See also Mencius on the "four germs" of virtue: "Mencius said, 'No man is devoid of a heart sensitive to the suffering of others.' . . . 'My reason for saying that no man is devoid of a heart sensitive to the suffering of others is this. Suppose a man were, all of a sudden, to see a young child on the verge of falling into a well. He would certainly be moved to compassion, not because he wanted to get in the good graces of the parents, nor because he wished to win the praise of his fellow villagers or friends, not yet because he disliked the cry of the child. From this it can be seen that whoever is devoid of the heart of compassion is not human, whoever is devoid of the heart of shame is not human, whoever is devoid of the heart of courtesy and modesty is not human, and whoever is devoid of the heart of right and wrong is not human. The heart of compassion is the germ of benevolence; the heart of shame, of dutifulness; the heart of courtesy and modesty, of observance of the rites; the heart of right and wrong, of wisdom. Man has these four germs just as he has four limbs." *Mencius*, D.C. Lau, trans. (New York: Penguin Books, 1970), Book I, Part A, 6, pp. 82–83.

317. "Hillel," by Solomon Schechter, Wilhelm Bacher, in *Jewish Encyclopedia* (1906), 396–400, 398, JewishEncyclopedia.com.

318. Matthew 7:12, Revised Standard Version.

319. Edmund Husserl, *Cartesian Meditations: An Introduction to Phenomenology*, Dorion Cairns, trans. (The Hague: Martinus Nijhoff, 1973), 90.

320. Ibid., 91.

321. Edmund Husserl, "Phenomenology and Anthropology," in Edmund Husserl, *Shorter Works*, Peter McCormick and Frederick A. Elliston, eds. (Notre Dame: University of Notre Dame Press, 1981), 322. Thomas Nagel makes a similar move in his rejection of solipsism in *The View from Nowhere* (Oxford: Oxford University Press, 1986), 20: "[T]he ordinary concept of mind contains the beginnings of an entirely different way of conceiving objective reality. We cannot make sense of the idea of other minds by construing it in a way which becomes unintelligible when we try to apply it to ourselves. When we conceive of the minds of others, we cannot abandon the essential factor of a point of view: instead we must generalize it and think of ourselves as one point of view among others. The first stage of objectification of the mental is for each of us to be able to grasp the idea of all human perspectives, including his own, without depriving them of their character as perspectives."

322. Husserl, *Cartesian Meditations*, 129.

323. Ibid.

324. As Colonel Thomas Rainborough insisted in the Putney debates of 1647, "For really I think that the poorest he that is in England hath a life to live, as the greatest he; and therefore truly, sir, I think it's clear, that every man that is to live under a government ought first by his own consent to put himself under that government; and I do think that the poorest man in England is not at all bound in a strict sense to that government that he hath not had a voice to put himself under." In A. S. P. Woodhouse, ed., *Puritanism and Liberty: Being the Army Debates (1647) from the Clarke Manuscripts with Supplementary Documents* (London: J. M. Dent & Sons, Ltd., 1992), 53. The related concept of the "suum," what is "one's own," played an especially important role in the development of liberal theories of justice. See Stephen Buckle, *Natural Law and the Theory of Property* (Oxford: Clarendon Press, 1991), esp. 29–37.

325. Andrew Sharp, ed., *The English Levellers* (Cambridge: Cambridge University

Press, 1998), vii. A closely related claim is that there is no obvious dividing line by which we may distinguish those with "more" claims from those with less. Such distinctions have been ritually asserted as part of a legitimation of the power of conquerors over conquered. As Alexander Rüstow notes: "[T]he distance between [upper and lower strata] can never be intensified to such gruesome, grotesque dimensions as in the . . . context of herdsmen-planter superstratification, where one finds court ceremonials in which a subject was permitted to approach the king only by groveling in the dust with a tuft of grass held in his mouth—truly a 'bestial servitude.'" Alexander Rüstow, *Freedom and Domination: A Historical Critique of Civilization* (Princeton: Princeton University Press, 1980), 22.

326. Thomas Jefferson to Roger Weightman, June 24, 1826, Library of Congress, http://www.loc.gov/exhibits/jefferson/214.html.

327. Francisco de Vitoria, *Political Writings*, Anthony Pagden and Jeremy Lawrance, eds. (Cambridge: Cambridge University Press, 1991), 247–248. (The passage does not appear in all editions of Vitoria's works.) According to Vitoria: "Every Indian is a man and thus is capable of attaining salvation or damnation"; "Every man is a person and is the master of his body and possessions"; "Inasmuch as he is a person, every Indian has free will, and, consequently, is the master of his actions"; "By natural law, every man has the right to his own life and to physical and mental integrity." The preceding statements are drawn from a variety of Vitoria's writings and are collected in Luciano Pereña Vicente, ed., *The Rights and Obligations of Indians and Spaniards in the New World, According to Francisco de Vitoria* (Salamanca: Universidad Pontifica de Salamanca, 1992), 17.

328. Robert E. Goodin, "Social Welfare as a Collective Social Responsibility," in David Schmidtz and Robert E. Goodin, *Social Welfare and Individual Responsibility* (Cambridge: Cambridge University Press, 1998), 99–100. (The "we" Goodin invokes refers to the state which, as I have noted elsewhere, is not always—indeed, never—well described as "we," unless "we" refers to a subset of the people subject to the state.)

329. Robert E. Goodin, *Protecting the Vulnerable: A Re-Analysis of our Social Responsibilities* (Chicago: University of Chicago Press, 1985), 1–2.

330. St. Thomas Aquinas, *Summa Theologica*, IIa, IIae, Q. 66, trans. Fathers of the English Dominican Province (Westminster, Md.: Christian Classics, 1981), vol. III: 1471.

331. Schmidtz, "Taking Responsibility," in *Social Welfare and Individual Responsibility*, 21.

332. Goodin also responds to counter arguments, not with reasons, but by asserting that "arguments against the welfare state couched in high-minded terms of 'personal responsibility' are often, quite simply, arguments in bad faith" ("Social Welfare as a Collective Social Responsibility," ibid., 114) and then launches the usual insults against those who disagree with him.

333. Almost all corruption is hidden behind claims of public good and often labeled as "aid to the poor," "help to local communities," or "assistance to developing countries," but persistent researchers can, with some work, discover which particular interests are benefiting from the transfers made in the name of our collective responsibilities. For a simple example, see "The United States of subsidies: The biggest corporate winners in each state," *Washington Post*, March 18, 2015, www.washingtonpost.com/ blogs/govbeat/wp/2015/03/17/the-united-states-of-subsidies-the-biggest-corporate-winners-in-each-state. James Madison anticipated the modern interventionist welfare state's empowerment of cronyism rather clearly in *The Federalist*: "It will be of little avail to the people that the laws are made by men of their own choice if the laws be so voluminous that they cannot be read, or so incoherent that they cannot be understood; if they be repealed or revised before they are promulgated, or undergo such incessant changes that no man, who knows what the law is today, can guess what it will be tomorrow. Law is defined to be a rule of action; but how can that be a rule, which is little known, and less fixed? Another effect of public instability is the unreasonable advantage it gives to the sagacious, the enterprising, and the moneyed few over the industrious and uninformed mass of the people. Every new regulation concerning commerce or revenue, or in any manner affecting the value of the different species of property, presents a new harvest to those who watch

the change, and can trace its consequences; a harvest, reared not by themselves, but by the toils and cares of the great body of their fellow-citizens. This is a state of things in which it may be said with some truth that laws are made for the few, not for the many." James Madison, "Concerning the Constitution of the Senate with Regard to the Qualifications of the Members, the Manner of Appointing Them, the Equality of Representation, the Number of the Senators, and the Duration of their Appointments," No. 62, in James Madison, Alexander Hamilton, and John Jay, *The Federalist Papers* (New York: Penguin Books, 1987), p. 368.

334. Jean-Jacques Rousseau, *The Social Contract*, trans. Maurice Cranston (New York: Penguin Books, 1968): 72.

335. Ibid., 64.

336. Isaiah Berlin, "Two Concepts of Liberty," in Isaiah Berlin, *Liberty*, ed. Henry Hardy (Oxford: Oxford University Press, 2002): 180.

337. The empirical literature on the consequences is, for each of the areas mentioned, enormous. With the advent of online archives and Internet search engines one can find a great deal of empirical social scientific research on such topics in a short time.

338. Michael Sandel, *Liberalism and the Limits of Justice* (Cambridge: Cambridge University Press, 1982), 172. I deal at greater length with such issues in my essay "Freedom Properly Understood," a paper originally presented at the 60th anniversary meeting of the Liberal International, Hamburg, Germany, November 17, 2007, reprinted in Tom G. Palmer, *Realizing Freedom: Libertarian Theory, History, and Practice*, expanded 2nd ed., (Washington, DC: Cato Institute, 2009), 23–42.

339. I address the issue in greater depth in "Myths of Individualism," originally published in *Cato Policy Report* 18, no. 5, September/October 1996, reprinted in *Realizing Freedom*, 43–50. Also available online at www.libertarianism.org/publications/essays/myths-individualism.

340. The historian Parker T. Moon explained the error and its source quite clearly in the case of international relations, but the insight is quite general.

"Language often obscures truth. More than is ordinarily realized, our eyes are blinded to the facts of international relations by tricks of the tongue. When one uses the simple monosyllable 'France' one thinks of France as a unit, an entity. When to avoid awkward repetition we use a personal pronoun in referring to a country—when for example we say 'France sent *her* troops to conquer Tunis'—we impute not only unity but personality to the country. The very words conceal the facts and make international relations a glamorous drama in which personalized nations are the actors, and all too easily we forget the flesh-and-blood men and women who are the true actors. How different it would be if we had no such word as 'France,' and had to say instead—thirty-eight million men, women, and children of very diversified interests and beliefs, inhabiting 218,000 square miles of territory! Then we should more accurately describe the Tunis expedition in some such way as this: 'A few of these thirty-eight million persons sent thirty thousand others to conquer Tunis.' This way of putting the fact immediately suggests a question, or rather a series of questions. Who are the 'few'? Why did they send the thirty thousand to Tunis? And why did these obey?

Empire-building is done not by 'nations' but by men. The problem before us is to discover the men, the active, interested minorities in each nation, who are directly interested in imperialism, and then to analyze the reasons why the majorities pay the expenses and fight the wars necessitated by imperialist expansion."

Parker T. Moon, *Imperialism and World Politics* (New York: The MacMillan Company, 1926), 58.

341. Karl Marx, "On the Jewish Question," in *Karl Marx: Early Writings*, trans. and ed. T. B. Bottomore (New York: McGraw-Hill, 1964), 31.

342. That essay is notable for its anti-Semitism; see Jerry Z. Muller, *Capitalism and the Jews* (Princeton: Princeton University Press, 2011) on the character of Marx's anti-Semitism.

343. Marx, "On the Jewish Question," 24–25.

344. Karl Marx and Friedrich Engels, *The Communist Manifesto* (1848; London: Verso, 2012), 37.

345. The stories of some of those victims are told movingly in Anne Applebaum's

*Gulag: A History* (New York: Doubleday, 2003); Timothy Snyder, *Bloodlands: Europe Between Hitler and Stalin* (New York: Basic Books, 2010); and Frank Dikötter, *Mao's Great Famine: The History of China's Most Devastating Catastrophe, 1958–1962* (New York: Walker & Co., 2010).

346. See for Heidegger's influence on the founding of the Islamic Republic of Iran Ali Mirsepassi, "Religious Intellectuals and Western Critiques of Secular Modernity," *Comparative Studies of South Asia, Africa, and the Middle East*, Vol. 26, No. 3 (2006): 416–433. See for Heidegger's general influence on "particularist" opponents of liberal individualism, Alexander S. Duff, "Heidegger's Ghosts," *The American Interest*, February 25, 2016. For Heidegger's involvement with the general movement that Jeffrey Herf calls "reactionary modernism," see Jeffrey Herf, *Reactionary Modernism: Ideology, culture, and politics in Weimar and the Third Reich* (Cambridge: Cambridge University Press, 1986).

347. See Emmanuel Faye, *Heidegger: The Introduction of Nazism into Philosophy* (New Haven: Yale University Press, 2009) and Hugo Ott, *Martin Heidegger: A Political Life* (New York: Basic Books, 1993).

348. Martin Heidegger, *Being and Truth*, trans. Gregory Fried and Richard Polt (Bloomington, In.: Indiana University Press, 2010), 3. The lectures in the book were delivered in 1933–34, after Heidegger's National Socialist German Workers' Party had come to power in Germany.

349. Ibid., 6. As he makes clear, "our western, German Dasein" refers to "our historical being-with others in the membership of the people." Whether "the derivative mock culture finally collapses into itself . . . depends solely on whether we as a people still will ourselves, or whether we no longer will ourselves," 11.

350. Ibid., 33.

351. Martin Heidegger, *Logic as the Question Concerning the Essence of Language*, Wanda Torres Gregory and Yvonne Unna, trans. (Albany: State University Press of New York, 2009), 45.

352. Ibid., 139.

353. Polylogism, in both its superficially distinct Marxist and Nazi versions, was subjected to withering criticism by Ludwig von Mises in such books as *Omnipotent Government: The Rise of the Total State and Total War* (1944), *Theory and History* (1957), and *Human Action: A Treatise on Economics* (1966), all of which can be purchased or accessed online at http://oll.libertyfund.org/people/ludwig-von-mises.

354. Robert Musil, "'Nation' as Ideal and as Reality" [1921], in Robert Musil, *Precision and Soul: Essays and Addresses*, ed. and trans. Burton Pike and David S. Luft (Chicago: University of Chicago Press, 1990): 104–5. Musil describes the state as the enabling instrument of such evasion of responsibility. "The active counterpart to this letting things happen is the summary, general, routine treatment of people. The legal document is the symbol of the indirect relationship between the state and the human being; it is life become odorless, tasteless, and weightless, the button you press; and if this causes a person to die you have not done it, because your whole consciousness was absorbed by the demanding task of operating the button," 110. (It is remarkable how much of the holocaust that was to come Musil intuited in his many writings.)

355. Heidegger, *Logic as the Question Concerning the Essence of Language*, 140.

356. Thomas Hodgskin, *The Natural and Artificial Right of Property Contrasted* (1832; Clifton, New Jersey: Augustus M. Kelley, 1973): 28–29.

357. See Gareth Evans, "Self-Identification," *Self Knowledge*, Quassim Cassam, ed. (Oxford: Oxford University Press, 1994). As Evans puts it, the judgment "*a* is F" is immune to error through misidentification if "it is based upon a way of knowing about objects such that it does not make sense for the subject to utter 'Something is F, but is it *a* that is F?', when the first component expresses knowledge which the subject does not think he has, or may have, gained in any other way" [than the normal way]. (The preceding is a quotation of Gareth Evans, *The Varieties of Reference*, John McDowell, ed. (Oxford: Oxford University Press, 1982): 189–190, cited in Gareth Evans, "Self-Identification," 194.

358. Evans, "Self-Identification," 198. Evans also allows certain forms of mental self-ascription to be immune from errors of misidentification, for perceptual states "must occur in the context of certain kinds of knowledge and understanding on the part of

the subject" (208) that will entail knowledge of a persisting self: "No judgment will have the content of a psychological self-ascription, unless the judger can be regarded as ascribing to himself a property which he can conceive as being satisfied by a being not necessarily himself—a state of affairs which he will have to conceive as involving a persisting subject of experience. He can know that a state of affairs of the relevant type obtains simply by being aware of a tree, but he must conceive the state of affairs that he then knows to obtain as a state of affairs of precisely that type. And this means that he must conceive of himself, the subject to whom the property is ascribed, as a being of the kind which he envisages when he simply envisages *someone* seeing a tree—that is to say, a persisting subject of experience, located in space and time," 208.

359. Epictetus, *The Discourses as Reported by Arrian*, vol. I, bk. I–II, trans. W. A. Oldfather (Cambridge, Mass.: Harvard University Press, 1998), I.27, 18–19, 173.

360. As Hugo Grotius notes, "It is the CIVIL law . . . which makes an owner answerable for the mischief or damage done by his slave, or by his cattle. For in the eye of natural justice he is not to blame." Hugo Grotius, *The Rights of War and Peace*, A. C. Campbell, A. M., trans. (London: M. Walter Dunne, 1901), 201. One can also, by means of consent, agree to take responsibility for the acts of others, as in a contractually assumed suretyship. See Albert Loan, "Institutional Bases of the Spontaneous Order: Surety and Assurance," *Humane Studies Review* 7 (Winter 1991–92) and Robin Chapman Stacey, *The Road to Judgment: From Custom to Court in Medieval Ireland and Wales* (Philadelphia: University of Pennsylvania Press, 1994), esp. chapters two ("Contractual Suretyship in Irish Law") and three ("The Social Context of Personal Suretyship").

## Chapter 11: Increasing and Improving Your Own Self-Control

361. John Lachs, *Meddling: On the Virtue of Leaving Others Alone* (Bloomington: Indiana University Press, 2014), 44

362. Steven Pinker, *The Better Angels of Our Nature: A History of Violence and Humanity* (London: Penguin Books, 2011), 726.

363. James Buchanan, "Natural and Artifactual Man," in *The Collected Works of James M. Buchanan, Vol. I, The Logical Foundations of Constitutional Liberty* (Indianapolis: Liberty Fund, 1999), 246–259, 259.

364. *Aristotle's Nicomachean Ethics*, trans. Robert C. Bartlett and Susan D. Collins (Chicago: University of Chicago Press, 2011), Book II, Chapter 1, 1103a–1103b, Kindle Edition (Kindle Locations 737–741).

365. Charles Duhigg, *The Power of Habit: Why We Do What We Do in Life and Business* (New York: Random House, 2014), esp. 60–93.

366. Ibid., 270.

367. For the deeper background of many of Dobelli's lessons, see Daniel Kahneman, *Thinking, Fast and Slow* (New York: Farrar, Straus, and Giroux, 2011); and Nassim Nicholas Taleb, *Fooled by Randomness: The Hidden Role of Chance in Life and in the Markets* (New York: Random House, 2005); and *Black Swan: The Impact of the Highly Improbable* (2nd ed.: New York: Random House, 2010).

368. For an understanding of the Buddhist religion and the theological context of Buddhist teachings, see Perry Schmidt-Leukel, *Understanding Buddhism* (Edinburgh: Dunedin Academic Press, 2006). For an approach to Buddhist meditation that rejects religion, see Sam Harris, *Waking Up: A Guide to Spirituality without Religion* (New York: Simon & Schuster, 2014). For a Christian-oriented approach to meditation and awareness of selfhood, see Joel S. Goldsmith, *The Art of Meditation* (1956; Longboat Key, Florida: Acropolis Books, 2013).

369. Some readers might find odd a positive discussion in a book on self-control of a work that concludes with a chapter on "Relaxing the Self," but Hanson's use of "person" in his book corresponds well to the use of "self" in this one. What is rejected by Hanson and other Buddhist practitioners is similar to the untenable notion of the self as a little person looking out through one's eyes on the world who sees what the eyes see; the Latin term is *homunculus*, or "little man," and it generates a problem of

infinite regress, for inside the homunculus there would have to be another homunculus seeing through the eyes of the first homunculus, *ad infinitum*. The idea of the conscious self as a mental construct—even as a product of the brain—that arises and changes depending on circumstances is consistent with the idea of self-control that I've deployed in this book. For interesting thoughts and research on the self as a process and a product of the brain, see Antonio Damasio, *Self Comes to Mind: Constructing the Conscious Brain* (London: Vintage Books, 2010).

370. I should note that I encourage those interested in making better decisions to explore the following programs, but it certainly does not follow that they would endorse everything I believe or advocate.

371. *The Dhammapada*, trans. and ed. by Valerie J. Roebuck (New York: Penguin Books, 2010), Chapter 1 ("Twins"), 4.

372. Ibid., Chapter 12 ("Self"), 34.

# About the Editor: Tom G. Palmer

Dr. Tom G. Palmer is executive vice president for international programs at Atlas Network, where he works with a global network of over 450 think tanks and research institutes to advance the principles of classical liberalism. Dr. Palmer is a senior fellow of the Cato Institute, where he was formerly vice president for international programs and director of the Center for the Promotion of Human Rights.

He was an H. B. Earhart Fellow at Hertford College, Oxford, and a vice president of the Institute for Humane Studies at George Mason University. He is a member of the board of advisors of Students For Liberty, a director of the Institute of Economic Studies – Europe, and a member of the Mont Pelerin Society, the international society of classical liberal thinkers founded by F. A. Hayek after World War II. He has published articles and reviews in scholarly journals, as well as in popular publications such as the *Wall Street Journal*, the *New York Daily News*, the *New York Times*, *Die Welt*, *Slate*, *Al Hayat*, *Caixing*, the *Washington Post*, and the *Spectator of London*.

He received his BA in liberal arts from St. Johns College in Annapolis, Maryland; his MA in philosophy from The Catholic University of America in Washington DC; and his doctorate in politics from Oxford University. His scholarship has been published in books from Princeton University Press, Cambridge University Press, Routledge, and other academic publishers, and he is the author of *Realizing Freedom: Libertarian Thought, History, and Practice* (expanded edition published in 2014) and editor of and contributor to a number of books, including *The Morality of Capitalism* (2011), *After the Welfare State* (2012), *Why Liberty* (2013), and *Peace, Love, and Liberty* (2014).

# Index

# Liberty at your Fingertips

Enhance your research ... become an active participant in the online community committed to individual liberty ... and jumpstart your career ... through the Cato Institute's vast online resources. From the global community on Facebook.com/CatoOnCampus, the insights and immediate-use analyses of Cato's policy experts on Cato.org, to the innovative perspectives on the *Cato@Liberty* blog, and the one-of-a kind material and multimedia content on Cato's Libertarianism.org project ... and so much more ... the value of Cato's work is now only matched by its immediate accessibility.

# About Atlas Network

Atlas Network's vision is of a free, prosperous, and peaceful world where limited governments defend the rule of law, private property, and free markets.

Atlas Network has partnered with Students for Liberty to bring you: *The Economics of Freedom*, *The Morality of Capitalism*, *After the Welfare State*, *Why Liberty*, and *State Control or Self Control?*, edited by Atlas Network Executive Vice President for International Programs Dr. Tom G. Palmer.

- Atlas Network has more than 450 independent, free-market partners in over 90 countries.

- Atlas Network provides its independent partners with coaching, competitive grant and award opportunities, and occasions to celebrate high-impact successes.

Learn how you can get involved:
AtlasNetwork.org

1201 L St. NW • Washington, DC 20005 • 202-449-8449
AtlasNetwork.org

# About Atlas Leadership Academy

Join a growing network of inspired and innovative think tank leaders as we build a freer world.

- Lessons in think tank management from industry leaders

- Courses in the basics of launching a think tank

- Strategic direction, practical tips, & real-world solutions through case studies of successful think tank projects

- Business school-style training on strategic planning, management, and project execution

- Mentorship with luminaries of the free-market movement

Enroll in Atlas Leadership Academy today:
AtlasNetwork.org/ALA

ATLAS
LEADERSHIP
ACADEMY

1201 L St. NW • Washington, DC 20005 • 202-449-8449
AtlasNetwork.org

"WHO AM I? What is freedom and how do I achieve it?"

"What is a good life and how do I achieve that? How do I live the life of a free and responsible person? How am I related to others? How should I behave and how should I expect others to behave?"

"For what am I responsible and for what not? Should some people use force to control others? How does control through the state function and what are its effects?"

"What is self-control, what are its benefits and its costs, and how do I achieve it?"

Young people may be especially likely to pose these questions, but these questions are not only for youth—they're for every stage of life.

They're what this short book is all about.

—Tom Palmer, Editor, *Self-Control or State Control? You Decide*

### Special Bulk Copy Discount Schedule

| | | |
|---|---|---|
| 1 book $12.95 | 25 books $ 75.00 | 500 books $ 975.00 |
| 5 books $25.00 | 50 books $125.00 | 1000 books $1,750.00 |
| 10 books $35.00 | 100 books $225.00 | |

*All prices include postage and handling.*

**JAMESON BOOKS, INC**
**Post Office Box 738**
**Ottawa, IL 61350**

**ORDER TOLL FREE**
**800-426-1357**

Please send me _____ copies of *Self-Control or State Control? You Decide.*

Enclosed is my check for $_____ or please charge my
     [ ] MasterCard     [ ] Visa or     [ ] Discover card

Card No. _____ Exp. Date _____

Signature _____ Telephone _____

Name _____

Address _____

City _____ State _____ Zip _____

Illinois residents please add 6.5% sales tax. Please allow 2 weeks for delivery.